Tend My Sheep

Figure A.1. Frances and Dr. Gerald Mitchum

Tend My Sheep

A Veterinarian in Mongolia

The Amazing Story
of How the Kingdom of God
Is Growing in Mongolia
Through Veterinary Missions

Gerald Mitchum, DVM

Tend My Sheep

–A Veterinarian in Mongolia by Gerald Mitchum

Printed in the United States of America

ISBN: 978-1-7328834-1-3 (hardback)
ISBN: 978-1-7328834-0-6 (paperback)
ISBN: 978-1-7328834-2-0 (ebook)

Book cover art design by Bob Brown. Artwork by Tamir Dugermaa, on staff of V.E.T. Net in Mongolia. Right to use acquired.

Published by KDP Direct, the purchaser of CreateSpace, a subsidiary of Amazon.com

Table of Contents

List of Drawings and Photographs

Dedication

> *Where you go I will go, and where you stay I will stay.*
>
> –Ruth 1:16b, NIV

Figure A.2. Frances Mitchum (on horse)

This book is dedicated to my wife, **Frances**. There was no other consideration to whom to make this dedication.

Frances left her family and friends and followed God and me to a land where the earth ended—exactly half-way around the world in a place called Mongolia. This was a place where lonely herders on distant hillsides had never heard the name, Jesus Christ. The nation was suddenly open to Westerners after being one of the most closed countries in the world.

"Frances," I said, "I believe God is calling us to this desolate place where there are waiting ears to hear the gospel. Come go with me."

And her thoughtful answer was, "Yes."

When God tapped Frances to be my life-partner, it was a perfect match. She is the love of my life. Describing her stretches my vocabulary—her eyes are so blue they appear to reflect the sky on a cloudless day; her hair is golden with just enough streaks of red to season her with a touch of fire; tender but tough; caring and compassionate; winsome spirit and bubbly personality; and strongly endowed with the gift of hospitality. And it was that gift of hospitality that played a central role in the start of V.E.T. Net. You see, it attracted the young Mongolian students to our home for a taste of Frances' cooking. This was part of God's plan.

Whether on her knees praying or cleaning floors or a combination of the two, Frances was driven to make people welcome and comfortable in our home. Her goal was to gain the opportunity to share her love of Christ with all who entered.

Earthly speaking, she gave up so much—and yet, unquestionably, without my dear Frances there'd be no V.E.T. Net, and thousands of Mongolians would not have heard of our wonderful Savior and the Word of God would not have found its way into their world. As has been said before related to doing God's will, "She gave up what she could not keep, to gain what she could not lose" (paraphrase of quote by missionary Jim Elliot).

Praise God for you Frances! Scripture tells us that when someone comes to salvation in Jesus, the angels rejoice in heaven (Luke 15:10). Thank you, Frances, for the part you played in so many coming to salvation in Mongolia and causing the angels to rejoice in heaven.

Acknowledgements

1. Jesus—We owe everything to you!
2. Dr. Joseph and Judy Lenard—General Editor;
   Technical Consultant
3. Francine Thomas—Manuscript Editing
4. Steve and Ann Kullberg—Leaders of Senders Group
5. Wes Harrison—Sending Church Representative
6. Our Sending Church, Other Churches, Individuals and Foundations
7. Tamir Dugermaa—Artist
8. V.E.T. Net Team
9. Short-Term Missionaries
10. Mongolia V.E.T. Net Advisory Board
11. Christian Veterinary Mission (CVM)
12. Bob Brown—Cover Designer; Technical Advisor

1. **Jesus**, indeed, we owe everything to you.

2. It was 1987 when we joined with a handful of families in Southern Pines, North Carolina as part of a new church plant. At that time, we met **Dr. Joe and Judy Lenard** and started a friendship that has lasted for over 30 years. It is no stretch to say that without Joe and Judy the publication of this book would have been unlikely. **Judy** has been the consummate encourager as she has said year-after-year, "Gerald, you have got to write down your experiences to share with others." And **Joe**—it is impossible to count the ways he has blessed me through this long and arduous process. He has served untiringly as the general editor and technical consultant on many areas of the book. But more than this, he has tirelessly urged me on to the

completion of this written record of my last 24 years of ministry in Mongolia. Frances and I are honored to be able to call Joe and Judy true friends.

3. I was praying on a particular Sunday that I might meet **Francine Thomas**, a member of our church, who had authored and edited books and publications and had served as a ghost-writer for military brass. We met providentially, and she volunteered to help with the editing of the manuscript. I am grateful for her gifts, her patience, and her contribution. She was a true gift from God.

4. **Steve and Ann Kullberg** brought a heart for missions and prayer with them when they began to attend our little start-up church in Southern Pines. God brought them for "such a time as this" to lead a Senders Group for Frances and me as we prepared to serve in Mongolia. Step-by-step, God was paving the path for us as we began this long journey. Thank you, Steve and Ann, for allowing God to use you in such a direct way in our lives and the ministry to the Mongolian people.

5. One of the great blessings in this life are good friends. I count **Wes Harrison** as exactly that—a very close friend. The miles have separated us physically, but distance and time have increased the strength of our relationship. During our absence, our church has grown from 50 to almost 2000, and we only know a handful of the members. Wes has been the connection between us and our local church. He has come to Mongolia many times, and his gift of discipleship has greatly blessed the V.E.T. team and countryside believers.

6. **Our sending church, other churches, individuals, and foundations** have been true "partners in the gospel." We look back with deep appreciation for these dedicated followers of *The Faith.*

7. God has poured a double portion of gifts on our good friend **Tamir Dugermaa (Tamara)**. We are grateful for his contributions of the drawings that make the stories in the book come to life. Thank you, Tamir!

8. The **V.E.T. Net team** is an amazing group of nationals and Western advisors. God has so blessed us to be part of this

vibrant group of men and women reaching across the nation of Mongolia.

9. I want to give credit to the **hundreds of Short-Term Missionaries** who have contributed mightily to the ministry of V.E.T. Net. Of course, that would fill a book in itself. Your deeds are already recorded in the only place that will live eternally—they are written on the hand of God. You have blessed me and Frances and the work in more ways that I can count—thank you! Some of you have even chosen to return as **Long-Term Missionaries**, and your commitment and service has been invaluable to Frances and me and V.E.T. Net—thank you!

10. The **western V.E.T. Net Advisory Board** are a special group of men and women from the US and Canada who are a critical part of the work and ministry in Mongolia. They meet annually at their own expense and support V.E.T. Net in unimaginable ways. Speaking for the whole team of V.E.T. Net, I want you to know how grateful we all are for each of you.

11. I am grateful to **Christian Veterinary Mission** (**CVM**) for making this ministry possible and for their valuable support over these many years. I am particularly thankful for those who manage the short-term missions program. Sending 50 or more short-term missionaries each year has been no easy task. Blessings to the CVM home-office team.

12. How do you design a book cover? I had no idea. But of course, God knows our every need, and he brought **Bob Brown** into our lives. Thank you, Bob, for expressing your creativity in ways that truly glorify our Lord. Thanks too for your help with converting the color images to B&W for the print version of the manuscript and other technical assistance. Also, thanks for helping to shepherd the book through the publication process.

Foreword

by Kit Flowers, DVM

Figure A.3. Kit Flowers, DVM

"Gerald and Frances Mitchum loved me to Jesus Christ," said Dr. Enkee as she began her talk with this bold testimony.

Dr. Enkee was sharing at the Christian Veterinary Mission (CVM) fellowship breakfast meeting at a major veterinary conference in the U.S., and she continued presenting the amazing story of His Good News coming to her through Gerald and Frances. She also shared about the open doors for effective service in Mongolia through veterinary medicine and rural school development. Dr. Enkee is just one of the many who have been loved to Jesus Christ through Gerald and Frances.

The apostle Paul wrote to the church in Corinth *"And now these three remain: faith, hope and love. But the greatest of these is love"* (1 Cor. 13:13, NIV). I have had the amazing opportunity to serve alongside Dr. Gerald and Frances as God stirred their hearts to mission service in Mongolia. They have served as instruments of faith, hope, and love to the people of Mongolia and to those who have joined them in that calling in short-term and long-term missions. They have served to mobilize an amazing team of co-workers in the V.E.T Net leadership and staff, the foreign advisor team, the hundreds who have served with them in short-term missions, and the hundreds who have been faithful to pray and give financially.

Each of us has experienced His love through Gerald and Frances. Each of us has also been inspired by their faith and challenged to take steps of faith in our own journeys. Their response in faith has mobilized others to do the same. We have also seen hope birthed in the hearts of their Mongolian teammates as together they have sought to understand God's calling to take the good news of the gospel to the remotest parts of the world.

Dr. Mitchum has always been a wonderful story teller. His gift will inspire you as you read this book and as you see the testimony of this work serving to bring glory to God. His gift will also challenge you to ask:

> "What am I doing? Am I listening for His voice and being obedient to His call? Are there those in my life whom I should be loving to Jesus Christ?"

Dr. Kit Flowers
Executive Director
Christian Veterinary Mission
19303 Fremont Ave N
Seattle, WA 9813
www.cvmusa.org

Preface

> *And this gospel of the kingdom will be preached in the whole world as a testimony to all nations, and then the end will come.*
>
> –Matthew 24:14, NIV

This book, *Tend My Sheep—A Veterinarian in Mongolia,* is God's story of reaching across the nation of Mongolia with the Gospel of Jesus Christ and the implications of that life-changing power that comes from walking with Him.

In 1995, Frances and I packed a few of our belongings in suitcases and moved to Mongolia—literally, the other side of the world. The nation had only recently opened to Westerners. Businessmen, developers and religious groups flooded in from all over the developed world.

The essence of the story is our spiritual walk with God guiding our plans. It is a story of the training of a group of nationals, being touched by God, who continue to carry the Gospel to the far corners of Mongolia—and beyond. They are a team of professionals and support staff with a heart to change the lives of their people forever. This little group is called *Mongolia V.E.T. Net,* a non-government, non-profit public service organization (NGO). It is a band of first-generation Christians driven by the command to go and make disciples.

Frances and I were sent by *Christian Veterinary Mission,* a U.S.-based organization focused on bringing a better life to thousands around the world through Christian development, outreach and discipleship.

We are sensitive to the importance of protecting the beautiful heritage of the Mongolian people as we work to help them achieve a better life-style for their families. We follow the lead of Jesus—we give the herders a helping hand with their physical needs, but we know that this is not enough. Without a change of heart through the gospel message, all influence is only temporary.

We applaud the men and women in veterinary medicine who view this profession as more than a livelihood. Veterinarians from academia, research, government and practice have donated their skills, time, and resources to assist the people of Mongolia in their recovery from the Russian era.

Christian Veterinary Mission, our parent organization, cares about all aspects of veterinary medicine, from the kitten on the exam table to the child that is infected with brucellosis. This "caring" has now reached half-way around the world into the "Land of Genghis Khan."

Figure 1.1. "Tend My Sheep"—herder feeding lamb

Chapter 1

Spying Out the Land

> *Send some men to explore the land of Canaan, which I am giving to the Israelites.*
>
> –Numbers 13:2a, NIV

It was November the 9th, 1989, and the Berlin Wall, symbolic of so much pain and suffering, was at last coming down between East and West. The success of democracy and capitalism had outlasted the failed utopian dream of communism and socialism.

On the other side of the world, the Mongolian People's Republic, a nation with its own rich history, was caught in a downward spiral with the old Soviet Union. Food was scarce and long lines at government shops led to arguments and fights over small amounts of rationed commodities. People resorted to eating livestock-feed to survive.

Eventually, government shops closed completely, and were slowly replaced by private businesses. Years of dependence on Russia and the Eastern Bloc nations were abruptly ending. The overnight exodus of the Russian military and industrialists eventually paved the way for the birth of a fledgling democracy that became the independent democratic nation of Mongolia, a land-locked country located north of China and south of the eastern extension of Russia. The world was changing, and with it came an influx of people from the West eager to share their knowledge and expertise with the people of Mongolia.

Pristine Paradise

God saw all that he had made, and it was very good.

–Genesis 1:31a, NIV

The sheer beauty of Mongolia is truly breathtaking. Its majestic mountains rise to form the northern border with Russia. They stand in distinct contrast to the vast Gobi Desert in the south and the lush grasslands in the east bordering China. The Kazakh area of Bayan Ulgii in the west adds to the grandeur of the land with its snowcapped mountains and rugged terrain. High meadow mountain passes are splashed with glorious colors much like an artist's pallet with its dabs of intense color and subtle hues.

Wild flowers die each year only to bloom again in the early summer. Crystal rivers cutting through grassy valleys teem with tasty fish appearing only too eager to flip into the frying pan. In autumn, larch trees gracefully scatter their needles to carpet the forest floor with layers of gold, while stars sparkle in the night sky undimmed by manmade lights. This remarkable country stretches across unending landscapes leaving the observer to stand speechless before the artistry of the creative God whose divine paintbrush brought such exotic beauty into existence.

Mongolia is called the "Land of Blue Skies" for a very good reason; it boasts of approximately 250 days of sunshine throughout each year. Mongolia has a population of only 3.1 million and has the lowest population density among all independent countries in the world with only 1.7 people per square kilometer. It is this vast and majestic emptiness that causes first-time visitors to feel a sense of awe.

In stark contrast, the capital city of Ulaanbaatar has a population that has grown from approximately 600,000 when we first arrived in 1995, to over one million today. However, that is relatively a small number for such a large region. Regardless, both the nomadic herders and Mongolia's natural beauty never fail to fascinate all outsiders who visit this enchanting land.

Up, Up and Away

It was 1994, and the Air China flight was packed with Asians returning to their homeland. We were flying at 30,000 feet sitting rather uncomfortably in a kind of fetal position. It's not that we were expecting a crash; there just was no room for our legs. Narrow rows of seats easily accommodated the shorter Asians, but the longer legs of the Western veterinarians onboard poked into the seats ahead of them inadvertently massaging the backs of fellow passengers as we crossed the wide Pacific.

Six of us had volunteered with Christian Veterinary Mission, an American-based organization, to travel to Mongolia to ascertain the possibility of future involvement in this recently opened country. We were a diverse lot of practitioners and academians, as well as industrial and laboratory veterinarians. Interestingly, it was my dubious reputation as a sheep producer that secured this invitation to the historic land of Genghis Khan. Mutton (lamb) was, after all, the Mongolians' favorite dish.

Our plans were to spend three weeks training Mongolian veterinarians while attempting to determine if this would be a place where Western veterinarians might be effective in helping to restore a once-vigorous animal economy. We could not help but wonder if we would be allowed to use our profession as a means to share the deep Christian beliefs and values we held dear. I admit there were moments during that first seemingly endless flight that I questioned why I had ever agreed to join this group.

First Things First

Our first days were filled with countless meetings between Mongolian officials and veterinarians in the capital city of Ulaanbaatar, but it was our visits into the countryside that we looked forward to the most. It was there that we witnessed the plight of herders firsthand. We were greatly impacted by the realization that this country was far behind the rest of the world in the teaching and practice of veterinary medicine and animal care. Yes, there were many practical lessons we could teach these veterinarians that would greatly improve production for their herder clients and allow them to offer safer, higher quality meat and milk products. We were overwhelmed by one singular impression: This was a land ripe for harvest, and veterinarians held the keys to God's heavenly combine.

At the end of our initial three-week stay, representatives from the government, the veterinary school, and the research and diagnostic laboratories hosted a special celebration in our honor. We gathered in excited anticipation of what we would experience. As it turned out, the other veterinarians from the West were seated with various groups around the room. However, I somehow was placed at the table of the Mongolian Director of Veterinary Services. While practicing veterinary medicine in a Gobi Desert state some years earlier, he had been kicked in the mouth by a camel. As a result, he now sported a row of shiny stainless-steel teeth. He looked like a character straight out of a James Bond movie!

Following the meal and obligatory speeches and usual words of appreciation, the entertainment began. Never had I witnessed such sights! One female contortionist displayed her ancient, seductive art of dancing while twisting her body into grotesque shapes. Then, an interesting-looking man took center stage swallowing fire like it was a part of his regular diet. As impressive as all this was to the naïve Westerners, it was the finale that shocked us the most. A number of women filed onto the stage and began to prance down the runway showing off the latest Mongolian fashions. All was going well until the last "lady" reached the end of the runway and had a complete wardrobe malfunction. She stepped out of her dress and high heels with a practiced and very dramatic flair. It was clear this was part of the show. As I quickly looked away from what I deemed an offensive show, I saw the mouths of the other Westerners fall open much as mine had done. My Mongolian counterpart seemed bewildered at our reaction. It was obvious that he appreciated this woman's "artistic" display.

What a predicament! I was just glad that no one was there to record our presence in the middle of a burlesque show as we sat with a can of beer on one side of our plates and a glass of vodka on the other. Each of us represented churches that would have been appalled if they had seen their short-term missionaries in such a compromising situation. As I left the hall, I felt disgusted and ashamed at having witnessed such a raunchy exhibition. Of course, our hosts had no way of knowing we would be offended. How could they? They had never met Christians before. I was determined to avoid similar questionable entertainment in the future.

Thankfully, we were able to make real progress on other pressing matters as we met with a number of Mongolian leaders in veterinary medicine during the final days of our stay. Our knowledge and vast experience would give us an inroad into this world—so clearly and principally in need of the Savior.

Where once I thought Frances and I had much to offer God, I

now realized that it was God who was the giver of all good gifts. I have learned to take my eyes off myself and focus them squarely on Him. It was a lesson in humility, one for which I am deeply grateful. We could not have known at the time the kind of sacrifices God would ask us to make, but in yielding to the Master Sculptor's hands, we found ourselves being shaped into vessels fit for His purposes.

The Spiritual Journey

> *Then I heard the voice of the Lord saying, "Whom shall I send? And who will go for us?" And I said, "Here am I. Send me!"*
>
> –Isaiah 6:8, NIV

On the return trip from Mongolia, our plane touched down in Los Angeles leaving the six veterinarians to find their separate ways home to various points across the United States. My flight continued to Raleigh, North Carolina where Frances eagerly waited to greet me. We had been out of contact for the three weeks I was in Mongolia, so as you might imagine, it was a sweet reunion.

"Frances," I blurted out, "I think God may be calling us to Mongolia as long-term missionaries!" Without missing a beat, she replied, "Perhaps He is calling you, but I am not so sure that He's calling me." We still chuckle about that even today, for little did we suspect this trip would change us forever. Only later would we discover that it would also change the lives of thousands of men, women and children in this beautiful land so far from everything and everyone we had ever known. God had far more in mind than we could ever have envisioned.

In the end, we were forced to ask ourselves if we would be able to walk away from family and friends and all the conveniences of our life in the States. Would we be able to leave our flourishing veterinary practice and move halfway around the globe? It is one thing to have a dream. It is quite another to act on it. I confess that while in Mongolia the impact of meeting these precious people, and what it might mean for our future, was a singularly personal adventure. I had no time to consider how all this might affect Frances who had yet to see this strange, new land, or meet its people. Over the next few days, though, I was able to share the totality of my experiences with her.

I was convinced that God had uniquely prepared both of us to reach these semi-nomadic herders using their close contact and dependence on their animals as a conduit. I prayed she would feel the same. As we sought God for His leading, every signpost pointed in one direction—Mongolia.

Looking Back

> *Consider it pure joy, my brothers and sisters, whenever you face trials of many kinds, because you know that the testing of your faith produces perseverance. Let perseverance finish its work so that you may be mature and complete, not lacking anything.*
>
> –James 1:2–4, NIV

El Toro…

There are a variety of dangers associated with this animal-doctoring profession. A rather large one was standing right before me at my practice in rural western Virginia. A massive black bull with rippling cords of rigidly tensed muscles stood defiant with strands of saliva hanging from his mouth. He had a foul disposition and fiery eyes to match, leaving no doubt as to his willingness to challenge anyone who might dare approach him.

It seemed this magnificent animal had been grazing around various pieces of old equipment when he accidentally stepped into the small center hole of a 50-pound metal wheel. Unfortunately, his hoof spread preventing him from stepping free of the heavy object. Obviously angry, he flailed about wildly swinging the chunk of steel encircling his leg like a tight wedding band. There was a great deal of reluctance to getting close enough to intervene as the poor beast dragged his enormous burden along with each step. Even when someone did muster sufficient courage to try to free the poor creature, his fierce reaction made us conclude that El Toro was completely opposed to the idea of us freeing him from his burden. He valiantly continued to fight the good fight until we were finally able to rope and anesthetize the bellowing creature. Ultimately, I was able to remove the massive encumbrance and set him free to roam the green pastures once again.

Like the bull, we sometimes balk and strain against God's attempts to set us free. It is only when He gives us a passion and desire to give up the very things that weigh us down that we realize He knows best after all. I am so glad Frances and I chose to give up the temporal things in our life to follow Him into a new and exciting life filled with rip-roaring, hair-raising adventure in His service.

Rare is the wife who is able to make the break from the security of home and move far away from children and grandchildren, parents, a much-loved church, and all things familiar and comforting. Frances, however, never wavered in her decision to do so from the moment we started the journey. Step-by-step, we moved together down a road we never dreamed we would be traveling.

Indeed, this land seemed like a land that time forgot. It was exciting for us to experience a life that had changed very little over the millennia. However, it was not the physical destination that was the most intriguing and satisfying to us, but rather the spiritual journey along the way with God leading us as a father leads his little children by the hand. Today, Mongolia is our home, and we deeply miss it when we are not there.

A Road Less Traveled

I was attending the University of Georgia School of Veterinary Medicine in 1967 when, during the summer break prior to my final year, Frances and I decided to visit Colorado State University Veterinary School. We also planned to search out other western points of interest to include Yellowstone Park and various attractions in Montana. We were in awe of the beauty of the mountains and valleys around Bozeman, Montana. Seeing those mountains made us realize we no longer had a desire to live and practice in the Blue Ridge Mountains of North Carolina. We had fallen in love with the wide-open West! There was only one problem: How would we, a naïve young couple from the east coast, find a reason to move across the United States?

I still have a clear memory of the day our answer came. It is as fresh as if it happened yesterday. On a cold Saturday morning in

February, a phone call brought an offer for an internship at Fort Collins, Colorado. Of course, I quickly accepted. This is what we had dreamed about! We could barely contain our excitement as we danced around the room. Our dreams were becoming reality.

Time passed quickly, and when my one-year contract in Colorado ended, we moved to Bozeman, Montana to open our first veterinary practice. Fortunately, Frances landed a teaching position with a salary sufficient to stave off starvation long enough for the business to take root and grow. As you might guess, I rarely had the opportunity to treat sheep during my veterinary training in Georgia. In fact, I only remember seeing a couple of these wooly creatures during my entire four years of school.

Who Could Fall in Love with a Smelly Sheep?

One early Sunday morning while in Bozeman, we received a call from a local rancher by the name of Charlie Sales. He had an unfortunate ewe in distress who was unable to deliver her young. "Sure, I will come have a look," I said, "but I really don't know very much about sheep." Well, it was love at first sight as I untangled what seemed like a plethora of tiny hooves to gently deliver two sparkling white lambs. In no time at all, the mother licked each one dry and nudged them up onto their unsteady legs before guiding them to their first meal. In gratitude for my assistance, Mrs. Sales caught a plump hen and prepared a scrumptious dinner of fried chicken and fresh garden vegetables. Over the meal, the conversation quite naturally turned to the subject of raising sheep. One thing led to another, and before we knew it, we had our own farm stocked with Columbian ewes and rams.

Some years later, our love of sheep took us to New Zealand where I secured a teaching position at Massey University Veterinary Department in the town of Palmerston North. This gave me a unique opportunity to research sheep-production diseases, a subject of which I knew very little. Although we didn't know it at the time, this knowledge would come in handy in the years ahead.

Two weeks after our arrival in New Zealand, we attended a service at Central Baptist Church with its newly completed building project. As only God could have planned it, the church was actively looking for ways to expand their ministries using this new facility. One day, at an after-church meeting, Frances and I shyly raised our hands to tell of our experience in working with international students while on faculty at Kansas State University in the late 70's. We wondered if this was a ministry the church might embrace. Indeed, they did so eagerly, and we made plans to launch a new hospitality outreach to campus students from Singapore, Malaysia, Indonesia and Mainland China.

As part of the ongoing ministry, we held Sunday morning meetings and scheduled visits to church members' homes where students were given the opportunity to taste New Zealand cuisine. In addition, we arranged for them to visit working farms and dairies. This ministry thrived and continued to expand even after we left New Zealand two years later. It was such a joy to learn later that the church decided to expand its reach by launching a new Chinese Church in order to better meet the needs of the students from that country. We were thrilled to know that we had been part of building God's Kingdom in New Zealand.

Tapestry of Life

In the late 1970s, we had the privilege of spending time on the Navajo reservation in Aneth, Utah assisting the people with their livestock. At the same time, we offered encouragement to their small church. Our new friends among the Navajo Christian population included a number of the *Begay* tribal families. I remember one grandmother by the name of Lucile, who could always be found sitting before her weaving frame making beautiful rugs. When we asked where she got her patterns, she told us they were stored in her head. The first part of each rug was always rolled tightly on the frame as she put the final touches on her masterpieces. It wasn't until she unrolled a rug that we could see its beautiful symmetrical patterns defined by threads of glorious color made from the dyes she extracted from local berries and plants.

I can't help but believe this is how God works with His children. It is only in the finished product that we see how each thread of our life is intricately fashioned into a tapestry worthy to carry out His master plan. In our case, each experience in working with sheep and the Asian international students became the backdrop for future ministry with the Mongolian people. The dark threads of pain and disappointment along with the bright hues of joyful experiences were required to complete a design capable of bringing glory to Him.

Figure 2.1. "Lost Again"—van lost in the night

Chapter 2

You Mean Me, God?

> *"Pardon me, my lord," Gideon replied, "but how can I save Israel? My clan is the weakest in Manasseh, and I am the least in my family."*
>
> –Judges 6:15, NIV

There is a myth that goes something like this: Missionaries are special, favored of God, a chosen people. One of our church families posted our prayer card on their refrigerator door. Their young son did a double-take one day as he stopped by for his milk and cookies. He screamed, "Mom, Mom, what are the Mitchums doing on our refrigerator door?" We had invaded the sanctity of that hallowed place reserved for those mystical saints of God who visit the church every three years when back on furlough. We had been elevated to the level of sainthood, but, you see, John really knew the truth about us—we were just like everybody else in the church. It was shortly after we moved to Mongolia as the New Year of 1996 began, that I wrote to John to explain why our photo was posted in his kitchen:

> Dear John,
>
> I've tried to change. Honestly I have. Every January I promised myself and sometimes God that I would be a more righteous person; I would care more for others; I would be less judgmental, and I would be more understanding. Unfortunately, those New Year resolutions were usually short-lived.
>
> You see, John, change doesn't really come from me. It comes from God. He promised that if I will allow Him, He will make me into a new creature. This happens when I ask Christ to live His life through me.

Then, John, once we trust Jesus, we become a new person in God's view. We want to be like you perceive the people on the refrigerator to be. God describes this as a potter working with a lump of clay. He wants to mold us into a useful vessel designed to fit His purposes. Of course, even after we have accepted God's offer of Jesus as our Savior, most of us want to continue to control our own lives. The hardest thing we must learn is to rest in Him.

Many years ago, I had an old black dog that stayed in my office. He was about the laziest thing you have ever seen. He stretched out on the carpet becoming one with the floor. I think God wants you and me to be like my dog, but in a spiritual sense. He wants us to totally rest in Him; to stretch out, relax and let Him take over our life.

I've thought a lot about it, John, and I think there are really only two differences between regular Christians and missionary Christians. The first one is that missionary Christians get their pictures put on refrigerator doors. The second difference is that God places foreign missionaries where we can't control our lives regardless of how hard we try.

Please pray that we will always lean on our Heavely Father.

Your friend,

Gerald

The Voice of God

If the Lord delights in a man's way, he makes his steps firm.

–Psalm 37:23, NIV

Listening to the voice of God is not easy in this world filled with the noises of modern life; children being bussed from soccer to violin lessons, basketball and football games being followed by a quick meal before youth night at church. During times of trouble, it is easy to remember to seek a quiet place with God. However, He wants consistent time with us even when everything is going well. He wants to share the smooth roads of our life as well as those marked by broken pavement and potholes. He longs to direct our lives to help us avoid unnecessary pitfalls.

After our move to Mongolia, we were returning from a long countryside trip and decided to stop at a particularly beautiful place to spend the night. It was a warm summer evening, and the wind had already gone to bed. In fact, it was so pleasant we didn't bother with tents but simply spread sleeping bags on the ground. On a hillside, several hundred feet away, a flock of sheep and goats was grazing under the watchful eye of their shepherd. The quiet was awe-inspiring in this serene paradise away from all the modern technology that fills our world with noise. Listening carefully, I could hear the faint sound of sheep and goats that I seldom hear when even closer to them.

Have you ever looked into the mouth of a sheep or goat? It is quite a surprise the first time you examine the front teeth of these small ruminants. They look like an old grandpa who has his false teeth soaking in a glass beside his bed for the night. It is almost as if God forgot to give these creatures upper front teeth. Instead they have a dental pad on top, and as they graze, they clamp the grass against this pad with their lower incisors. They can't bite the grass off, so they twist their head quickly to snap the grass. It was this sound I heard in the distance that night under the stars. Just as we were able to hear their sounds in the stillness of the night, we can hear God's still, small voice when we remove ourselves from the hustle, bustle and noise of everyday life.

Ruminants are mammals that are able to acquire nutrients from plant-based food by fermenting it in a specialized stomach prior to digestion, principally through microbial actions.

Jesus set the example for His disciples and for us. He often went away to a quiet place to be alone with His Father. When the world was on His shoulders and He faced His greatest trials, He slipped away to be with God. Mark records this in his Gospel: *"They went to a place called Gethsemane, and Jesus said to his disciples, 'Sit here while I pray,'"* (Mark 14:32, NIV).

When God had a message for the prophet Elijah, He did not come to him in the deafening noise of the wind, nor did He come in the violent sounds of an earthquake, or the crackling of a roaring fire. He came quietly as if in a low whisper. We may want to see great events, signs and wonders to impress our sensibilities, but if we are going to hear from God, we must turn off the noise and tune in to Him.

A New Land

> *The Lord had said to Abram, "Leave your country, your people and your father's household and go to the land I will show you."*
>
> –Genesis 12:1, NIV

This daunting sound, a clarion call from God, reverberates through the prospective missionary. "Come follow me to a land that is completely foreign to you in every way," He says. "Come away with me. Leave your mother and father, sisters and brothers, children and grandchildren, friends and church, work and your country. Come—and follow me."

There has always been a great need in the United States and other nations for Christian witnesses. This was part of the struggle we faced as we looked to God for direction in a decision that would take us into a strange culture in this faraway land.

A farm one-third the size of the United States with no cross-fencing became my new veterinary practice area. In fact, there were virtually no fences in the entire country of Mongolia except those needed to keep the flocks of sheep and goats, vast herds of cattle and yak and camels and horses from venturing onto the railroad tracks. Sometimes the ground appeared to be moving as flocks and herds moved off the hillsides into the night protection of ger-dotted valleys. (A ger is a tent like structure used by Mongolian herders. see notes) Herds of horses drifted across the steppe in a solid mass.[1]

Imagine for a moment an earlier time across the western prairies and mountains of America when Native Americans roamed freely through the oceans of waving grass. It was a time when buffalo were not merely intended for the pleasure of summer spectators in parks, but were, instead, a necessary food source for the inhabitants of the land. Like the early natives, Mongolians also depend on grass to fatten their animals so that they, in turn, can provide enough meat, fiber and hides to sustain the semi-nomadic way of life. This life of much beauty and harshness, laughter and pain is as different from today's American suburbs as the distant planets in the night sky.

Unlikely Choice

When I read about the hardships of the missionaries of past eras, I can't help but think how easy we have it today. It is possible to fly back and forth from the mission field to our homeland where we are surrounded with support and lots of encouragement. We also have instant access to email service anywhere on the globe. If need be, we can Skype with people across the ocean to see the faces of our families in real time. However, with all the conveniences of technology and rapid travel, a call to global missions remains intimidating.

I once had an English Pointer dog named Beck. Now, this dog proved to be a great friend to help me through my turbulent high school years. On any given afternoon, after the last school bell of the day, I could be found following Beck over the fields and through the dales of my native North Carolina. She crisscrossed in front of me with a beauty and grace that only a bird hunter could appreciate. As much as I loved her, Beck had an aggravating habit that frustrated me to the point of exasperation. If the birds were scarce, she would wander farther and farther away from me. I could scream until my throat was raw, but to no avail. Oh, Beck heard me well enough, but chose to act as though she was stone deaf. She responded to my commands at close range, but when the distance between us increased, I had absolutely no influence on her.

So it is with God's call. When we are far from Him, we are less likely to hear, much less respond. "I'm doing fine out here by myself," we say. "I will come back when I feel the need." Even when we do want to hear His voice, we expect an instant response to our questions concerning what He wants us to do and what direction He wants us to take. God's clear and concise answer is simply, "I want you closer to Me. I want you walking by My side, and then the place will not be so important. You will be with Me."

All to God

> *As they were walking along the road, a man said to him, "I will follow you wherever you go." Jesus replied, "Foxes have holes and birds of the air have nests, but the Son of Man has no place to lay his head."*
>
> –Luke 9:57–58, NIV

We knock on the door of global missions. When it opens, we enter carrying all our earthly belongings with us, and nail them to the Cross. Yes; we respond to the call of Christ, but it still takes time to adjust to having little of our former selves along with us. In truth, it is the same whether you stay in America, or like us, move to Mongolia. What He wants from each of us is far more than our earthly possessions, family, or friends. He wants all of us on the altar—mind, body and spirit. Oswald Chambers expressed it this way:

> "You were looking for a great thing to give up. God is telling you of some things; but at the back of it there lies the central citadel of **obstinacy**; I will not give up my right to myself—the thing God intends you to give up if ever you are going to be a disciple of Jesus Christ." [2]

Bound to Earth

> *A certain ruler asked him, "Good teacher, what must I do to inherit eternal life?" ...When Jesus heard this, he said to him, "You still lack one thing. Sell everything you have to give to the poor, and you will have treasure in heaven. Then come, follow me."*
>
> –Luke 18:18, 22, NIV

We do not suddenly become super saints by giving up what should have never controlled us in the first place. Think for a moment of what Jesus was asking of the rich young ruler. (See Matthew 19:16-26; Mark 10:17-27.) He was trying to draw him away from everything that kept him bound to the earth and away from Him. Jesus requires the same of us today. He wants us to break ties with anything that prevents us from following Him.

A number of our Mongolian staff have visited the United States over the years. They are always amazed as they tour the homes of their hosts. Often, they choose to sleep on the hard floor beside a comfortable bed with its soft, inviting mattress. They feel the bed is just too luxurious for them.

One of the young veterinarians we sent to the States to study for a month returned with an interesting observation. He visited several hospitable families in their average American homes. The part of the house that he found most fascinating was not the kitchen with all its time-saving gadgets and well-stocked shelves, nor was it the fancy dining room, or the opulent living room. It wasn't even the cozy den with the glowing fireplace, or the private bedroom with an indoor bathroom. No, the part of the house that most intrigued him was the garage. Yes, the garage! He was absolutely shocked with the overflowing two-car garages with no room for the cars. They were inevitably filled with mowers, golf clubs, bicycles, and boxes and boxes of things long since relegated to storage. He could not believe all the extra things that Americans accumulate and seldom use.

Get Ready, Go!

> *We are therefore Christ's ambassadors, as though God were making his appeal through us. We implore you on Christ's behalf: Be reconciled to God.*
>
> –2 Corinthians 5:20, NIV

One of the last books we read before leaving America was *Experiencing God* by Henry Blackaby and Claude King. I was certain this book was written just for Frances and me because it came off the press shortly before God began speaking to us about going to Mongolia. There were seven realities covered in this book, and, although all were important, two of them spoke loud and clear to us.

Reality Number One: God is at work around you. God was in Mongolia long before we arrived there. Atheism was a foreign concept to the Mongolian herders who lived so close to the land and saw God in the wind, the trees, the sky and their animals. These people of the land knew how to see God in all of His creation:

> *Since what may be known about God is plain to them, because God has made it plain to them. For since the creation of the world God's invisible qualities—his eternal power and divine nature—have been clearly seen, being understood from what has been made, so that people are without excuse.*
>
> –Romans 1:19–20, NIV

In the 1920's, Russians marched into this defenseless country and stole the soul of the Mongolian people. They tried to force their brand of atheism on them and began to systematically destroy everything that suggested there might be a god. They killed most of the Buddhist lamas or filled concentration camps with these peaceful religious leaders. Hardly a family was left untouched by such a ruthless practice. Only a few Buddhist temples remained standing as testimony to the time before the Soviet Empire swallowed up much of Mongolia's history.

The idea that the Soviet Union could expel God was ludicrous, yet that is exactly what they attempted to do. Buddhism was the dominate religion before the Soviets took control of Mongolia. Although this was a religion in which followers tried to achieve status with their gods through their own works, it did, at least, recognize the existence of a god.

A Mongolian man sat across from me in a ger one day and lamented,

> "The Buddhists were here, and they said that the way to 'God' was to follow the teachings of Buddha. The Russians came and said there is no God. Now you Christians come and say that Jesus Christ is the only way to God. *I just want to know the truth.*"

A second principle that impacted us was *Reality Number Three* of *Experiencing God*: *God invites you to become involved with Him in*

His work. This God of the universe was asking us to join Him in His plan to reach the people of Mongolia with the love and message of His Son. [3] Imagine that!

Gideon is one of my favorite Old Testament characters. It is not because he slew thousands with only a handful of men, or even because of his leadership as a judge. Rather, it is the humble beginnings of this man God chose to deliver his people from camel-riding, relentless aggressors that speaks to my soul. The book, *Hearts of Iron, Feet of Clay* by Gary Inrig, describes the pitiful state of this man God called to carry out His purpose:

> There was never a less likely liberator than **Gideon**, the son of Joash, a man from the tribe of Manasseh and the clan of Abiezer.
>
> But, when we met Gideon, he was threshing wheat by beating it with a stick in a winepress. Normally, a man would thresh wheat on a wooden threshing floor, using a threshing sledge pulled by oxen. The floor would be by a wheat field, in an exposed place, so that the wind could carry away the chaff. Only the very poorest people would have so little wheat that they would thresh it by beating. Yet that was exactly what Gideon was doing. In a hidden winepress, under a tree, beating out a few sheaves of wheat, he desperately tries to save the little bit of food that he had from the Midianites. It was the picture of a defeated, discouraged man filled with doubts and fears. The man under the oak in Ophrah was no hero! [4]

I Am Not a Prophet

> *Amos answered Amaziah, "I was neither a prophet nor a prophet's son, but I was a shepherd, and I also took care of sycamore-fig trees.*
>
> –Amos 7:14, NIV

Why was God directing us to Mongolia, and how would He

use a veterinarian and a teacher in what He was doing there? These were the questions ringing in our ears. We were to learn that our credentials were not a priority with God. If God could use Amos, a sheepherder, was it possible that He could also use us? Dr. Charles Stanley has a list of forty principles in his *Life Principles Bible.* Principle number ten is: "If necessary, God will move heaven and earth to show us His will." He lists nine areas that God may use to get our attention as He desires to give us direction. 1) A restless spirit, 2) A spoken word, 3) An unusual blessing, 4) Unanswered prayer, 5) Disappointment, 6) Extraordinary circumstances, 7) Defeat, 8) Financial troubles, 9) Tragedy, sickness, and affliction. [5]

It is unthinkable that a loving God who cares deeply and wants a close relationship with his children would ever hide His will from us. What we often fail to realize is that while God may not always speak to us directly, He may very well choose to use difficult circumstances to prepare us and guide us to our next assignment. No matter how He communicates His will, He will never fail to reveal His will to us in His time. Make no mistake; He is always on time.

A Roadless Path

The constant twisting and jarring of the Russian vehicle on countryside trips without roads takes its toll on both human and truck bodies. These vehicles are similar in design and construction to American cars made in the 1930s and 1940s. They are prone to breakdowns, so it is essential to have a driver who is also a skilled mechanic.

Drivers in Mongolia are part of a strong and proud profession and are paid more than doctors in many cases. Their value is hard to estimate since sometimes they are all that stands between the traveler and death. Extreme winters, temperamental springs, along with autumns and their unexpected early snowfalls can result in life-threateningly harsh conditions just over the next rise, or around the bend.

Lost Again

It was a cold day as we drove through the valleys on our way to a small village. Getting lost was not all that uncommon.

In fact, it happened to us almost every time we traveled to a new place because there were no road signs to direct us. Some of my fondest memories are of those adventures we had while lost in the Mongolian countryside. When all else failed, we would stop at a ger along the way to spend half an hour drinking suutei tsai (salty milk tea) while listening to the lengthy instructions of an old herder as he pointed with his chin to show us how to reach our destination.

The single door of each ger always faces south and serves as a compass when the sun or stars are behind the clouds. During one particular trip, all the herders had already moved away from their summer grazing sites in the valleys. There were no "ger-compasses" and no one to give directions. The sky darkened, and it soon became difficult to follow tire tracks in the deeply rutted road. Eventually, we saw a pinpoint of light on the side of a mountain. We turned from the valley to find its source while winding our way up a steep grade where two gers were nestled on the side of the slope. It was indeed a relief to find someone who could give us directions. One woman came to the door, and we greeted her from our van with the usual question, "Does your dog bite?" Wolves were common, and dogs were kept to protect the livestock. These dogs sometimes mistake strangers for thieves, so we wanted to make sure the dog was friendly, or at least securely tied. The woman graciously gave us directions, and soon we were on our way arriving only an hour past the time the anxious herders expected us.

We completed our work in a few days, so we decided to get an early start back to Ulaanbaatar the next day. It was pitch black when we left, and we soon found ourselves hopelessly lost. Again. We drove back and forth looking for the road that we had followed on our way to the village. Once more, we saw a ger in the distance and drove to it to ask for directions. The door flew open, and to our utter surprise there was the same woman who had given us directions several nights before. She was incredulous when she saw the same lost faces. "Just wait a few minutes while I get my things, and I will just go with you and show you the way." We were never lost again on that trip. Our guide gave clear directions at every turn making sure we successfully arrived at our destination.

We often struggle to know God's will for our lives and His plan for our future. That is not really a preeminent need. With God at the wheel, we don't really have to know His plan or His will. If we are walking beside Him every day, we don't have to know where He is going. We simply need to stay close to Him and hang on to His hand. Following Jesus is much easier than trying to anticipate and navigate every twist and turn of life without Him.

For if you remain silent at this time, relief and deliverance for the Jews will arise from another place, but you and your father's family will perish. And who knows but that you have come to your royal position for such a time as this?–Esther 4:14, NIV

The story of Esther is a great account of deliverance for God's people. This Hebrew woman was thrust into a position of royalty in Persia at exactly the right time to save her people whom the Babylonians took into exile after their destruction of Judah. If she had said no to her divine mission, God could certainly have found another way to accomplish His purposes. However, because she was willing to face extreme danger and had the courage to step out in faith, Esther has become a symbol of strength and obedience for thousands of people through the centuries.

I think about God's timing for Frances and me, and how we fit into His plan for us. We went to Mongolia at exactly the perfect time. Perhaps, we were prepared for such a time as this after all.

Although Frances had reservations when I first told her about God's call on my life, she willingly took the plunge with me. We have now been in this ministry for more than 23 years, and our partnership has been a major reason for our success. God has used her in quiet ways to accomplish extraordinary things for Him. We have no doubt that we were called to be a missionary couple on His mission field in Mongolia.

Why would God choose us with all our blemishes and warts, inabilities and inexperience, lack of training and theological education to carry the precious gospel message to a people who had not yet heard His good news—we cannot fathom. What we do know, however, is that God does not look for perfection, but rather for availability. Author Mark Batterson wrote in his book, *The Circle Maker–God doesn't call the qualified; He qualifies the called.* We have definitely found that to be the case.[6]

Notes:

1. The Mongolia ger (or yur*t* in Russia) is made for mobility. These nomadic herders usually move at least four times each year as they follow the grass to feed their animals. The *ger* has a wooden frame that is easily assembled and disassembled. A wheel with 81 spokes radiating from the wheel forms the top. The top rests on a lattice wall. Inside the *ger* there is a central stove, one door, and no windows. The diameter is 22 feet, and the wall is 5 feet high with two posts supporting the central wheel. The frame is covered with felt for insulation and canvas to help shed rain. The outside covering is made of white cotton.

2. Chambers, O. (1992). *My Utmost for His Highest*. (Discovery House Publishers, Grand Rapids, Michigan), devotional for September 24, p. 268.

3. Blackaby, H. T., & King, C.V. (1994). *Experiencing God: How to Live the Full Adventure of Knowing and Doing the Will of God*. (Broadman & Holman Publishers, Nashville, Tenn) Pp. 33, 35.

4. Inrig, G. (1979). *Hearts of Iron, Feet of Clay*. (The Moody Bible Institute, Chicago, Illinois) Pp. 88–89.

5. Stanley, C.F. (2009). *The Life Principles Bible, NASB*, II Chr. 20:12, loc 35302–35345, (Thomas Nelson Publishers, Nashville, Tennessee), Kindle Book.

6. Batterson, Mark (2014). *The Circle Maker*. https://goodreads.com/quotes/1233972.

Figure 3.1. "Hooked for Life" —Ganzo catching one fish

Chapter 3

Touch Down

> *Trust in the LORD with all your heart and lean not on your own understanding; in all your ways submit to him, and he will make your paths straight.*
>
> –Proverbs 3:5–6, NIV

It was a disconcerting day when Frances and I arrived at the airport in Ulaanbaatar, Mongolia in August 1995. We entered a dark, dreary building—the Mongolian International Airport. It was an old structure, and it had no electricity at that time. The luggage conveyer belt was disabled, so the luggage was delivered by truck and unceremoniously dumped in a pile. We scrambled between the other travelers to claim our bags before they followed another passenger out the door of the terminal.

We knew that supplies were limited in the meagerly stocked stores after the exit of the Russians, so we came prepared with our household collection of essentials packed in ten suitcases. Sheets, dishes, towels, and silverware were scattered among our warm winter clothing. No smiling face waited at the gate to greet us. No one held a sign, "WELCOME MITCHUMS." Eventually, though, a timid, American man sauntered into the airport to meet us. He put our treasures in a van and took us to our fourth-floor apartment in an old, drab Russian building. We soon discovered that homeless people frequently slept in the stairwell. It reminded us of American slums. We thought, "Welcome to Mongolia—what have we gotten ourselves into?"

Even though our initial welcome at the airport was less than we might have liked, a more enthusiastic greeting committee was waiting for us at our new home. Unfortunately, we also had a welcoming committee of big, nasty roaches that scurried about in the night. Although we did try, we soon learned that it was impossible to eradicate these permanent pests because they travelled from apartment to apartment through breathing holes in the concrete walls. Spraying one room only caused them to move to the next-door neighbor only to return after the pesticide had run its course.

Our apartment with its two small bedrooms, living room/dining room, and tiny kitchen was noticeably unkempt at first. Actually, we were surprised the roaches would even choose to live there. Several months after our arrival, we painted and wallpapered the entire apartment and bought colorful Mongolian rugs, pictures of the countryside and decorative curtains to hang on the windows. This was going to be our home for the next eight years, so we might as well make it pleasant.

The Roach and the Missionary

One evening, as we curled up in our cozy apartment, a little rhyme in honor of our permanent guests flowed from my pen:

The Roach And The Missionary

What of the life of the chosen of God,
Those who would serve Him on foreign sod,
Those who could help fulfill His commission,
This is the call to a strange distant mission.
How holy it seems and how sacrificial,
This godly life that's so consequential,
As we strive for a witness without reproach,
We open the cabinet and there is that roach.

Roach:
For over a month the water's been cold,
No heat in the building forthcoming you're told,
Why do you stay in this difficult place,
It is weary and tired that I see in your face.

Missionary:
The days run full with the many requests,
There's cooking and cleaning along with the rest,
For time with Him my spirit does yearn,
But when all is through, there's still language to learn.

Roach:
Things will slow down now or that's what they think,
Watch as I push them right over the brink,
Some problems with health, just one more small blow,
It's homeward I'll send them on early furlough.

Missionary:
Oh, how wonderful to serve Him here,
His Word may never have touched their ear,
God loves them more than we can know,
He has asked that we come and tell them so.

Roach:
Hot water at last, you're the luckiest ones,
With bubble bath in, what glorious fun,
Of course, you know I will have the last laugh,
Just look at me now here I am in your bath.

Missionary:
Don't you look now but you're caught in the whirl,
Good-bye little friend, you're starting to twirl,
With God's help we'll stay here and He'll be our coach,
We'll not be dismissed by a tiny cockroach.

When Frances opened the refrigerator that first day, she found our fare for the weekend. Bread, jam and strange-tasting cheese decked the shelves. Oh yes; a jar of precious coffee was placed next to the fridge on the counter. As we were obviously on our own, we left our apartment on Monday morning in search of some meat and veggies.

The walk into the city took us over broken pavement, uncovered manholes, large puddles from recent downpours, dilapidated buildings with peeling paint, and broken windows. Stucco exteriors were crumbling, and every faded-gray apartment building was an exact replica of the one next-door. Street signs hung precariously from posts. Garbage lay stacked against the apartment walls or strewn around by packs of stray dogs as they fought over rotting morsels. Small flocks of sheep, goats, horses, and scrawny cows mowed the patches of grass along the medians. A few men on horseback travelled deserted streets while antiquated Russian vehicles languished on the concrete. Some were under repair right where they gasped their last breath, while others were stopped in their tracks without fuel. It was a rare one that rolled along the road. Ulaanbaatar was a neglected city.

Frances and I entered sagging doors of unnamed stores to inspect the few items that rested on rickety, sparsely-stocked shelves. There were multiple stalls with individual vendors who ignored the waiting customers competing for the limited supply of food. Hours later, we found ourselves exhausted but contented. It had been a profitable hunting trip. We returned to our new home with backpacks partially filled with gritty bread, cooking oil, butter, eggs, a large jar of Bulgarian cabbage-veggie mix, potatoes, measures of sugar and rice scooped into bags and a much-needed broom and cleaning detergent. We elected to become temporary vegetarians after eyeing the market's unrefrigerated, smelly meat covered with flies on blood-splattered tables.

A few days after our shaky arrival, our guardian angel appeared in the person of a sturdy, young Danish lady who lived a couple of stairwells away from us in the same building. Greta proved to be a blessing beyond description as she taught Frances the ropes of shopping and general life in Mongolia. She was with Joint Christian Services—a consortium of 16 mission agencies working under the same umbrella. This was the same organization that had invited us to this country. Greta would become a dear friend to us over the years.

I was initially asked to work with the *Mongolian Herder's Association*, a group organized by the Konrad Adenauer Foundation, to assist the privatized herders. During the Soviet era the government owned all livestock. Later, this herders' organization deteriorated into a cooperative with a dubious mission. However, during the time we worked with the association, it was an enormous benefit to us as we explored the countryside. This experience gave me a much-needed education on how to survive and work in remote Mongolia.

One early adventure took us to the Middle Gobi where we treated hundreds of cashmere goats. Their beautiful hair makes a soft, scratch-proof fabric. The hair from these goats is not sheared like sheep wool but is raked with a wire comb. This cashmere is the most valuable livestock product in Mongolia, and it is sold all over the world. When we first came to this country, we discovered that Chinese traders were cheating many of the herders. Instead of paying them with money, they gave them trinkets and vodka in exchange for their precious cashmere.

On one trip to visit a Gobi family, we stopped at a ger along the way. During the warm months, the interior of gers becomes unbearably hot as the sun bears down on the insulating felt. It is the practice of these nomadic herders to roll up the skirt of their home to allow air to circulate across the floor. Meat and butter are often stored under the beds just inside the circular perimeter. As we approached, I watched a dog grab a juicy leg-of-lamb from underneath the side of the ger before running for his life. The children poured out the door in hot pursuit of the poor canine criminal. Eventually, they ran him to ground. You guessed it; the chunk of meat that was retrieved from the dog was cooked for our evening meal.

Mongolia Veterinary College

On my first trip to Mongolia in 1994, after meeting with faculty of the Agricultural University, I was invited to help the Mongolian Veterinary College with their development. Now, having come back to Mongolia with my wife, but with no organized project, we decided to visit the dean of the school who invited us to teach English and veterinary medicine. A month after arriving in Mongolia, I had a class of veterinary students, and Frances had one English class for students and one for the faculty.

The school building was in need of fresh paint. Its classrooms were dirty and dark with poor lighting and old, broken desks. Floors were covered with uneven planks, and rooms were always uncomfortably cold. Primitive bathrooms were indescribably nasty. Frances didn't dare drink coffee before her teaching sessions. She avoided having to use the toilet at all costs.

Magsar was a veterinarian working as a part-time translator for the *Mongolian Herders Association*. I needed a translator to accompany me on remote trips, and Frances needed one for her English lessons at the veterinary school. Thankfully, Magsar took on the responsibilities as our first full-time translator. He had an old, burgundy Mercedes that was likely stolen in Germany and driven thousands of miles across Russia to Mongolia. At least, that was a common practice after the fall of the Soviet Union. Money was scarce, and Magsar's car was always running low or out of fuel. He kept a jug in the trunk and would frequently leave Frances to watch his vehicle while he ran to a station to get another few liters. It was November 1995 when Magsar asked Jesus into his life and became the first of our Mongolian friends to embrace the faith.

One cold, October day in 1995, Frances entered the classroom and looked for a place to hang her coat. She saw two stout electrical wires protruding from the smoky wall and thought, "This is the perfect place." As she reached out with her coat, Magsar grabbed her arm—possibly preventing her execution. The wires turned out to be a dangerous, albeit convenient, light switch. It only required putting the two ends together to turn on the lights.

We discovered that there had never been a Christian influence at the school. It was obvious that a great ministry opportunity awaited us with students who came from almost every state in Mongolia. Reaching these students with the gospel was a strategic way to disperse the Good News throughout the country as many eventually returned to their families and homeland. We were warned, however, to be careful about sharing the Christian message.

Frances decided to highlight American holidays in her classes leading up to Christmas as a natural way to share the Christmas story. October brought lessons on Halloween with Trick or Treat for students and the opportunity to cut squashes into jack-o-lanterns. Thanksgiving lessons focused on the Pilgrim's trip across the Atlantic Ocean, hardships on land, the celebration dinner with Native Americans as they thanked God for safety and provisions for the coming long winter. It was hard to believe the Mongolians were not familiar with anything about Christmas, yet that was the case. The students were introduced to Santa and his reindeer, decorations and presents, and colorfully decorated cakes and cookies. The emphasis, however, was on the real reason for the celebration of Christmas—Jesus.

Frances twisted my arm to teach three Christmas songs to my class and acquaint them with the story of Christmas in preparation for the party being planned. Our kitchen was tiny with no room for wasted steps. We could literally reach out and touch everything while standing in one spot. Small as it was, the room was filled with the wonderful aroma of holiday cooking as Frances plied her gift with the newly cleaned oven working overtime to turn out cakes and cookies in mass quantities.

Regardless, we were excited to learn that a new bakery had just opened a few blocks from us. We splurged and bought dozens of fried apple pies to supplement Frances' goodies. Our temporary driver at the time was a former KGB officer. His main job had been to train policemen in the skills of martial arts. Sometime during his career, his head had collided with an immovable object, and now a metal plate replaced a section of his skull. We sent him to get the bakery goods, and as he navigated our stairs, he tripped causing the fried pies to race down the stairway. Being resourceful, he quickly gathered them and blew off any debris. Thankfully, no one was the wiser.

It was an exciting time as our students created a Christmas extravaganza in one of the dreary classrooms. Faculty members were just as jubilant as the young veterinary students when the party began with the singing of Christmas songs. There were various competitions staged between the classes. Christmas crossword puzzles were handed out, games were played and gifts were shared. Frances made certain there was plenty of festive food to savor. Our afternoon ended with the most important part—a non-apologetic presentation of Jesus' birth. This was the start of their knowledge of Christ. The party was a huge success.

When Frances first began to teach, unsmiling faces stared at her each time she entered the classroom. One of those faces belonged to a young student named Zolaa. She was intelligent, attentive, and ambitious. Over time, she began to trust Frances more and more. An occasional smile graced Zolaa's face. It was during our first Christmas season in Mongolia that Zolaa first heard about the miraculous birth of this Savior born in Bethlehem. Curious to know more, she started attending one of the few churches in the city along with us, and later became the first Christian at the Veterinary School and worked with us after graduation.

During one summer school holiday, Zolaa led a group of Christian American and British veterinary students and professionals in an outreach to students and faculty at the Mongolian Veterinary School. These were some of the first short-term missionaries to work side-by-side with our national staff.

English classes, computer training, and veterinary terminology classes were taught, and close relationships were forged. Camping trips, dinners and games uniquely opened the door to share deep Christian values and truths. A number of students even accepted Jesus as their Savior. Eventually, these students graduated and were dispersed over Mongolia where they had the opportunity to share their life-changing experience. Zolaa included a recorded conversation with a student in her report:

> "One student asked if she could talk with me and ask some questions. She asked me if I really believed in Christ. I told her, 'Yes.' Then she asked, 'How do I worship Him, and how do I believe in Him?' Then she started to talk about her life, and she said she wanted to have a sister like me. I told her that if she would become a Christian, then she would be my sister. We talked for about two hours. At the end of this conversation, I prayed for her, and she received Christ. Now, God is changing her life."

What a joy it was to see these young disciples reaching their own people for Christ. Zolaa also shared the gospel with her sister, Manda, who was a veterinary student and the president of her class. She became a believer, and both helped us start our new organization. Some years later, Manda moved to Sweden with her husband and children where she attended Bible school. Today, she is a church leader and focuses on discipling the large Mongolian group of believers living in that country. Manda is modeling the Great Commission as she reaches out to Mongolians living in Sweden.

> An **NGO** is not directed by the federal, state, or local government, and is not-for-profit. NGO's are usually funded by donations from individuals, churches, trusts, and foundations; in our case, we established a business to move toward sustainability.

Zolaa continues to train rural people in public health using her extensive experience. She also serves on the Mongolian Board of Directors of our organization. A lot of water has passed over the dam since we first met Zolaa in 1995. She grew strong in her faith and became a leader of our organization. A few years later, Zolaa was invited to study at

Sydney University in Australia where she was involved in intensive training in campus ministry. She returned to Mongolia with her Master's Degree in Public Health on fire to share her faith with fellow countrymen.

V.E.T. Net Is Born

We called our little group of followers "Vet Net." At first, our outreach was mainly to veterinary students, but as we expanded and added teachers, accountants, artists, economists and translators to our team, we needed a name change. When we chose to become an **NGO (Non-Government Organization)** in 2003, we toyed with new names, but kept returning to the name "Vet Net." We already had name recognition throughout much of the country—it was our trademark. Finally, we chose to alter the name (and add a byline) to an acronym to represent the broader group.

Mongolia V.E.T. Net is registered as a public service non-government organization (NGO). The acronym stands for a *Network of Veterinarians and Educators Training professionals throughout Mongolia* to gain the opportunity to share the hope that is within us. The board of directors, leadership team, and staff are all Mongolians with Westerners serving as advisors.

In January 1996, we began inviting veterinary students to our apartment for Sunday dinner. We might as well have been clucking as we walked along the road from church to our apartment because a string of students began to follow us like a clutch of chicks might trail an old mother hen. Some went to church with us, but many just showed up for home cooking, fun, and fellowship. They were hungry for anything Western—English language, food, jeans, songs, games and movies. At that time, there was little in the way of entertainment—no cell phones or computer games, few television programs or videos.

One Sunday after Christmas, Enkee, one of our young female students, said to us, "My mother is a committed Buddhist. I don't want to dishonor her by going to church, but I would like to learn more about the Bible." That was the beginning of a Bible study that became part of our Sunday lunch meeting. This continued for several years until it completely outgrew our tiny apartment.

We discovered that Enkee's English was excellent. She and her father had studied this language together before our arrival. As a result, she was invited to accompany a Mongolian poultry producer and his wife when they visited America. When Enkee returned to Mongolia, she burst through the door of our little apartment with a glowing smile on her face. She had exciting news to share. On her return flight, she was seated beside a couple that befriended her and gave her a bible. She was thrilled as she told us about them and showed us her brand-new book. When we saw her treasure, our hearts skipped a beat in unison. The book she cuddled was not the Bible, but a copy of the *Book of Mormon*. We carefully explained to Enkee that this was not the real Bible, but instead, a false teaching with little historical evidence for its claims. Without hesitation, she relinquished her new book to us.

Some weeks later, Enkee sat in the corner of our living room as she listened intently to the message of the Living Savior from the genuine Word of God. Never have I seen the Holy Spirit so visually grab hold of a person. We experienced God's invisible presence in our home as she struggled between the darkness of Buddhism and the light of Christ. Enkee chose Christ, and her life was gloriously illuminated by the power of the resurrection. God may have saved her that afternoon in our little home, but He "forgot" to remodel her mischievous personality.

Let me illustrate Enkee at her mischievous best. During our first year in Mongolia, we tried to keep up with our young friends, but soon learned that we could not stay up half the night and still meet the challenges of the next day. However, we decided that a sleepover would be interesting, and we were open to almost anything to gain the opportunity to share our Lord with these eager students. After a night of Uno and Skip-Bo, movies, snacks, and singing, we sneaked into our bedroom for a few winks to discover our bed was already occupied by three girls. We scratched the idea of waking them and snuggled instead on the floor surrounded by a roomful of peacefully dreaming students.

Early in the morning, I awakened with my ears full of white foam. Enkee had discovered my shave cream and was busy filling the ears of sleeping victims. She also had an irritating habit of hiding one shoe of our student guests.

One afternoon, as we enjoyed our new-found friends from the

university, I sat beside a young woman named Rachjama—Argai for short. My Bible was literally falling apart from old age and the constant, demanding trips to the countryside. I told Argai that I needed to get a new Bible since mine was in such poor condition. My Bible was full of valuable notes and phrases underlined, and I regretted the thought of starting over with a fresh book. She was appalled that I would even consider replacing my Bible. Bibles in their language were few and difficult to get. She told me that her mother restored old books at the central public library. Argia was delighted to ask her mother to repair my Bible.

A couple of weeks later, she came to our study group with a refurbished Bible. Her mother had done an excellent job of restoration. I was pleased that I had not discarded my old friend and companion of many years. But then, I looked on the front cover and there embossed in bold letters were the initials HBG. Well, of course those are not my initials; I quickly opened my Bible to see if her mother had mistakenly sent me the wrong book. No, it was mine for sure. There were all my scribblings in my own hand that no one could counterfeit. I was a little embarrassed and unsure if I should even mention the mistake on the front cover. Finally, my curiosity overcame my good judgment, and I said to Argia, "Your mother did a wonderful job on restoring my Bible, and I am so grateful. However, I believe she made a mistake on my initials on the front cover. My initials are GDM not HBG."

"Oh," she said, "That is not a mistake. We first thought we would put GHB for Gerald's Holy Bible, but it did not seem right to put your name in front of God's Word. So, we changed it to HBG for Holy Bible Gerald's."

The Right Bait

> *"Come, follow me," Jesus said, "and I will make you fishers of men."*
>
> –Matthew 4:19, NIV

Enkee and Argia shared the same question: Where are the boys? Our group of students was made up of almost all girls, so we knew we had the premier attraction. The boys would come. We recognized it was the women, including those in the countryside, who responded first to the gospel. It wasn't unusual for them to live an authentic life in Christ for many years before the husband, family, or friends would even begin to show an interest in the faith.

One Sunday, as we met with our university student group, we scanned the room and were amazed to see more boys than girls sitting around the circle in our living room! This was a good place for young Christian women to find a prospective Christian husband. Mongolian dating is quite different than in the West. It is usually a slow process, at least in the beginning. Sometimes we were clueless about a boy and girl's interest in each other until the announcement was made that they were going to be married.

Enkee and a young man we named OB (short for Onolbattar) had the very first Christian wedding of our group. Enkee's mother was a devout Buddhist and was deeply offended that her daughter would not be married in a Buddhist ceremony conducted by a lama. These ceremonies were usually accompanied by excessive alcohol consumption and drunkenness. Enkee's mother refused to come to the wedding. We shared Enkee's sadness. At the last minute, however, her mother had a change of heart. It was a strange wedding, indeed, with beautiful Christian marriage vows substituting for the monotonous Buddhist chants and with no alcoholic beverages to serve.

Enkee's mother was truly impacted by the entire wedding from preparation to the formal ceremony. She was touched by the amazing efforts of our student group as they prepared the food, decorated the room, and made her relatives and friends feel special and part of the occasion. There were no drunkards stumbling into other guests. She couldn't miss the fact that the ceremony honored God, respected marriage, and offered a blessing for this beautiful couple and their families.

Some years later, sadness struck OB and Enkee while they were living in Sacramento, California. She had recently finished her Master's Degree. Enkee was expecting and their first child was due soon when she sensed there was a problem. They rushed to the hospital and a motionless, perfectly-formed beautiful baby girl was delivered with the umbilical cord wrapped around her neck. Devastated and alone in a foreign country, they were carried through this life-shattering time by the Jesus they loved. Fortunately, they were active in a local church that put its arms around Enkee and OB and lived the love of

Christ as they helped them shoulder their heavy burden.

OB and Enkee have since returned to Mongolia and are now leaders in the veterinary profession. Enkee is director of a major project and OB has been a high official in the veterinary sector of the Mongolian government and worked for other important projects. They now have three lovely, healthy daughters who have brought laughter and happiness back into their family.

Argia became the soul of V.E.T. Net as its chief accountant. Her honesty and integrity were the cornerstones for the future success of our organization. Many nights, she worked into the wee hours until she finally fell asleep at her desk. We would find her the next morning sleepily readying herself for the day's challenges. Argia was a bit more cautious about staking her claim on one of these suitors than Enkee and some of the other girls. Finally, though, she cast her net and caught Ganzo (Ganzorig) to become her lifelong partner.

Ganzo began to attend our English class and home group while at university. He was short in stature but made up for his lack of height with a very sharp mind. This young man excelled academically making him one of the top-students in the Veterinary School. He was so soft-spoken that Frances had him sit in her classroom where she could encourage him to speak loudly. "I can't hear you—speak up!" Frances would say.

Ganzo and a couple came by our office to interview for a job. We offered all thee employment following graduation with the couple accepting immediately. We never heard a word from Ganzo about the job, so we assumed he had found another opportunity. After graduation, the young couple showed up for their first day of work dressed to perfection. Minutes later, the door swung open and in strolled Ganzo—dressed in suit and tie and ready to work. Ganzo became a conscientious veterinarian who worked in the projects to train countryside veterinarians and herders. He was like a sponge soaking up the teaching by Western consulting veterinarians.

Hooked for Life

In late summer, Ganzo accompanied two American short-term missionaries, a veterinarian, and a physician and other team members, to several remote sites. After a few days of work, the group spotted a river and thought, "Yes, fresh fish would be a nice change from mutton." Everybody on the team, including the girls, caught fish after fish. Poor Ganzo. He did not have a single bite. He threw the lure and reeled in the line time after time until his arms grew weak. Being shorter than most of the girls, he was the recipient of constant ribbing, and now his lack of fishing prowess was an added insult.

Ganzo decided to stroll down the riverbank plunking his lure tirelessly in the flowing river. When he was out of sight from the rest of the group, he bowed his head to this God he was just learning about. "God," he said, "just one fish, and I'll not ask You for more. If I can just catch one fish, I will believe in Jesus and give my life to You." It was on the very next cast that the water exploded. Ganzo had the first fish of his life on the end of his line. His nerves were strung as tight as the line until the flopping Tiaman fish was finally secure on the bank. No matter how many times he cast after that, there were no more fish for Ganzo that day. You see, one fish was all he had asked God to provide.

The fish were fried to a golden crisp and placed on plates—one per person and two for the American from Texas who sat on Ganzo's right. However, Ganzo's plate was left empty as a practical joke. "Why don't you give thanks, Ganzo?" the Texan drawled. When heads were bowed and eyes closed, Ganzo reached out with his fork, stabbed his neighbor's fish and put it on his plate. Then he thanked God for the bounty of the meal and the little miracle he had experienced that day.

As we listened to **Ganzo's testimony, he credited the miracle of the fish for steering him toward an acceptance of Christ** as his Lord. Ganzo had been "hooked for life" by Jesus. Just as Jesus used the miraculous catch of fish on the sea of Galilee, He is still changing lives through His miraculous power. Today, Ganzo is rapidly growing in his faith. He is reaching out to veterinarians in remote parts of Mongolia through his personal story of how God reached out to him on the bank of a river in Mongolia that beautiful summer day.

Although the romance and courtship of Argia and Ganzo was the best-kept secret in V.E.T. Net, we rejoice with them that they are doing so well. We never saw them speak to each other, much less hold hands or smile. It was quite a shock for all of us when the announcement of their intended wedding came. Now, they have three wonderful daughters and one precious little boy. Ganzo is currently the CEO of V.E.T. Net, and Argia is a leader in the financial department where she continues to be the gold standard of honesty and integrity for all the staff.

These are some of the original disciples of V.E.T. Net that God used to start an organization that is changing a nation. They are as diverse as the original 12 that walked along the shores of Galilee following the Christ. The truth is, we are still following that same Jesus who led His disciples, and just like them we, too, have seen Him perform many miracles. Our non-government organization has become a major provider of veterinary training across the entire country, and Christ is being proclaimed to thousands. Praise God.

A God-Size Work

> *The LORD answered, "I will be with you, and you will strike down all the Midianites, leaving none alive."*
>
> –Judges 6:16, NIV

I found myself in the center of a circle of men and women representing mission organizations that served in countries around the world. I had never even heard the word "missiology" and had little idea how missions was implemented through development. I felt like a Spanish bull surrounded by matadors with swords drawn. "God, we don't want to stay unless, unless this is something You are doing and we can be part of Your plan."

In this circle of men and women, it was impossible for me to keep eye contact with everyone. As I turned round-and-round while speaking, I completely forgot what I was going to say. My mind was totally blank. Finally, I said to this group of seasoned missions leaders, "Frances and I want a God-size ministry that we know with certainty that we are not able to do by ourselves." God has answered that prayer and taken us to new heights we didn't dream were possible.

Figure 4.1. "A Savior on Horseback"
—Frances being rescued by herder in river

Chapter 4

Listen to the Animals

> *They have left the straight way and wandered off to follow the way of Balaam son of Bezer, who loved the wages of wickedness. But he was rebuked for his wrongdoing by a donkey—an animal without speech—who spoke with a human voice and restrained the prophet's madness.*
>
> –2 Peter 2:15–16, NIV

Perhaps the strangest story in the Bible revolves around a talking donkey and a conversation she had with her owner, Balaam. Balaam was a prophet of God who was influenced more by wealth than by God's plan.

The Israelites had been in bondage hundreds of years and were returning from Egypt to the promised land of Canaan. They were great in number, and the Moabites panicked at the sight of the hordes of Jewish exiles. They feared the people of Israel would destroy them, so they sent for Balaam to come and curse God's people. God told Balaam clearly that he was not to go. When the second request came from the Moabite leaders, Balaam succumbed to the temptation to name his own price for his services. He then started down the road to the land of Moab.

During the journey, Balaam's donkey saw the Angel of God with drawn sword standing in the middle of the road. The donkey veered into the ditch to avoid the Angel and was promptly beaten by her master. This happened three times. Finally, the donkey simply laid down in the middle of the road. She was not about to confront this armed Angel. Balaam's eyes were closed to the presence of this heavenly messenger. He beat his poor, faithful donkey unmercifully.

The donkey said to Balaam, "Am I not your own donkey, which you have always ridden, to this day? Have I been in the habit of doing this to you?" "No," he said.

–Numbers 22:30, NIV

Balaam must have thought he was losing his mind. Not only was this poor donkey talking to him, but he was also answering his donkey. Can't you just see Balaam looking around to see if anyone was watching him? Then Balaam saw the angel. He had some serious apologizing to his loyal donkey!

Veterinarians learn to listen to their patients. Owners often give information about their animals that is steeped in misunderstanding, prejudice and sometimes guilt. Of course, the sick animals don't usually verbalize their maladies, but they have numerous ways to communicate their problems to their astute doctor. Listening to the owner instead of the animal may be misleading and lead to a misdiagnosis.

Give Me a Dog's Life!

This is how we know what love is: Jesus Christ laid down his life for us. And we ought to lay down our lives for our brothers.

–1 John 3:16, NIV

I never thought that Mongolians would become as completely attached to their animals as Western pet owners are, but it has surely happened. We see the very same thing in Mongolia that we see in America. Pets are treated like children and sometimes better than the kids.

My mother was a prime example of what I'm talking about. She was a godly woman who set a great example as a mom. She loved all five children, but also had a great love for her dogs. One of her favorite dogs was a Chihuahua named Jigger that we boys despised. The little pest would bite our fingers at the drop of a hat, and only reluctantly would he let us sit on the other end of the sofa far away from him. It wasn't a matter of whether he could get on the furniture, but whether he would allow us to sit with him. Did my mom ever love this worthless dog!

Jigger was wise in the ways of manipulating people. Like Balaam's donkey, Jig could express himself fluently. He learned to say "haaamburger" and "huuungry" as clear as that. He talked himself into an early grave as he begged himself into obesity. Mom buttered his biscuits and hand-fed him. After all, who could deny a talking dog? Well, I reckon Jig tipped the scale at twenty-five pounds when the vet recommended euthanasia for his geriatric patient. Poor Jig looked like an overstuffed sausage as he lay in his coffin with his little toes pointing heavenward. I never quite knew if the vet really thought he should be put to sleep, or if he was just tired of being bitten by Jigger.

Veterinarians are often asked whether animals go to heaven. Well, I don't know the answer to this question with certainty, but I can tell you this; I don't expect Jig to be waiting expectantly for me at the Pearly Gates. At least I hope he's not.

Tragedy of Sin

> *Now the Lord God had planted a garden in the east, in Eden; and there he put the man he had formed.*
>
> –Genesis 2:8, NIV

The Bible begins with the description of an idyllic place where the first man and woman lived. It was a perfect environment with everything they needed. Adam and Eve lived in this garden with no sickness or death. They had an intimate relationship with their creator God, but something terrible happened that destroyed this utopia. Genesis 3 tells us that the man and woman rebelled against God and broke their relationship with Him. This rebellion is called *"sin,"* and it is that which separates us from God to this day. Unfortunately, since the beginning of mankind, people have been in rebellion against God.

God is very frank about this word that causes such discomfort to our modern ears. This little three-letter, single-syllable word so affects our lives that we are inclined to shudder as we consider its impact. The Bible tells us in Romans 3:23 that every one of us has sinned. This is a serious problem. In Romans 6:23 we are taught that this sin leads to death—separation from God. Matthew 25:41,46 teaches that God's punishment for sin is eternal separation from God.

Enter the Plastic Bag

> *The heart is deceitful above all things and beyond cure. Who can understand it?*
>
> –Jeremiah 17:9, NIV

There is still much beauty in this great nation of Mongolia, but something has changed. With modernization has come the family car. Now, in the city many people have personal vehicles, and families take outings into the countryside. The once pristine nation is now littered with plastic bags and empty bottles, particularly around the small towns and cities.

Cattle eat these indigestible bags and must have surgery to correct the ensuing blockages. Mining companies operating without enforceable environmental regulations have polluted the beautiful rivers where we once caught freshwater salmon from crystal clear water. Many fish have disappeared from the waters that are now laden with heavy metals.

As better roads extend into the countryside from major cities and travel becomes much easier, we must go farther and farther out to escape the plastic bags that catch the wind only to sail to distant places where they become snagged by low growing shrubs.

Heart Disease

> *"I the LORD search the heart and examine the mind, to reward each person according to their conduct, according to what their deeds deserve."*
>
> –Jeremiah 17:10, NIV

To paraphrase Jeremiah 17:9–10, our hearts are littered with plastic bags and all sorts of garbage. There is nothing good that comes from them. Plastic clogs the arteries and prevents us from running the race that God has set before us. We sit in our easy chair struggling for oxygen—awaiting our fateful end. When God does a cardiac exam, He looks at the inside. Pride is one of the sins common to all of us—one of the plastic bags that litters our hearts.

A Proud Horse Called Absalom

> *In all Israel there was not a man so highly praised for his handsome appearance as Absalom. From the top of his head to the sole of his foot there was no blemish in him. Whenever he cut the hair of his head—he used to cut his hair once a year because it became too heavy for him—he would weigh it, and its weight was two hundred shekels by the royal standard.[added-about 5 pounds]*
>
> –2 Samuel 14:25–26, NIV

We were driving across the flatlands of Mongolia to the furthermost eastern state of Dornod. Dornod tapers into a finger that reaches far into the western side of China while Russia adjoins it on the North. We always take care to stay away from these borders to avoid problems with the wary border patrols. Contraband is commonly transported in both directions, and strangers are always under suspicion. The grass this particular year was up to the horse's belly. It was a welcome reprieve from the droughts and starvation of the last few years. We thought of numerous Biblical analogies as we crossed this land of the nomads.

> *You crown the year with your bounty, and your carts overflow with abundance. The grasslands of the desert overflow; the hills are clothed with gladness. The meadows are covered with flocks and the valleys are mantled with grain; they shout for joy and sing.*
>
> –Psalm 65:11–13, NIV

What a beautifully poetic picture of the joy that comes to herders as they see the land dressed in waving green and dotted with their contented animals.

The young stallion had thundered across the endless plains of Mongolia. He had raced in the wind with his long flowing mane that was the envy of all. Absalom of the equines pranced with his head high as young fillies stared at such a galliant steed. Unexpectedly, the grand stallion collapsed into a pitiful heap. From the freedom of racing across the endless steppe with effortless strides, he now lay pawing the air pathetically in arched sweeps as he struggled in vain to regain his feet.

As we approached Absalom, he raised his head with fear in his eyes and tried desperately to right himself. With our help, he managed to rise slightly only to fall back on his side again. A casual examination revealed a very simple, but exotic problem. The pride of Absalom, his flowing mane, had grown so long that the ends had knotted; his right rear hoof was entangled in the hair and would have been the death of him had providence not prevailed. Just in time, we released this poor beast from his bondage. The young stallion was freed from his entrapment with a quick pocketknife haircut, and he was once again riding the wind. When we are freed from the sin that so easily entangles us, we too, soar like our new-found equine friend.

When we look at our lives we may think, "I am not such a terrible person. I take care of my family, help my neighbors, and I'm responsible at my work. It is only occasionally that a little white lie slips past my lips." But you see, we all suffer from this sin of pride that infects us at various times in our lives. Resting on the past successes wrapped in pride, we become entangled just like our equine patient was entangled in his own mane.

> *Now Absalom happened to meet David's men. He was riding his mule, and as the mule went under the thick branches of a large oak, Absalom's hair got caught in the tree. He was left hanging in midair, while the mule he was riding kept on going.*
>
> –2 Samuel 18:9, NIV

Joab, the commander of the troops, saw David's son, Absalom, hanging by his hair from the tree. He speared him through the heart. Absalom was very proud of his beautiful flowing hair, but in the end, it led to his death. His pride stood in stark contrast to the humility of his father, King David—the man after God's own heart. The gospel is the pocketknife that cuts the strands that allows us to know the One True God which frees us to run like the wind.

Pride Before the Fall

Before his downfall a man's heart is proud.

–Proverbs 18:12a, NIV

Proverbs is just as true today as it was thousands of years ago when it was first written. It is certainly as true in our modern world as it was before we became so sophisticated in our technology and lifestyle. Unfortunately, modernization and education have not been the cure for spiritual congestive heart failure. We need a heart transplant with God as the surgeon.

We are seeing God reach all across this vast land of Mongolia with a loving arm. There are days we pridefully think this is enough. We don't require anything else. We can lean back and enjoy the fruit. But there are still many who have not heard a clear explanation of the gospel in a loving, caring way, of why Jesus came to earth as a man. There are those who gasp when told that the reason Jesus came to earth and died His horrible death by crucifixion is because of our sins. When we recognize the pride in our lives, we lay helpless in our own spiritual heap struggling powerlessly to rise, hopeless without the power of Christ. Pride is the universal sin, and Christians are susceptible as well as non-believers in Christ.

The Gospel According to Rover

See what great love the Father has lavished on us, that we should be called children of God!

–1 John 3:1a, NIV

It is difficult to understand God's amazing love for us and His desire to have a personal relationship with me and you. This is especially challenging for the millions of people in other religions whose god is a distant one. How does God have the capacity to love each of us so intimately? Rover's master gives us a glimpse into God's love as we observe the relationship between pets and pet owners:

A gentle herder was forced to move to the city following the death of all his animals after a severe "zud" (a destructive, severe winter/spring storm). He found a comfortable apartment and made the uncertain move. He desperately missed his animals and mostly sat dejected, staring out the window from his urban prison. One day he went to buy some necessities at the black market. An elderly woman dressed in her warm del (Mongolian traditional coat) and felt boots, sat by the gate in the sub-zero weather holding a sign, "Puppies for Sale." The old herder looked at the wiggly fuzz balls and quickly made his decision. He thought, "I will buy one of these puppies to fill my life with the joy I knew when I was herding my flocks."

The man took his new puppy home and made him a warm, cozy box where he could feel secure. The herder named him Rover and gave him the run of the house, all except for the dining room with its spotless, white carpet. They walked together on carefree strolls in the park. Rover chased the ball that was thrown again and again, and he was never tired of being with this man who loved him deeply.

Rover grew restless one night and began to chew on his comfortable box. He soon had a hole just large enough to squeeze his little body through. He couldn't resist. With his owner sound asleep, he crept into the dining area and frolicked and rolled on the wonderful snow-white carpet. He was so excited that he forgot himself and began to chew on the soft floor covering. Before he knew what had happened, there was a hole right in the middle of the beautiful carpet. Regardless of how hard he tried, he could not cover the huge hole. Little Rover crawled back into his box and waited for the footsteps of his master that were sure to come. Sure enough, there were no more walks in the park; no long evenings in his master's lap. The relationship was broken. How he longed to be close to his loving master again.

One afternoon, the herder sent his son to find a way to cover the ruined carpet. He returned with a fine red rug made of pure wool with intricate designs. The rug was rolled out under the table to completely cover the hole. The herder couldn't see it at all. He went to his precious puppy and held him tightly. Once again, they frolicked and played together in the park. The relationship between the master and his beloved puppy was completely restored.

If a mere human being can love a worthless, snapping, overweight dog like Jigger, or a mischievous rug-destroying Rover, perhaps God really can love me, too. In fact, that is exactly what God is all about. He is love. He loves us and made us for fellowship, but He also gave us the free will to decide if we will have our own way and chew through the box, or if we will trust Him. As Charles Stanley said, his number one *Life Principal—Our intimacy with God—His highest priority for our lives—determines the impact of our lives.*[1]

Man chose to rebel, and he broke the relationship with this creator and loving God. So, God sent the solution—His only son, Jesus Christ—to cover our sins with blood from the cross. God will completely forgive our sins if we accept His offer and believe on Jesus as our Savior. Try as we might, we can never cover our own sins, for that is a works religion—man trying to be so good that God will accept him. Only by recognizing our sin, turning from it, and asking for the blood of Jesus to wash us clean can we have a relationship and fellowship with God. It is impossible for us to do this by ourselves, and only through His sacrifice can this be a reality. Many have tried to reach God by being good only to find they are never able to bridge the gap.

The Gathering of the Vultures

> *Therefore, just as sin entered the world through one man, and death through sin, and in this way death came to all people, because all sinned.*
>
> –Romans 5:12, NIV

Some years before we moved to Mongolia, I had a veterinary practice in the western part of Virginia. Much of my work was in the Appalachian Mountains that are so reminiscent of the Mongolian mountains. It was a lengthy trip on serpentine roads from my office to the farms where I treated beef and dairy cattle, some pigs, goats, and horses. We lived nearby in the sleepy little mountain town of Independence, Virginia. The surrounding districts of Mouth of Wilson, Elk Creek, and Flatridge were a step back in time to an era of rocking chairs on front porches, and an occasional Sunday dinner on the ground at one of the local primitive Baptist churches that took place just after the foot washin'. This was a place of simple beauty capable of imprinting the soul with indelible memories.

It was a warm summer afternoon and the office had closed

at twelve o'clock on Saturday, but we were always available for emergency calls. I was working in our garden when I received a phone call. On the other end of the line was a farmer-client who spoke with barely controlled panic evident in his trembling voice.

Driving the winding road on the way to the farm, my mind was replaying the conversation on the phone that had me hugging the curves at speeds on the the edge of disaster. "Doc," the old farmer had said, "You got to get up here right away—all of my cows are dyin.'" Emergency is one of those words with a number of meanings for a veterinarian. To a rural practitioner, it can be anything from a laceration on a foal to a cow with milk fever, or maybe even a broken toenail on a Chihuahua. "My cows are laying around all over the place, and a bunch of them have already stopped breathin,'" said the desperate farmer. Now that is a real emergency.

I never quite knew what I might encounter on those rural farm calls. Modern veterinary medicine still competed with local folk medicine, and the condition known as "hollowtail" was often diagnosed before I arrived. The treatment was to split the tail with a knife. It was common for the poor cow to have a dirty old rag wrapped around the inflicted wound. If the cow was down, she might also have received a generous dose of moonshine—a temporary cure for any malady. But, there was no question about this one being an emergency. It was the most devastating sight of my practice career—a regular bovine armageddon. There were, indeed, dead cows everywhere cluttering the grassy meadows along the stream that trickled by the barn. Some neighbors were gathering awaiting a resurrection from my black Pandora's bag of modern medicines. Shadows sailed across the carcasses from the circling vultures as I listened to the tale from this pitiful farmer:

> "You know doc, it's a long way to town, and I just haven't been in to get salt for the last couple of months. My cows were starving for salt, and when they couldn't get it, they started looking for something else. We pushed over that old barn with a bulldozer yeste'day, and all of the cows started lickin' at the dirt. We'd stored fertilizer in there over the years, and I reckon some of it had sifted down between the planks. Seems like they were looking for salt, and just licked up some of that fertilizer."

A few cows still struggled for breath, but most were already dead. It was not likely that any of the remaining would survive the massive amount of poison they had ingested. I withdrew some blood, and instead of the normal red color, it was a light chocolate brown. The nitrate in the fertilizer had blocked the oxygen carrier sites on the red blood cells and prevented the life-sustaining oxygen from reaching the tissues.

I grabbed a bottle of ink-colored medicine from my bag and began to inject it into the veins of the dying cows. It was incredible! Their breathing became even, and soon my bovine patients rolled up on their sternums, bellowed loudly, and stood up. The methylene blue freed the transporting sites on the red blood cells that allowed it to carry the life-sustaining oxygen. Unfortunately, most were beyond help, but those that responded were miraculously cured. Soon enough, they were back to grazing around the dead bodies as if nothing had happened.

The farmer gained an important, but costly lesson in the necessity of providing good nutrition, including salt, for his animals. I drove home with stained hands from the methylene blue, knowing but not caring that it would take some time to wear off. I was pleased that we saved some of the animals but saddened by the farmer's huge loss.

We use many veterinary drugs as we treat animals for multiple maladies. These drugs are quite different in many ways, and each have specific uses for various problems we encounter as veterinarians. But, there is one thing that all drugs have in common—they all have an expiration date. And so it is with each of us. We, too, are born with an expiration date. Though we may believe that we have many years to live, some of us are very short-dated. Death is an eventual reality for each of us, and we must make a choice about what we will do with and for God.

The Blood

. . . and the blood of Jesus, his Son, purifies us from all sin.

–1 John 1: 7b, NIV

An old hymn by Robert Lowry paints a clear picture of 1 John 1:7:

What can wash away my sin?

Nothing but the blood of Jesus;

What can make me whole again?

Nothing but the blood of Jesus.

O! precious is the flow that makes me white as snow;

No other fount I know,

Nothing but the blood of Jesus. [2]

Our modern grocery stores blind us from the horrendous reality of an animal's sacrifice. We choose meat from a refrigerated counter in a tray wrapped in cellophane. A pad absorbs any seeping blood, so blood doesn't drip from our grocery bag, or soil other items in our cart. Meat markets are quite a different enterprise in Mongolia. Slabs of meat lay on unrefrigerated tables in grocery stores. Blood is a part of the everyday shopping adventure.

Watching the slaughter of sheep and goats in the rural areas is not a spectacle for a queasy stomach. It's not pretty. The poor, bleating victim is placed on his back while a quick incision is made into the abdomen. A hand slides through the wound and grasps a major vessel, rupturing it and spilling the blood into the abdominal and pleural cavities. The blood is then dipped from the abdomen and thorax into a container to fill the washed intestines in preparation for making blood sausage. Bits of various organs float in the blood adding to the mystery of this dish. Such a sight appalls Westerners, but it does give us a better idea of the suffering Savior and His sacrifice for us.

The prophet Isaiah didn't shop at the local supermarket. When he wrote of the sacrifice of the lamb, he was only using a snapshot of everyday life—something his readers understood perfectly. This is the context in which they lived.

A Lamb Was Born

The smell of stable filled the air, Shepherds huddled 'round their *ger*, Resting livestock unaware,*A lamb was born.*

Velvet fleece unblemished white, Innocent yet born to strife, Destined to give his life, *A lamb was born.*

The gore of death cannot be told, One's heart must feel this scene unfold, The flow of blood did all behold, *A lamb was born.*

The blade was thrust in hand unshaken, That we might live, his life was taken, Scattered flock they felt forsaken, *A lamb was born.*

These verses might describe the Lamb of God, or they might portray a scene repeated continually in the Mongolian countryside. If a herder read this, he would immediately think of a scene that is a familiar part of his life. Isaiah 53 is the most vivid picture of the death of Jesus in the Old Testement. The ancient prophet used the familiar slaughter scene for the description:

> *He was oppressed and afflicted, yet he did not open his mouth; he was led like a lamb to the slaughter, and as a sheep before her shearers is silent, so he did not open his mouth.*
>
> –Isaiah 53:7, NIV

The lives of herder families are entirely dependent on the sustenance provided by their animals. Since their diet lacks many of the components of a balanced diet, the nutritious blood is important to them. Isaiah witnessed this process many times around the temple just as it is played out in the life among the herders today. Only in the West are we kept from seeing the reality of sacrifice.

There was one time when we had traveled for days, and our meat supply was gone. An old herder stopped by our campsite wanting to sell us a sheep. Fresh meat is something our Mongolian friends always crave. We stopped to replenish our larder and were able to negotiate a great deal. They would keep the skin and intestines, and we would get the head and meat, and, of course, the fat tail. Later, we shared the head and snacked on the eyeballs with another herder that stopped to visit. We found that hospitality is a great ministry tool.

It is easy for the Mongolians to understand the language that Isaiah uses as he describes the sacrifice of the coming Messiah. In our sterile environment, it is, of course, much harder for the

Westerner to be confronted with the reality of the unbelievable price the Son of God paid for each of us. The life is, as the Bible tells us, truly in the blood, and when we forsake the sharing of that truth, we have moved from gospel revelation to religion. We must accept the reality of the Lamb of God. There is clearly no other way. The evidence of Christ's power to transform is evident in the lives of the Mongolians who have accepted Him as Lord and Savior.

Why Blood?

Since the beginning of God's revelation, He has required the blood of acceptable animal sacrifices for the forgiveness of sin and reconciliation. It is His plan. It is He who has set the requirements with Christ as the ultimate fulfillment of His plan.

Wayne Grudem describes the significance of the blood of Christ:

> Scripture speaks so much about the blood of Christ because its shedding was very clear evidence that his life was being given in judicial execution (that is, he was condemned to death and died paying a penalty imposed both by earthly human judge and by God himself in heaven). Scripture's emphasis on the blood of Christ also shows the clear connection between Christ's death and the many sacrifices in the Old Testament that involved the pouring out of the lifeblood of the sacrificial animal. These sacrifices all pointed forward to and prefigured the death of Christ.[3]

A Savior

> *For all have sinned and fall short of the glory of God, and all are justified freely by his grace through the redemption that came by Christ Jesus.*
>
> –Romans 3:23–24, NIV

One day, we were in our Russian truck on the way to Bat-ulzi, a county in the western mountains of Mongolia. The river was swollen from frequent, heavy summer rains to several times its normal width. We usually crossed the rickety wooden bridge over the Orhang River, but a few months before, it collapsed and was washed away. We knew the river was dangerous, but we needed to get to the other side, and did not want to drive to the nearest bridge in Kharhorum, a four-hour trip.

A large truck, hauling Mongolian racehorses from an adjacent state, was parked along the riverbank. The passengers and driver were weighing the risks of the crossing, just as we were. We decided to put Frances in the back of the truck with the horses, thinking it was more likely to safely cross the flooded river. Our driver, a visiting veterinarian and I left the horse truck behind to ride in the smaller truck, knowing that we could swim out if something went wrong.

We splashed into the river and had almost made it to the other side before the motor gulped a carburetor full of water and died. Not to worry; our driver had been in this situation many times. He used the starter motor and the flow of the river to pull us far enough to elevate the engine above the water so that he could crank the sputtering motor.

We were now safely on the far shore as the old blue horse truck, with Frances in the back, plunged into the water to join us. Near the middle of the river, the truck's electrical system shorted out and the engine died, leaving the truck stranded in the treacherous waters. I had gone through several frightening experiences in Mongolia, but this was by far the worst. Frances was stuck in the middle of the river with darkness rapidly approaching.

Standing safely on shore, I felt totally helpless, so I began to pray. About that time, a young herder on a small sturdy horse approached us and surveyed our worsening dilemma. We pleaded with him, "Please go and rescue the woman from the back of the horse truck." "Oh no," he said. "If I do that and something happens to this foreign woman, I will be in trouble with the police and may even be imprisoned."

Finally, after understanding our desperate situation, he agreed to take the risk of rescuing Frances on his little horse. He made his way through the surging water and, after several attempts, Frances was securely seated behind his saddle on his horse holding on for dear life. Ever so slowly, the two made it across the long stretch of dangerous, swirling water. When Frances was safely on the riverbank, we stopped to give praise to God for providing the caring herder and for preserving Frances' life.

> *Jesus answered, "I am the way and the truth and the life. No one comes to the Father except through me."*
>
> –John 14:6, NIV

There is only one way that the Bible shows us how we can have our sin-slate wiped clean and establish a relationship with the creator God. You see, the story about the brave young herder who saved Frances from the flooded river is much like the story of what Jesus has done for you and me. Just as the herder on horseback was our only hope to deliver Frances, Jesus is our only hope of salvation. Agreed, it is an exclusive arrangement. However, it is God's plan, one He made long ago. In John 14:6, Jesus assures us that He is the only path to a relationship with God. If we fail to accept His offer, we will be separated from God throughout eternity. We will forfeit the huge blessing of being His child, one who is free to enjoy an abundant life in Him.

A Relevant Message

> *Yet to all who received him, to those who believed in his name, he gave the right to become children of God.*
>
> –John 1:12, NIV

The nomadic herder lives in a world of isolation. This is especially true for women and children. When asked for directions, they may not even know the way to the closest village. They find it difficult to understand things with which they are not familiar, such as the message of Jesus who was born over 2000 years ago in a land far away.

We needed to communicate the Christian message to herders and their families on a level they could easily understand. Our solution was to produce a simple pamphlet designed to speak to them in familiar terms in their own language. It is the language of the herders—of sheep and shepherds and things that surround their everyday life.

I remembered my experience with the cows I treated in Virginia on that memorable Saturday afternoon so long ago. One minute they appeared dead, and the next moment, it was as if nothing had ever happened. They were transformed from a pitiful state—unable to stand, barely breathing, and hopeless—to new life. They were free to enjoy the lush, green pastures. The following was inspired by the same vivid imagery:

The Good Shepherd
by Gerald Mitchum

The good shepherd is constantly caring for his flock. He protects them from storms and predators and finds the best grass and clean water for them.

Sometimes the good shepherd risks his life when he goes out in severe weather to check his flock. The harsh weather in Mongolia can be risky for herders and their flocks. The herder often loses sleep when the wolves are prowling around the flock. He must be vigilant to protect the sheep from these dangerous predators.

There is a story about a good shepherd who was missing a lamb. The lamb had crossed a shallow stream, but since then the rain came—the creek was flooded, and the lamb was stuck on the other side. He was wet and cold and there were eyes glistening in the trees near him, and the howl of wolves rang in his ears as the pack of predators started to encircle him.

Dressed in his winter del the shepherd searched for the lost sheep until he saw it across the creek. The stream was torrential, and he knew the dangers, but he plunged into the racing water and tucked the lamb into his warm del. He crossed the stream and carried the lamb back to his ger where he warmed him and gave him some milk. When the lamb was full and warm he was placed back with the other sheep in the protection of the shed.

There is a parable about the Good Shepherd that has been passed down for thousands of years. It goes like this:

I am the good shepherd. The good shepherd lays down his life for the sheep. The hired hand is not the shepherd and does not own the sheep. So when he sees the wolf coming, he abandons the sheep and runs away. Then the wolf attacks the flock and scatters it. The man runs away because he is a hired hand and cares nothing for the sheep. I am the good shepherd; I know my sheep and my sheep know me.

–John 10:11–14, NIV

When we accept God's offer of salvation as our hope, and believe in our heart that Jesus is Lord, things begin to change for us. We are renewed and made strong to build our house on a solid foundation that will withstand the storms of life.

Notes:

1. Stanley, C.F. (2009). *The Life Principles Bible, NASB,* Life Principle 1, loc 881. (Thomas Nelson Publishers, Nashville, Tennessee), Kindle Book

2. Lowry, Robert, (1986) *Hymns of Faith,* "Nothing but the Blood" (Tabernacle Publishing Company, Wheaton, Illinois), p. 264.

3. Grudem, Wayne (1994). *Systematic Theology: an Introduction to Biblical Doctrine.* (Inter-Varsity Press, Leicester, England), p. 579.

Figure 5.1. "Caught in a Sandstorm"—tent in sandstorm

Chapter 5

Solid Granite

> *Therefore everyone who hears these words of mine and puts them into practice is like a wise man who built his house on the rock. The rain came down, the streams rose, and the winds blew and beat against that house; yet it did not fall, because it had its foundation on the rock.*
>
> – Matthew 7:24–25, NIV

It was time to fold up camp. There was absolutely no one to blame but ourselves. Sandy grit irritated our eyes and crunched between our teeth. We were gathered around a dual-fuel Coleman stove and had just finished our dinner with our little team. As we basked in the warmth of a Mongolian evening, we savored the serenity of the Gobi Desert with its enormous spaces and endless blue horizons.

We had chosen this sandy, desert knoll to erect our tents in the shadow of a rocky hill. Hardy, drought-tolerant plants decorated the sand. Ungainly camels occasionally lumbered across this harsh desert and disappeared into the distant glistening heat waves that danced in the late afternoon.

Suddenly, we saw in the distance a heavy, dark curtain hanging from the sky and reaching to the ground. We were almost lulled into a trance as we stood watching it thinking the whole time that it would go around us. Our driver, Zorgoo, and veterinarian, Batsukh, climbed up the rocks near our campsite to get a better view of this approaching monster.

Frances and I came to our senses and began to hurriedly wash and stow the dishes. We ran as quickly as we could to sit in the truck where we could watch the devastating storm. The sandstorm hit with such speed and furry that there was no time to take the tents down. They were pulverized into the ground. Zorgoo and

Batsukh held a canvas over the side of the truck to keep the wind from sandblasting the paint off the metal and pitting the windows. Thankfully, our windshield was protected because it was facing away from the wind. When the storm finally weakened, we quickly recovered our packs and damaged tents, and stuffed everything into the truck—broken poles and all.

Covered with sand, we crawled back into our truck and drove through the dark night to a vacant, three-sided shed. It wasn't much, but it was better than nothing. We were relieved to find that the herder had moved his animals to another site. Only the smell of sheep lingered inside. We managed to straighten the poles and erect our tent in the shelter of the shed. While the storm blew outside, we were warm and cozy, away from the reaches of the fierce fingers of the wind.

The next morning, Frances awoke from a deep sleep to the sound of music; Zorgoo and Batsukh were singing "Happy Birthday, dear Frances."

Now, it is one thing for Frances to celebrate her birthday in a sheep shed, but think about the Son of God beginnning his earthly life in a stable. It is difficult to even imagine such a thing. God, our absolute all-knowing, all-powerful God sent His Son to be born to a poor, young couple in a stable.[1,2] The manger scenes we see at Christmas almost appear sanitary and comfortable, but it wasn't that way in our shed. The ground was caked with several inches of manure, and the smell of sheep permeated everything, including us. So, why would God allow His only Son to be born in such a place? The only possible answer is His incredible love for each of us. There is no other reasonable explanation.

He wants us to return that love to Him, and share it with those around us. We certainly felt His love for us that night as the sand pelted us relentlessly. Isn't this just like God? He is always there for us in every storm of life we encounter. Sometimes the storms do not abate as quickly as our sand storm did, but we know that His hand is always there to cover us.

As I look across this vast, sparsely-populated nation of Mongolia, I see many people standing outside who are caught in the storms of their own lives. Yes; a spiritual sandstorm is sweeping across this nation, and people are dying without the truth of Christ. So, how can we stand mesmerized as if waiting for the storm to go around us? We have the escape plan, so we must share it with others.

Christ's birth was heralded by great joy. His death, as unimaginable as it was, made salvation possible for each of us. He was the great storm-calmer on the Sea of Galilee, and He continues to be that for those who trust in Him today.

Firm Foundation

> *For no one can lay any foundation other than the one already laid, which is Jesus Christ.*
>
> –1 Corinthians 3:11, NIV

A few years ago, our team came upon an accident involving a gasoline truck on a short stretch of paved road. The vehicle was turned on its side with the petrol pouring from its tanks. The poor driver had obviously tried to claw his way out of the burning truck attempting to escape the disaster. Sadly, the roaring flames engulfed him before he could reach safety. His charred body lay locked with arms outstretched grasping for life at the time of his death. No doubt, he had begun his day as any other without the slightest thought of impending disaster.

Like this man, our lives can be over just as quickly. Each of us must be prepared to meet our Maker at any time.

Orthopedics on Our Truck

In the 1990's, fuel was often in short supply in Mongolia, especially in the distant rural areas. We were experiencing one of those times of fuel scarcity. We were forced to haul huge barrels of gasoline to the countryside for our teams to refill for their return trip to the city. The truck was loaded to capacity with 55-gallon drums brimming with the highly flammable fuel. We knew it was extremely hazardous, but we needed the gas, and this seemed the only way to solve the problem.

During one trip, we turned off the main road, but the shoulder ended abruptly and caused the truck to torque grotesquely. The frame was totally broken on one side; the other side was severely bent. Our vehicle looked like a dump truck tilted at a dangerous angle. If we had been driving faster, the outcome might have been far worse. We would have needed to be towed to the nearest junkyard if our resourceful driver hadn't taken control. He jacked up the back of the truck and bolted a metal splint to the side of the broken frame. I couldn't help but think this was exactly what I would have done to repair a broken leg on an animal. Thankfully, we were able to limp along the next 15 miles to a small town where there just happened to be an old man with a welding machine. Thank you, Lord.

This man was 80 years old and nearly blind from age and from watching the welding flame during his many years of work. Our driver offered to guide the old man's hand as he welded the metal along the fractures of the frame. The two of them were able to make a temporary fix to last us until we returned to the city and had it replaced with heavy-duty steel. Amazingly, we only missed one day of travel and were back on the road the next day.[3]

This was a good lesson for us. A vehicle may be beautiful on the outside with shiny paint and sparkling chrome reflecting the sunlight. However, if the frame is weak, there is a very real risk of a serious accident. Whether you are building a house, or buying an automobile, the foundation, in our case the vehicle frame, is the most important factor.

A solid foundation is even more important when we consider our social, emotional, and psychological wellbeing. Without a firm foundation, there is no stability in our life.

Building on the Rock

> *So this is what the Sovereign Lord says: "See, I lay a stone in Zion, a tested stone, a precious cornerstone for a sure foundation; the one who trusts will never be dismayed."*
>
> –Isaiah 28:16, NIV

The remote village of Muren Bag boasted a small school for herder children and two or three small stores. During the school year, students lived in a small dormitory, or with other family members residing in the village. About a hundred families lived there, but the population varied with the seasons. In the summer, it became almost a ghost town when students returned to their families in the countryside to help herd their animals.

Tavin Olzi was the name of a little girl born near the distant mountain village of Muren Bag. Tavin was the first of ten children born into a herding family. With nine siblings to help care for, there was little time for fun and games. She started herding and milking the yak when she was only six years old.

At the age of 12, a little yak calf died that she had been bottle feeding, and it touched her heart. "When I grow up," she thought, "I will learn to care for these little ones so this doesn't happen again."

Tavin, whose name means "peace and blessing," decided to become a veterinary technician after graduating from high school. Much of the practical veterinary work in this country is done by technicians. She was offered a job in the Gobi Desert, but she decided to return to her home in the mountains. Tavin married her childhood sweetheart who had also come home to Muren Bag after college. They began herding as a way of life and had their own herds and flocks. She worked with their livestock, and they soon had two precious daughters.

Sadly, tragedy struck when her husband contracted hepatitis. In those days, needles were not always sterilized, and the disease was often spread by medical personnel. Tavin was devastated when her husband died, leaving her to care for their two children by herself. Her husband's parents were committed Buddhists, and they were oblivious to the needs of their distraught daughter-in-law. In fact, they were so out of touch with her plight that they took back the ger they had given to the couple as a wedding gift. At the same time, Tavin made the decision to return the family idols as well, knowing that while they were valuable to her in-laws and of no help to her.

Now, without any hope or idea of how to go on, she stumbled down to the old bridge near her birthplace and looked into the cold, black water. "This is where all of my pain will end," she thought. Rather than ending her life that day, she uttered the words, "Oh, if there is a real God, please come to me."

Tavin turned away from the bridge to begin her search for this God. V.E.T Net veterinarians were able to share the love and message of Christ with her and present her with her very first Bible. The V.E.T. Net teachers told her of a loving God who could bring real peace to her life. Tavin accepted Jesus Christ into her life and received His peace. Indeed, God came to her, as she had prayed at the bridge. She is now involved in bringing peace and blessing to her whole practice area.

Tavin treats the animals and shares the gospel with these most remote people. Eventually, she received training to be a discipleship leader so that she could show others how to grow in their faith.

After some time, a large group began meeting in Muren Bag on Fridays for prayer, songs and praise, and on Sundays for Bible study. The gathering usually included the school principal, the dormitory house-mother, some teachers, herders, and others who had become Christians through the V.E.T. Net ministry. The group invited a well-respected local herder to be their pastor.

The believers needed a church building where they could meet and worship together. The former county governor helped them secure a section of land for the church, and the surrounding mountains furnished the trees for the log building. Donations provided metal for the roof and glass for windows. The glass was framed by the local carpenter, and most of the other work and materials came from people in the community.

As construction began, we noticed that all normality in building practices ceased—at least what seems normal to the Western mind. The church building started to take shape, and from a distance it looked perfectly fine. On closer observation, however, something was obviously missing. There was no foundation. They were building the structure like they would erect a ger—right on top of the ground.

However, in the end, the builders dug a ditch around the building one section at a time. They mixed concrete by hand in a tub and poured it into the ditch to flow through the deep trenches until they were filled. At last, the building was resting comfortably on a firm foundation. The church would stand firm and withstand storms after all. Paul's words affirm the need for a firm foundation:

> *By the grace God has given me, I laid a foundation as an expert builder, and someone else is building on it. But*

each one should be careful how he builds.

–1 Corinthians 3:10, NIV

Raising a building without a foundation may work for gers in Muren Bag, but it doesn't work spiritually. A solid frame—or foundation—is essential if we are to have a healthy, personal walk with God. Paul clearly tells us that there is no other solid spiritual foundation than Jesus Christ. Of course, the believers in Muren Bag had things backward. You don't build a building and later add the foundation. So it is with life in Christ. Everything we've done before we trusted our life to Him has no eternal value and will eventually crumble. We must build on a firm foundation capable of withstanding the wind and storms of this life, or our own house will crumble.

Fortunately, the congregation in Muren Bag had a firm spiritual foundation long before the idea of a church building was ever conceived. Their foundation was the Lord Jesus Christ, the chief cornerstone. Studying the Word of God, prayer, experiences with God, worship, acts of kindness and fellowship with other believers were all important aspects of building on this foundation for the Muren Bag Christians. Jesus was the bedrock of their salvation.

If anyone builds on this foundation using gold, silver, costly stones, wood, hay or straw, their work will be shown for what it is, because the Day will bring it to light. It will be revealed with fire, and the fire will test the quality of each person's work.

–1 Corinthians 3:12–13, NIV

V.E.T. Net's driving force is always our need to answer the question: "How can we truly help these people who have been neglected for far too long?" Many funded projects offer temporary assistance, but as the funds disappear, we sometimes see that positive changes are short-lived. God's plan is to have an impact with eternal consequences. Once we choose Christ to be Lord of our life, we get out the hammer and saw and begin to build with materials that will last forever. We build on the Rock who is our immovable, indestructible foundation.

Water from the Rock

When the church has a solid foundation, it begins to make a real impact on the community.

> *"Strike the rock, and water will come out of it for the people to drink."*
>
> –Exodus 17:6b, NIV

The spring at Muren Bag had been dry for over two years. The other water source was foul and unpleasant to taste. Many thought of the old spring and longed for a return of clear, pure water.

Our small group of V.E.T. Net teachers and the local veterinarian walked to the pile of dry, dusty rocks, and asked God for a cold, clear drink of water. It didn't happen immediately, but 15 days later the life-giving water miraculously began to flow. Muren Bag now had a fresh supply of water.

There is a healthy group of believers in this distant place in the countryside, but they are not the only ones affected by this wonderful blessing from God. The whole community is blessed by this precious water that bubbles constantly from the rocks, creating a tiny stream that trickles down through the valley. The gift of this spring water and the gift of the Living Water, Jesus, is changing this entire village. We have witnessed all these things.

> *And do not forget to do good and to share with others, for with such sacrifices God is pleased.*
>
> –Hebrews 13:16, NIV

The spring is only one of the many blessings that came at the hands of the Christians in this community. We provided heat for the dormitory as well as much-needed new bedding. We painted the school and prayed with the locals for the rain to hold off until it dried. We offered teachers and the principal training to improve education.

Yes, the changes to Muren Bag were many, but when multiplied by those who were being changed, the impact was truly eternal.

Projects Built on the Rock

So, what brings success to a project? It is the partnership with God to do all things according to His will.

In considering a project, we should always ask a few key questions: Will this honor God, and if so, how? Can it be advanced with integrity and righteousness? Will it bring genuine long-term help to those it targets? We have learned that God will carry out the plan through us because it will be built on His Son, Jesus Christ.

We have watched solid Christian organizations in this country falter and yield to the temptation to get out in front of God. From international contributions, they collect millions of dollars every year in the name of Christianity, and yet, they have only a small percentage of Christians on their staff. This may be an excusable practice in some countries where believers undergo extreme persecution, but not now here in Mongolia. Several of these organizations have been completely taken over by non-Christians. As a result, they are increasingly secular and frequently anti-Christian.

An organization based in the United States funded some of our early work with a yak project. God used this in a miraculous way to save V.E.T. Net from early extinction. At that time, the organization had a man in a high-level of leadership who was a committed Christian. With his positive influence, we received the grant. When he was no longer with the organization, the organization's Christian focus changed. We applied for funding for another animal project but were summarily rejected.

One of our short-term volunteers visited this organization to thank them for the earlier grant given to our project. An administrator informed him that there would be no more funding for the V.E.T. Net animal programs. Our friend then told her that he had received a card informing him that his brother had donated, in his name, a yak for a Mongolian family. "This can't be true," she said, "We have no such program." He showed the administrator the gift card. The administrator was certain there was some mistake. Our friend asked her why they no longer featured their organization's Christian heritage on their website. She answered, "This organization has now grown beyond their Christian beginning." What a dangerous place to be!

Keeping V.E.T. Net on track spiritually has been a primary commitment. One policy we have never deviated from is starting the day with morning devotions with our staff. It has been a battle to maintain this effort because of the "tyranny of the urgent." However, our devotional time is an integral part of the DNA of Mongolia V.E.T. Net. By resisting the temptation to forego devotions in favor of other activities, we ensure that our staff is prepared for whatever the day may hold. If anyone even mentions forgoing it, the rest put up a fight. Our major responsibility is to assure that the foundation of V.E.T. Net remains a focus on Jesus Christ. We have a duty to live out that faith, for as James, the brother of Jesus, said, *"What good is it, my brothers, if a man claims to have faith but has no deeds?"* (James 2:14a, NIV).

True faith in Christ must lead to results with a life that reflects Him. V.E.T. Net has an extraordinary opportunity to make a difference in Mongolia. We are able to help herder families across this land have a better life. Through animal care training, this can become a sustainable transformation. It is not just the herders and their families that we are able to assist; it is also the students, the veterinarians, the teachers, the doctors, and principals, as well as village leaders. Like the Christians of the early Church, the opportunity to witness to a whole population is often through public service. I believe that it is because we are a public service NGO and focused on Christ that we are able to make a huge difference.

All this seemed impossible when Frances and I first arrived at our dreary apartment all those years ago. But now, we see that it is through V.E.T. Net that we are able to take the story of God's amazing love to every district in this country. We believe we are called to reach this entire nation for Him as we depend on Him to lead us.

There are shepherds standing out there tonight gazing up at the same stars you and I see, but no one has told them of the creator God and His love for them. No one has told them that God became a baby and was born in a shed just like the one near their ger. No one has told them that this same God wants to have an intimate relationship with them—to walk side-by-side with them even as they herd their animals. They need to know that even in the remote countryside of Mongolia, they can walk with this God of love, both now and for all eternity.

Notes:

1. The traditional Christmas stable with a manger for the baby Jesus may not be the way it was in reality. However, regardless of the exact type of stable, we know that it was a place where animals were kept and not a suitable place for the birth of a King—except for this King. For interesting thoughts on the possible type of stable where Jesus was born, read *Mysteries of Jesus' Life Revealed–His Birth, Death, Resurrection, and Ascensions,* by Joseph Lenard (see details in note 2 below).

2. Lenard, Joseph (2018). *Mysteries of Jesus' Life Revealed–His Birth, Death, Resurrection, and Ascensions.* (Wordzworth Publishing, www.wordzworth.com; also available at www.Amazon.com) Pp. 99–113.

3. On our next trip to the community where our truck was welded, we took a pair of reading glasses to the old welder. He was back in business once he was able to see again.

Figure 6.1. "Heart Felt"—making felt for a ger

Chapter 6

Traveling a New Road

> *Wash me, and I shall be whiter than snow.*
>
> –Psalm 51:7b, NIV

We startled a remarkable rabbit one day while tramping through a pine-nut forest in the mountains of Mongolia. This bunny was unusual because he turned a brownish color in the summer. But when winter comes, he adapts to the color of his environment with a snow-white coat that blends perfectly with the patches of snow. It is a challenge for predators, whether on wing or pad, to see him as he sits motionless.

This is a picture of what happens to us when we choose to believe in Jesus and give our life to Him. We turn snow-white in God's eyes. He transforms us and sets us on a new path for Him and graciously forgets that we had been motley brown from sin. We may not always escape the attacks of the spiritual predator, but we have the knowledge that God is greater than any assault Satan may send our way.

Heart Felt

> *Consider it pure joy, my brothers, whenever you face trials of many kinds, because you know that the testing of your faith develops perseverance.*
>
> –James 1:2, NIV

Sheep are a critical part of the herder's way of life. Milking the ewes is a prime example of Mongolian efficiency. The ewes' heads are roped together as they stand in two long lines facing each other. The herder women squat behind the sheep and move along the line milking each of the patient ewes. In fact, all of the livestock in Mongolia are milked by the women—yak, horses, camels, cows, sheep and goats.

Mongolians truly love their mutton. They only butcher older sheep; lamb is never on the menu. These fat-tail sheep have a blob of fat attached to their backside that bounces as they run across the grasslands. Fat is important for the animal's survival, and without this dietary staple, Mongolian herders would also waste away. In such an extremely cold climate, it is impossible to maintain healthy body condition without a very high caloric intake. It may be unhealthy for Westerners to eat fat meat, but it is an essential part of the diet for Mongolians who tirelessly follow their livestock in subzero weather. I was once served a T-bone steak size slice of fat with no streaks of lean meat and fried in butter. It was not for the faint-of-heart, that's for sure.

Over twenty products are made from **milk:** cheese, butter, yogurt, and others including milk vodka.

Some *gers* have a small **still** that fits on top of the stove. The wife distills the soured milk to produce drinking alcohol for her husband and guests. Traditionally, milk vodka is served to visitors as they drop by to visit. It is culturally unthinkable to be without vodka to offer these guests.

Another product is a rock-hard **cheese** that Mongolians eat throughout the winter—an essential source of calcium and phosphorus for growing children.

The sheep serve another function as well. During our first years in Mongolia, we noticed there were no plastic toys for herder children. After the family had eaten the meat, the innovative parents dried the ankle bones and cleaned them until they gleamed to use them for many challenging games. To this day, children and adults compete for bragging rights in a game called "shagai." Depending on the particular version of the game, the ankle bones may be tossed like dice, flicked like marbles, shot at with arrows, caught in the hands or simply collected according to the roll of a die.

While all parts of Mongolian sheep are important, the wool is absolutely critical. Herder wives and daughters make sweaters, gloves, caps and other articles of clothing to keep the family warm. However, the most essential wool product is **felt**. Without it, it is impossible to survive in gers during the artic weather. Covering the frame of the ger with layers of felt insulates the nomadic home from severe cold.

Felt is made from wool that has been cleaned, washed, dried and then beaten with flexible sticks. In this way the white wool is fluffed and made ready to prepare the felt. This process is often a social event with a group of Mongolians sitting around a large hide or piece of canvas as they craft the felt. Patches of clean wet wool are patted down on the hide in a quilt size rectangle. When finished, the wool is rolled in the hide around a long pole with the animal skin serving as a protective wrapper. Ropes are then placed on the two ends of the pole and attached to a horse. The horse pulls the roll of wool over rocks and bumps to crush the fiber and compress the fluffy wool into compacted felt. Once this process is completed, the family is finally ready to cover the frame of the ger.

Perhaps God views us as a pile of dirty wool filled with trash and cockleburs, briars, and mites. After He makes us clean and white, He begins to fashion us into something useful for His purpose using a carefully planned progression. Oh, yes; it hurts all right, but as we go over those rocks and bumps, God's hand is constantly holding us. In time, we, too, become His well-crafted masterpiece. We can take comfort in knowing that the painful process is necessary for God to make us into His spiritual felt.

A Veterinarian Changes Colors

At age 14, Tserendorj saw the Jesus Film on television, but didn't really understand the story. He thought it was just another fictional movie. In 2001, he was invited to our office in the old Russian apartment building where we lived. As he entered the office, he saw Bibles on the shelf. "This is just a foreign religion," he thought. He even ridiculed some of his friends who were working with V.E.T. Net for reading their Bible.

After he graduated from veterinary school, Tserendorj agreed to join one of our V.E.T. Net countryside trips. When he returned from the trip, he made a decision that would change the course of his life. "I will work with V.E.T. Net," he said. On his first day at work, Tserendorj attended devotions and was rather shocked to hear the singing of praise songs. Later, he was invited to attend church with us. "These people are crazy," Tserendorj thought "They teach that I am a sheep and Jesus is my shepherd. There is something seriously wrong with these Christians. They are all abnormal." [1]

Tserendorj had a very inquisitive mind and soon began to compare the Bible to books on philosophy. He asked many difficult questions. When our drivers told him that if he didn't become a Christian, he might lose his job, he started to act the part. He said, "I prayed, but I knew that I was living a lie."

After traveling to the countryside again, one of the short-term volunteers asked the group to share their testimonies. Tserendorj said, "I can't do this, and I can't keep living this lie." Finally, he told the truth and felt better for having done so. As he went along on other countryside trips, he began to be influenced by the teaching of both the long- and short-term missionaries working with V.E.T. Net.

At the time, a young woman named Undraa was attending our Sunday Bible study group. In fact, she was one of the first teachers to work with our organization. She had first come to faith while attending her parent's homegroup. She said, "I really didn't understand what I had done until I started attending the V.E.T. Net home group." She grew quickly in her faith as she continued to study her Bible.

Undraa was attracted to the young veterinarian, Tserendorj, but she knew she could not date a non-believer. One day at the office, Tserendorj was exhausting teacher Nara with his constant, impossible questions. He was definitely the "Doubting Thomas" of V.E.T. Net who needed to put his fingers in the nail prints of Jesus' hands before he would believe. As it happened, Undraa was in the kitchen preparing lunch when Nara said to her, "You come and answer his questions, and I will be glad to do the cooking." Undraa spent an hour talking with Tserendorj and finally told him, "It is not how much you know because knowledge will never save you. It is a matter of the heart. I can't talk you into believing. There will be a moment when you will know the truth. When that time comes, don't harden your heart."

In 2005, after many months of searching, Tserendorj made the decision to follow God. He is now a leader at V.E.T. Net and one of the best-trained veterinarians in Mongolia. God is using him in many ways to share his story of faith with Mongolians across the nation. He is a great example of how God can take a little country boy and mold him into a man capable of changing his country.

Oh, yes; What about Undraa and Tserendorj? Some of Tserendorj's friends at V.E.T. Net had already told him that he should marry Undraa. At the time, though, he thought, "I will never marry this crazy girl; she is one of those Jesus freaks." Well, it turned out that they lived close to each other, so they began to walk to the bus stop together. On one of these walks, Tserendorj asked her if she would consider dating him. She responded by saying that he needed to ask her father, a pastor at Holy Way Church. When he gathered his nerve to ask her dad, he said, "Yes." They were married in 2007. Their three children certainly kept the V.E.T. Net daycare full and lively.

Driver Education

> *Therefore, if anyone is in Christ, he is a new creation; the old has gone, the new has come!*
>
> –2 Corinthians 5:17, NIV

From the beginning, we used many different drivers. This was considered to be an important profession in Mongolia, and they were a valuable part of our organization. The drivers were a tough lot with a leaning toward bad habits. We employed six of these important team members before we found anyone remotely resembling a Christian. I had my doubts at times that there would ever be a believing driver.

Because the weather is so severely cold and unpredictable in winter, it is unsafe to travel without a skilled driver who is also a capable mechanic. Our vehicles are mechanically simple making it easy for our drivers to repair them. The drivers' ability to be innovative increases the chances of our survival on winter countryside trips. Occasionally, some people use tires from a disabled vehicle to serve as fuel for an outdoor fire during emergencies to warm the passengers and prevent frostbite, or worse, death.

Our Russian vans and trucks are similar to the American vehicles of the 1930s and 1940s. They are somewhat uncomfortable with stiff springs and no seatbelts. The heaters make a nice humming noise that gives the impression they are working, but, unfortunately, they produce little heat. The good thing about these vehicles, however, is that they are built high off the ground which allows us to travel almost anywhere regardless of whether it's over rocks, up and down steep mountain passes or through rivers and deep snow.

About 1999, a dental team worked at one of our countryside school sites in Ulaan Am (Red Mouth), a tiny village near a beautiful waterfall in Mongolia. It is close to the mouth of the Red River from which the village gets its name. Dr. Bill Pratt was the first dentist to join in any of our community projects, and he and his wife Peggy returned to work with V.E.T. Net many years. Unfortunately, at first the locals were afraid to get into his chair. You see, Mongolians have a history of bad experiences because sometimes teeth are extracted without anesthesia. Understandably, they wanted no part of a dental ministry. Finally, a brave soul got into the dental chair and experienced painless care made possible by the use of modern, local anesthetics. The news flash of painless dentistry reverberated through the surrounding area eventually resulting in endless lines of waiting patients.

And so, a routine was established: The dentist would examine the patient and give an injection of local anesthetic to deaden the offending teeth. While the anesthetic took effect, the patient was seated in another chair to wait for the area to become numb all the while listening to the Good News from a Mongolian team member. Talk about a captive audience!

Teacher Aggii previously attended a military university in Moscow. His Mongolian language was so polished that the rural herders could barely understand him. On one occasion, our driver named Jagaa was sitting nearby. He quickly recognized that there was a language problem even though they supposedly spoke the same language. As Aggii shared the gospel with the herder patients, Jagaa decided to translate proper Mongolian language into countryside Mongolian. After working on this for some time, Jagaa led himself to Christ—coaxed by the Spirit of God, of course.

The Great Mongolian Race

Over the years, we have had hundreds of short-term volunteers work with us. The value of these missionaries to V.E.T. Net has been immeasurable. One of the first groups to help our ministry was a small team consisting of a doctor, nurse, physical therapist and two other assistants from a church in Virginia. They arrived at the airport in the evening and spent the night adjusting to jetlag. For some of them, this was their first trip outside of the United States.

The following morning, they were herded into our van and sent with our translator to a remote district in Owerhangai, one of the western states. They were scheduled to work with the community in the tiny medical clinic and would also be working with students in the dormitory. Their driver was the jovial Jagaa who had led himself to Christ at Ulaan Am. Everything was quite new to these visitors as they swerved along the road filled with potholes that forced the driver to dodge a rare oncoming vehicle. The roads, where they existed, proved to be treacherous stretches of broken pavement and deep holes.

The drive to the team's destination was 12 hours. About halfway there, an approaching vehicle forced Jagaa off the road and down into the roadside ditch. Jagaa's temper flared as he tried to slip the grating transmission into four-wheel drive to regain the road. He managed to execute a sliding U-turn, and the race was on between both vehicles as they veered from side-to-side speeding along the road our team had just traveled. The new short-term missionaries were forced to hang on for dear life with white knuckles as they prayed without ceasing. Our team was gaining in the race, and finally, the other vehicle was forced from the road. Jagaa jumped from the van, extracted the other driver and began to preach a spicy sermon on driving etiquette to his captive audience.

The trip continued with the passengers visibly shaken, making their way to the small village of Jaragalant. When the work was completed in the community, the team returned to Ulaanbaatar. Afterwards, they all came to our apartment to share their stories over a Western meal. These short-term missionaries had scarcely entered our home before the leader of the team said to me, "We need to talk." I knew that was a bad sign, so I sat down to hear their frightening experience of the *great Mongolian race*. After listening to their harrowing tale, I assured them this was not acceptable behavior for a driver, and that I would meet with Jagaa the next day. I guaranteed this would never happen again.

"Jagaa," I began, "I heard the story about your race down

the road chasing the car into the ditch just to tell the other driver what you thought about his driving habits. You know, Jagaa, these foreign short-term missionaries are not accustomed to our Mongolian roads, and they were nearly frightened to death." Jagaa looked up from checking his shoelaces and mumbled, "Yeah, but they should've seen what I would've done to him before I became a Christian."

Well, since that time, Jagaa has been a faithful, even if more careful, driver for the V.E.T. Net Team. He realizes that he has been changed. There is a difference in the way he responds now compared to the way he would have reacted before he came to know Jesus as his Lord. He is not perfect and will no doubt sin again, but God is always willing to forgive and will gladly renew His relationship with Him. Jagaa is growing in his faith, and it is showing in the way he lives. Admittedly, he still has a mischievous side to him that sometimes gets him into trouble.

Driverless Cars

> *Jesus answered, "I did tell you, but you do not believe. The miracles I do in my Father's name speak for me, but you do not believe because you are not my sheep."*
>
> –John 10:25–26, NIV

Although a number of auto manufacturers are now working on driverless cars in the West, years ago we had the first one right here in Mongolia. Unfortunately, unlike Jagaa and Zorgoo, several of our drivers insisted on following the wide road that leads to destruction. A rock-throwing man named Orchraa was one of those who never turned his life over to God.

Orchraa was almost midget-sized and had to sit on a thick pillow just to see over the steering wheel. He was a holdover from the old Soviet system and continued to be a staunch supporter of the Revolutionary Party—an offshoot of the former Communist Party. Many Mongolians still missed the old ways. They especially missed the monthly checks they used to receive irrespective of their personal productivity. These people were intensely loyal to their past life which slowly disappeared when the Russians walked out of Mongolia.

After several problematic countryside trips, we discovered that Orchraa was a poor mechanic. When we were far from the city, I always shuttered when he fumbled with malfunctioning parts. Regardless of how hard he worked on the van, we continually sputtered along with the same old skipping engine. He also had some issues as a driver. For example, he refused to use the headlights until darkness was completely upon us, often driving at full speed without lights. I know that we were supernaturally protected on many occasions.

On one occasion, we were returning from one of our trips and were almost back to Ulaanbaatar. The two Mongolian men in the back seat, members of the newly formed Democratic Party, were at least twice as large as little Orchraa. As we drove down a stretch of pavement with vehicles approaching in the other lane, a heated political argument erupted. Orchraa suddenly took his hands off the steering wheel and began swinging at the men in the back seat.

The concept of driverless cars may be a desirable advance in some situations, but this one was not equipped with auto-drive. I seized the steering wheel, and fortunately managed to get to the shoulder of the road. I immediately got out of the van to take over the driving. Just as my feet hit the ground, Orchraa slammed into first gear and shot back onto the road. I grabbed the door and struggled to climb back into my seat. All were silent as we drove into town. Orchraa got out of his padded driver's seat, took his pillow, and walked away from the van. He never drove for us again. Unfortunately, there is an unwritten law among drivers that if you are fired from your job, it is your responsibility to get even with your former employer. Orchraa took this rule very seriously. He was committed to seeing that he evened the score.

It was late one night shortly after our return to Ulaanbaatar, and Frances was getting ready to retire. She had just left the kitchen and was standing at our bedroom door. I was already in bed, but not yet asleep. Everything was calm and quiet, and we were on track with our evening routine, when suddenly we heard a crash. We could not immediately determine the cause of the loud noise. Soon after the first crash, there was another one accompanied by shards of glass scattering throughout our kitchen and into the hallway. Fortunately, we were in the back bedroom protected from the missiles and flying razor-like pieces of glass. Orchraa had, indeed, evened the score.

The remarkable part of the story is that our apartment was on the fourth floor and the "rock-ets" were thrown from ground level. The first rock tore a hole in the outer glass pane. Then, our fastball pitcher threw another strike right though the first hole breaking the second pane before it sailed into our apartment. Accurately hitting the window four stories up from where he stood on the ground would have been quite a feat the first time. But, the real challenge was putting the second rock right in the same small strike zone. Somehow, he managed to do just that.

Orchraa didn't stand a chance in the earlier fight with the two men in the backseat of the van, but he could have won a much larger battle if he had chosen well. Instead of accepting Christ, he made the decision to continue on his own path of destruction. Today, all of our drivers are dedicated Christians committed to safe driving practices for V.E.T. Net and our Lord. For this we are very thankful!

The Wall Came Tumbling Down

The principal of the small school at the village of Jaragalant asked us to help with the construction of a building to house the kindergarten classes. Marty Boehm, a builder and general jack-of-all trades from America, came to oversee the construction process. Shortly after he arrived, the principal was called away for several days. In his absence, we proceeded with construction without his guidance or approval.

Marty was from northern Montana, so he knew a thing or two about cold weather. He had been scouring the cold weather construction literature and found an interesting concept that proved to be very functional in Siberia. The process entailed cutting firewood-length pieces of wood from a log. These short pieces were then stacked on each other at right angles to the length of the wall. Sawdust was used as insulation between each of the mini-logs before the joints were sealed both inside and out with cement. As the wall increased in height, the cut ends of the short pieces of logs made a beautiful rustic-finish surface.

The wall was completed, and our builder left Mongolia to return home. When the principal retuned, a representative body of townspeople met him. It seems the whole village was upset! No one had ever seen anything like this kind of construction. It simply could not stand—and it didn't. A demolition crew was formed, and the wall came tumbling down.

Just as the people rejected the strange new wall of the kindergarten, the Mongolians sometimes reject the new message of Christ's love even though they have nothing else to fill the deep longing in their hearts. Some say, "Buddhism is our traditional religion, and Christianity is strange to us. We will not accept this foreign religion." Sadly, those who reject the truth miss the abundant blessing of having Jesus live in their hearts.

The Road Not Traveled

His divine power has given us everything we need for life and godliness through our knowledge of him who called us by his own glory and goodness.

–2 Peter 1:3, NIV

Mongolian herders are considered semi-nomadic because they move seasonally to traditional grazing sites. Herders leave these grazing areas to allow the grass to catch-up and get ahead of the grazing livestock. They return each year to the same sites. When unoccupied, these areas can be quite desolate with the nearest people miles away.

It was a beautiful morning one summer when we left Hangai, a county in the mountains of Owerhangai. The name, "Hangai," means uplands, and it distinguishes this part of Mongolia from the vast Gobi Desert. This day, we decided to take a shortcut by following a wagon track across a mountain pass thereby saving many miles of travel. Unfortunately, we encountered problems along the trail with patches of mud.

We were able to successfully negotiate the first risky stretch of soft track and were peacefully moving along when the wheels unexpectedly fell away from beneath us. The frame of the truck settled solidly on the ground with the wheels stuck firmly in thick, black mud. Frances took over as our newly appointed driver and got behind the wheel so that all the men could get out to push. We soon discovered that the combined strength of the four of us was not enough to even rock the truck much less free it from the tight suction of the mud. When we realized the futility of our efforts, we gave up and lay exhausted in the grass to catch our breath.

It appeared that we were in yet another seemingly hopeless situation—miles from any help in a place untraveled by herders this time of year. Unfortunately, cell phones had not yet been introduced to Mongolia. Even today, we are out of range of cell towers in many parts of this country. We had food, tents and clear water was running near the spot where we were stuck, so we were in no immediate danger. Still, it was a major inconvenience! Since we were expected in another village the next day, we decided it was time to earnestly pray for someone to pass by who could rescue us.

"What's that noise?" I thought. "Are my ears playing tricks on me?" From a distance came the sound of chains dragging, animals scraping through the brush, leather creaking and hooves striking the ground. Before long, we noticed a string of yak tied together traveling in a caravan. They were plodding up the valley on their way to the town we had left earlier that morning. Men on horseback were driving the yak as they made their way ever closer to our disabled truck.

We later learned that every two weeks these men went into the forest to cut logs for their families who lived in the small town some ten miles away. On this day, they were returning with firewood to heat their homes and cook their food. As God would have it, this just happened to be their day to travel the lonesome route. They would not pass this way again for another two weeks.

What had been a somber occasion quickly turned into jubilation. There was laughter and much talk as the herders joined our team to help us out of our dilemma. The wheels were levered from their entombment by strategically positioning long logs under the axles. Once the tires were released from the mud, the powerful yak were chained to the truck and coaxed into pulling the vehicle out of the muck. We added our shoulders and the motor to the effort, and our vehicle was moved back onto solid ground at last.

Pastor/author Dr. Gene Getz explains II Peter 1:3 (this Scripture is given at the beginning of this subsection) this way: *"Drawing on God's power, we are to do all we can to become mature followers of Jesus Christ."* [2] Although the yak did the pulling, we still had to do our part. And so it is with our spiritual walk. God requires us to be part of the process as we become more Christ-like. He does not force us to leave the mud, but when we choose to do so, He will give us the power to change and spiritual resources—like prayer—to achieve victory. It is the power of God that moves into each of us when we invite Christ into our lives. The Holy Spirit now dwells in us to give us direction—what an amazing truth: *"Christ in me."*

Driven by the Spirit

> *In the same way no one knows the thoughts of God except the Spirit of God.*
>
> –1 Corinthians 2:11b, NIV

We had driven many miles and were now passing the village of Ondor Cant. We had never worked in this region before, and we had no intention of becoming involved there now. This time, however, Frances and I both felt the pull to go into the tiny town to at least meet the people. We asked our driver to stop the van so that we could talk more about what this diversion might mean. We also felt the need to pray.

As long as the Russians were in control of Mongolia, the country was divided into states and counties much like in the United States. The counties were sub-divided into districts, and some of these districts had small villages. Ondor Cant was one of these district villages with only a few hundred residents. It existed to serve the herders living in the surrounding area and to provide a dormitory school for their children.

We met Pagamkhand who, at the time, was the community leader and school principal. The mayor happened to be a veterinarian, but Pagamhand was clearly the one in charge. Like Orchraa, she was another leftover relic of the past communist system, and as such, she ruled with an iron fist.

We quickly developed a close relationship in Ondor Cant and for several years, church groups, teachers, a principal, builders, veterinarians and medical teams worked with Pagamkhand's school. Even though she had multiple contacts with Christian people, her heart still seemed hardened, and we saw no response to the message of Christ.

Our team offered to teach preschool and summer school students in Ondor Cant where Pagamkhand's daughter, Nuda, was a teacher. Before long, Nuda became a believer, and the Holy Spirit instilled in her the gift of evangelism. She began to enthusiastically share her faith with her family and friends. Although it took many years, Pagamkhand also accepted Christ. Now all five of Pagamkhand's children, as well as other relatives, have come to know Jesus. Pagamkhand's husband was slower to accept Jesus as his personal Savior, but before he ever believed he told others about Jesus. He had witnessed such dramatic changes in the lives of his family that eventually he, too, made a decision to follow Christ.

It took some time, but ultimately Pagamkhand destroyed her Buddhist idols that once held a prominent place in her home. This was no small thing since religious statues are precious family keepsakes and considered to be very valuable to the Mongolian people. Releasing these prized possessions represents a very real sacrifice for the family. By destroying family idols, they sever their last ties to Buddhism. What a tremendous testimony!

Pagamkhand started a little Ondor Cant Bible study/home group in her home. About 20 people met in the ger on Sunday afternoons to sing praise songs and worship God. Only a short time before, no one in this small town had met Jesus. One of our teams returned to Ondor Cant where they disassembled our V.E.T. Net ger to move to another site. "Please," the people begged, "don't leave our little town. We want you to continue to teach us more about the Bible."

Pagamkhand has retired as the school principal, and she and her husband have moved to the county center. They opened a store to sell groceries and other necessities to the community. She has a license to sell alcohol and cigarettes but refuses to put these on her shelves. These products are an important part of the income of most small stores, but she wants to set a Christ-like example for her town. She has used part of the store income to support a national missionary serving in another area. Pagamkhand has been changed from a harsh communist dictator, to a loving, caring person. Only God can do this kind of heart transplant.

Nuda moved to Ulaanbaatar and began to work at V.E.T. Net as a teacher. She had a personality that bubbled over and infected all the people around her, but she also inherited some of her mother's traits and could be quite difficult at times. God did a work in her life, and she has now become an integral part of the V.E.T. Net outreach ministry to rural communities. Over the years, we have seen her entire state come to understand the truth about Jesus. Many small churches have established roots as a result of Nuda's ministry. Her brother is now the governor of Ondor Cant, and the Christian influence continues in the little village.

Nuda was not a believer when she had a common-law relationship with Muugii, who is now her husband. When she became a Christian, she was living with her young daughter from that relationship. I want you to hear Muugii's story about God totally changing his life:

> "I heard about Jesus from Nuda. I said, 'You can go your way with Jesus; I will go my way without Him.' I didn't like for my Nuda to love Jesus more than she loved me. Nuda became very sick and was diagnosed with lung disease. She had surgery, and after that my parents-in-law took away my Nuda because they didn't believe I cared for her. I was often drunk, and I became degraded in life. I left Mongolia and went to Korea to work. I was there illegally, and I worked very hard for money. At that time my life's goal was just to make more and more money. Now, I understand that my purpose was wrong:
>
> *Do not work for food that spoils, but for food that endures to eternal life, which the Son of Man will give you.*
>
> –John 6:27a, NIV
>
> I really missed my Nuda and my daughter, and I went to the countryside where they were staying. I only spent two days there because my parents-in-law didn't like me. At that time, I met a V.E.T. Net dental team. They extracted my bad teeth and shared the Good News. Then, I went back to Ulaanbaatar to live. After a year, I heard that my Nuda was starting to work with V.E.T. Net, and that she would be living in Ulaanbaatar.

My life was terrible; I was drunk much of the time, separated from my family. I missed my daughter, and I had conflicts with my parents. I felt lonely, and I didn't have money. Sometimes I wanted to die, but God protected me. I began asking and praying to the Unknown One—"What is the meaning of life? Why am I living? What is the purpose of my life?" One day a girl gave me an invitation to go to church. I visited her church and felt very peaceful.

I really missed my daughter, and I decided to meet my wife and my daughter in Ulaanbaatar. I visited their home, but to my surprise and disappointment—there was my mother-in-law. This was not my plan and she scolded me and gave me some work. This work was to repair a little addition to the house for my daughter. I agreed and started to do my new job. I thought that my mother-in-law was a very hard person. Now, I know that this was the beginning of my life's recovery and I began to turn from my sinful ways.

Three months later, some of the V.E.T. Net leaders met me and said that I could work as a veterinary technician. I couldn't believe my ears. After this meeting my tears were coming from my heart because I had never felt loved like this. They hugged me, they trusted me, and they gave me a job. It was amazing, and I was feeling God's amazing love through them. This was July of 2005 and in August Nuda's pastor met me and shared with me about life's meaning. Then I accepted Christ into my heart.

In October of 2005 we were married in Christ. We were surprised that Nuda's parents agreed to our marriage and even helped to organize the wedding.

The last seven years God's plan for my life has been realized through my wonderful support team at V.E.T. Net and direction from my pastor. I am now also serving as assistant pastor of my church. I have

> just completed my 5-year veterinary degree and am now a veterinarian at V.E.T. Net.
>
> Now we have Nuda's two nieces and a nephew living with us. These three teenagers really like to live with us and my daughter. I am thankful to God for their spiritual growth day by day, and they have joy and peace. Every evening we share with each other about what has happened that day and we spend funny time and studying many things too. These last several years God has completely changed my whole life. I never imagined before that these things were possible in God."
>
> –Muugii

Muugii continues to work with V.E.T. Net, and today Nuda is a leader in our teaching department. The couple is very active in their church as they continue to disciple younger V.E.T. Net staff. Their family stands as an amazing testimony to the power of God and how He dramatically changes lives.

Nuda has a younger sister, Oyunaa, and both have become essential members of the V.E.T. Net team. When we first met Oyunaa, she was herding sheep and goats. After she finished high school in Ondor Cant, her parents wanted her to continue her education. She was happy to stay with the family and help care for the animals, but eventually she agreed to move to Ulaanbaatar and live with Nuda to attend university.

Oyunaa visited our Sunday fellowship group, but she was extremely shy, and she came infrequently. She continued to hear the gospel from her sister and others. In 2000, she accepted Christ through her own personal study of the Bible. She worked as a summer teacher for V.E.T. Net during the summers of 2002, 2003, and in 2003, became a full-time staff member in our organization. Now this shy, young woman is one of the most outgoing members of the team. She currently serves as the Chief Operational Officer for the organization with a staff of 75 full-time and more than 100 part-time Mongolian personnel under her direction. God has taken this young sheepherder and shaped her into one of the most important members of this ministry in reaching across the nation of

Mongolia for Him.

> *Still other seed fell on good soil, which it produced a crop—a hundred, sixty or thirty times what was sown.*
>
> –Matthew 13:8, NIV

God Is Preparing Each of Us to Carry Out His Plan

God has a purpose for us. Just as He is growing Tserendorj, Zorgoo, Jagaa, Oyunaa, Nuda and Muugii, and Pagamkhand, He is able to shape you and me into harvesters for His kingdom. He plants some of us right where we stand, and others, He uses to prepare the soil in a far-off land such as Mongolia where they plant seeds and nurture their growth. Then, when the time is just right, He gathers in a bountiful harvest—a cornucopia of herders and villagers of every possible description. These too will be planted to produce an additional rich harvest for God. We praise God that this is a part of the ongoing story of V.E.T. Net as it continues to spread throughout Mongolia.

We would do well to take note of the fact that Joshua had conquered much of the Promised Land and was getting some years on him when the Lord said to him, *"You are very old, and there are still very large areas of land to be taken over,"* (Joshua 13:1, NIV). This is pretty amazing, isn't it? God did not say to him, "Joshua, what a wonderful job you have done; you can retire now." He didn't reach down with a holy pat on the back. Instead, He said, in effect, "Get on with it! You will have all of eternity to rest, rock in your chair and retire. There is still a lot of land to take" (See Joshua 13:1).

There are many Mongolians who have not yet heard of this wonderful Savior, Jesus. This is a significant time in the history for the Mongolian people as many hear about Him for the first time and trust Him for their salvation. What a wonderful experience it has been to play even a small part in His plan. May He receive all the glory forever and ever. Amen.

Notes:

1. The church we attended was started when a home group of adult couples, along with their young children, met with our Sunday college group one weekend. We were on a camping outing on the *Tuul River,* about an hour from the city. Soon, there were sermons offered at the riverside followed by baptisms in the river. Before long, the *Holy Way Church* was born. This quickly became a dynamic group of believers making a lasting impact on Mongolia. The church has grown, divided numerous times and has started its own mission churches in distant towns.

2. Getz, G. A. (2011). *Life Essentials Study Bible,* II Peter 1:3, loc. 151009–151024, (Holman Bible Publishers, Nashville, Tennessee) Kindle Book.

Figure 7.1. "Parable of the Runaway Horse" — two horses tied together

Chapter 7

The Field Manual

> *As the rain and the snow come down from heaven, and do not return to it without watering the earth and making it bud and flourish, so that it yields seed for the sower and bread for the eater, so is my word that goes out from my mouth: It will not return to me empty, but will accomplish what I desire and achieve the purpose for which I sent it.*
>
> –Isaiah 55:10–11, NIV

An early autumn blizzard in 1995 blew horizontal darts of snow that streamed across the windshield. Our Russian van crawled over the rough, unpaved tracks as we made our way to the city of Muren, the capital of Khovsgol—one of the most beautiful states in northern Mongolia.

We drove into Muren and made our way to the only gas station in this city of 27,000 people. There were few vehicles on the road in those days, yet we still had to sit in a line waiting for fuel. "As soon as you fill your tanks, follow us to the police station—we are taking your vehicle," the brusque officer blurted. He was looking for vehicles to be used in an emergency search for a missing airliner that had been expected at the Muren airport earlier in the afternoon. Our Russian van was just the type of vehicle they wanted for the search.

Our freedom in America and familiarity with our police system did not prepare us for the intimidating post-Soviet police departments still remaining in Mongolia. The Mongolians themselves were terrified of the police, and that feeling was slow to dissipate. Respect for the men and women in blue still borders on abject fear.

We obediently followed the police and arrived at the ancient government building filled with smoke from rank-smelling Russian cigarettes. As we waited patiently, filled with apprehension, word came that the crashed airliner had been found, and everyone onboard was dead except for the pilot. We learned that the Mongolian Airline domestic flight had flown into a mountain in the blinding snow storm. Death hung in the cold air that night as 47 people were flung out into eternity.

What a feeling of emptiness to realize that 47 people had been killed in the blink of an eye—people who very likely had never heard of Jesus Christ and his loving message of salvation. This thought was continually before us: "How would we ever reach this nation with the message of Christ?"

Once the location of the crash site was identified, the police allowed us to continue our travels. Ironically, we were scheduled for meetings the next day in the hometown of the pilot who had miraculously survived the crash. The little village was understandably stunned by the impact of the disaster, so organizing any kind of meaningful meeting was impossible. We spent the night in the small town, and the next day I walked down to investigate the river that skirted the community.

The river flows from Lake Khovshol some 75 miles to our north. This is a long, picturesque lake that begins on the border of Russia before moving deep into this northern state of Khovshol. A crystal-clear river spills from the lip of the lake to begin its arduous trip south. From there it flows east and finally north to Russia and into the famous Lake Baikal. It supplies the village with clean water and abundant fish.

It was a gorgeous river with sparking water bouncing over smooth rocks. It was too wide to wade across, so I paused to flip my artificial grasshopper fly along the ripples at the river's edge. The fishing was poor, and I soon turned my attention to a group of men surrounding a tiny object. I watched intently as they unwound a long cord attached to a toy boat. The little boat was carved from a small block of wood about 12 inches long. It had a fixed rudder that caused it to cut into the current and drive to the middle of the river as it was held from the shore by the cord. Spaced along the cord every couple of yards was another short line about a foot long. On each of these lines was a sharp hook with a plump, juicy grasshopper attached to the end. As the little boat bounced in the river currents, the grasshoppers skipped on the surface of the water in a most irresistible dance. The fish lurking below the surface of the river were in a feeding frenzy as they watched the native grasshoppers issue an invitation to dinner.

The men had prepared each hook carefully with sharpened points and just the right bait. One man held the line with its many hooks in the river. The fish were driven to insanity as the hoppers bounced on the water while the contented fishermen shared their interesting stories. As the line coursed through the water, sleek, silver fish were firmly caught on their hooks, and the fisherman pulled the little boat to shore to collect their bounty. They carefully prepared the hooks once again and launched the boat for another bountiful catch.

I cast my line along the edge of the water with a bit of hair and feathers shaped into a hopper that I hoped would capture the attention of a fish. Unlike the other fishermen, I knew my success to snare a fish would require a wrist-wrenching battle. Looking upstream, I saw the Mongolian men stretched out on the bank resting on their elbows and paying little attention to their tiny, bobbing boat. They smoked their rolled cigarettes and laughed at this foreigner who thrashed the water with his phony grasshopper catching little for all his effort.

Fishin' for Men

> *Then He said to them, "Follow Me, and I will make you fishers of men."*
>
> –Matthew 4:19, NIV

Jesus visited with the fishermen along the shores of Galilee. I believe he built strong relationships with these men before he ever encouraged them to make a commitment to follow Him. Through the lives of these weathered fishermen of Galilee, Jesus teaches us how to put out many hooks as well. He put feet to some of his closing words.

With the vastness of this country, it was unlikely that Western missionaries could ever share the gospel effectively. But, Jesus modeled the perfect plan: It is called discipleship.

I have reflected back on this beautiful river scene many times and on the spiritual lessons I learned on the bank that day. Regardless of how diligently I fished, I only snagged a small number. The same is true of us as we serve as fishers of men. If we are able to build a team and disciple its members, the catch can be limitless. Organizations spend a great deal of time in strategic planning, but Jesus already has the strategy. We should follow His example. You see, in His humanity, Jesus understood that He could only manage a certain number of close relationships. Dr. Lynn Anderson, President of Hope Network, put it this way:

> Jesus didn't have the same level of intimacy with all twelve of his disciples. Like all normal human beings, Jesus had special friends—
>
> In other words, the relationships through which Jesus' equipping ministry flowed were natural human relationships. Normally, human beings can manage only a limited number of intimate relationships. Not even Jesus was capable of an unlimited number of intimate relationships. [1]

The Mystery

> *I tell you the truth, anyone who has faith in me will do what I have been doing. He will do even greater things than these, because I am going to the Father.*
>
> –John 14:12, NIV

The statement Jesus made in John 14:12 is not easily understood. We think, "Oh, what did he mean? How could I possibly do more than Jesus?" But in fact, Jesus meant these words for you and me living in the here and now. It is a principle to be implemented today. Jesus prepared his disciples until they were ready to be *fishers of men*. Then, He sent them out two-by-two. Soon there were others, and eventually 72. Throughout the years, millions and millions have been reached by this simple strategy of multiplication. It is Jesus who wrote the Field Manual—the Bible—and He passed it along to you and me. He crystalized the plan into one simple sentence: *Go and make disciples*.

By ourselves, John 14:12 is not possible, but with the Holy Spirit, we can do greater things than Christ did while on earth. One person may not make a great impact by himself, but what if he places many hooks in the water? This is the secret of how discipleship exemplifies the grasshoppers in the water.

> *The next day John was there again with two of his disciples. When he saw Jesus passing by, he said, "Look, the Lamb of God!" When the two disciples heard him say this, they followed Jesus.*
>
> –John 1:35-37, NIV

As we read further in John 1, we notice that the first thing Andrew did was to go and tell his brother, Simon Peter, about Jesus. Then, Jesus called Phillip. Phillip found Nathanael and told him. Soon Jesus had the 12 together, and He began the process of discipling these men. It wasn't in a stuffy classroom setting, but rather it was training where the rubber meets the road—experiential.

These men walked with Jesus and learned from Him as He cared for the needs of those who pressed around Him. They even cleaned up the leftovers after a meal of fish and loaves. He was building a team and preparing them to carry the gospel message to a dying world.

At V.E.T. Net, we do everything Jesus modeled. We simply follow Him as we develop teams of disciples and prepare them to be fishers of men. We follow His *Field Manual.*

The Parable of the Runaway Horse

> *We proclaim him, admonishing and teaching everyone with all wisdom, so that we may present everyone perfect in Christ.*
>
> –Colossians 1:28, NIV

Surely, the heartbeat of the Mongolian man sounds like a horse galloping across the steppe. Whether he works in a bank in the city, or lives in a ger in the countryside, his close affinity with horses was built into his DNA—even before Genghis Khan conquered most of the known world on horseback.

There was once a Mongolian herder who loved his fast horses above everything. He was aware that his neighbors often remarked about his swift animals whenever the subject of racing was debated. He always stood tall in his saddle and rode with great pride across the land where his animals grazed. He was continually searching for ways to improve his herd and breed them to run just a little faster.

One day, this herder received word about a man in a distant land who had extremely fast horses. He thought to himself, "I must see those horses and buy one of the stallions to improve my breeding stock." This thought was always on his mind. He had trouble sleeping because he thought about owning horses that could fly like the wind.

When he could stand it no longer, he asked his wife to pack some dried yak meat and hard cheese for a long trip. He rolled his food in a small pack and tied it to the back of his wooden saddle on his favorite work-horse. His wife threw a dipper of milk into the air to encourage the gods to bless his trip and return him safely to her. The airborne drops of milk sparkled in the morning sun as the herder began his long journey in search of the extraordinary horses he'd heard about. The woman loved this crusty old herder husband of hers even though she knew he spent more time thinking about his horses than about her. After all, he was a good provider, and they always had plenty to eat.

The herder rode hard each day. During the late evenings, he snuggled in his warm winter del and looked at the beauty of the vast Mongolian landscape. It seemed endless—much like what a sailor would see when scanning the open sea. The horseman struck his flint against the steel and sparks leaped to the kindling he had gathered. The wood began to smolder as he protected it from the breeze with his cupped hands. Blowing gently on the glowing tinder, he nursed a little flame into a larger fire fueled by the dung he had collected around his meager camp. After chewing awhile on his store of homemade jerky, he packed his pipe full from the valuable pouch of tobacco he always carried. He lit it and exhaled the fragrant smoke slowly. This was a man consumed by a dream, a man who, at the moment, was reveling in the beginning of its fulfillment.

After several days, the tired herder arrived at the famous horse trainer's ger and was warmly welcomed by this hospitable family. "Come in! Come in!" the horse trainer called. A cup of salty-milk tea was quickly placed in the traveler's hands. He sat in the back of the ger, the place of honor, with Buddhist idols staring over his shoulder. Three jiggers of milk-vodka brought a warming sensation to the visitor's cold, weary body. Small decorative snuff bottles were exchanged with his new-found acquaintance. They sat together around the crackling **stove**—a welcome change from the cold days and nights on the trail.

Inside the ger, the horse trainer's wife rolled dough on a board that was placed on the bed as she prepared fresh homemade noodles for dinner. A delightful odor from chunks of boiling mutton wafted across the ger. The mouth-watering smell was a tantalizing reminder of the herder's wife's familiar cooking. The men peeled the freshly cooked mutton from the bones with their knives. Not one shred of meat was left clinging to the polished bones that collected in a pile on the table.

Every ger has a small **stove** in the center of a single, circular room. Dung or wood is fed through a door in the side of the stove. The round lid forming the top of the stove can be removed and replaced by a large pot that fits through the opening. In this way, the flame comes in direct contact with the pot—very efficient.

With the completion of traditional formalities, it was now time to get down to the business of horse trading. The old herder could hardly wait to see the young stud he had traveled so far to buy. He tried to hide his anxiety because he knew this would give the horse owner the upper hand in the dealings ahead. Together, they walked outside to untie their horses from the rope hitch and mounted up for the ride to the place where the herd grazed peacefully on the hillside. As they rode slowly through the group of horses, the herder examined each young stallion carefully. Finally, his eyes locked onto a sleek, smooth, two-year old sorrel. When he watched this young stallion run, it was as if his hooves barely touched the ground. This was the horse he must have to improve his herd! After much dickering, a deal was finally struck.

The next morning, with great pride, the herder placed the lead rope on his new treasure, and the long trip home began. The young stallion was excited throughout the first day's travel. There were new vistas to see as he inhaled the cold air mile after mile. By the second day, he was beginning to miss his old friends he used to frolic with as they played the days away in his pleasant homeland. Each day took him further and further from the horses he knew and his old way of life. He longed to return to the place he knew so well and the comfort of familiarity.

The herder finally arrived at his home in the valley and approached his ger with his new, glistening horse. He was tired and ready to rest from the long journey, but he knew that he could not leave this energetic, young stallion alone with his complacent herd. He was certain his new horse would quickly take flight and not stop until his hooves felt the earth they had plied in his youth. He would whinny as he topped the last hill to alert his old friends of his return.

The herder had a problem. There were no fences to hold his new horse. With the open range of Mongolia, there was nothing to keep the horse at his new home—no friends, no familiar surroundings, no memories. This fast young horse had been taken completely away from his world and placed in another one totally alien to him. No wonder he craved his old friends and the pastures he knew so well.

The wizened herder took a short length of rope and fashioned a loop to slip over his new horse's head—loose enough not to choke, but tight enough to keep him from slipping free. The other loop was placed on an old, reliable home-range gelding. The old horse led his new burden down to where the clear water coursed through the rocks, and he showed him where to find the best grass in the valley. After the old gelding had been tied to his new, annoying, frolicking friend for many days, the young stallion learned the ways of his new home enough to help him forget his past life. Then one day, the rope was no longer needed. The joy of being accepted and feeling at home in the new herd brushed away the loss of his old life. Even though the old gelding was exhausted from the lack of privacy and the grind of always having someone grazing beside him, he took pride in knowing that he now had another close friend who was adjusting well.

Some months later, the herder left on a second trip, and soon returned with another new horse to add to his developing herd. The young sorrel bought on his last trip exploded with pride when the loop was slipped over his head to tie him to the newly purchased horse. Now it was his turn to teach the new young addition the lessons that helped him forget his old life.

The analogy of the horses can be applied to any new believer, whether Mongolian or Western, when suddenly jerked from a familiar environment into a completely foreign world. He is faced with the new world of Christianity with its own language, words, and values he does not understand and is not ready to embrace. There is even a whole new set of friends to make with different habits, different life styles and a different future eternal address. People read the same Book year after year and ponder its pages with wrinkled brows. They meet regularly to sing, to worship, praise God and encourage one another. The newcomer finds himself in a very strange world, indeed, and wonders nervously how to fit into his totally new surroundings without appearing hopelessly out of place. Like the young stallion, our new Christian friend may also be likely to flee. He may sit stoically in his padded pew, but the pads will not comfort or protect him from the lonely feeling of being displaced from what he has known in his past. He will thirst for his old life and long for things left behind.

This is the essence of the *Great Commission* Jesus Himself gave to us when he said, in effect, "Go and tie yourself to a young believer and lead him closer to Me." He also encouraged young believers to seek a mature Christian who would be willing to become their mentor. This need exists in our Christian organizations, churches and anywhere we encounter young Christians. By partnering together, we can produce multipliers and strong, sustainable churches. This challenge that Jesus gave to us before leaving this earth is the only way faith in Christ will truly impact our world.

The Parable of the Runaway Horse was presented to a group of countryside church leaders from many parts of Mongolia. At the end of the presentation, we gave each participant a four-foot length of rope with loops on the ends. Then we demonstrated what it was like to be physically tied to another believer—men to men and women to women. After the demonstration, the participants were challenged to spiritually tie themselves to another believer when they returned to their communities.

The next year, one of the ladies who had attended the training told me that after hearing *The Parable of the Runaway Horse,* she returned to her home and tied herself to her husband. Pointing to the man standing beside her, she said, "This is my husband. I brought him with me for training this year. He is my disciple." She learned well the lesson for spiritual multiplication.

The Book

> *Do not let this Book of the Law depart from your mouth; meditate on it day and night, so that you may be careful to do everything written in it. Then you will be prosperous and successful.*
>
> –Joshua 1:8, NIV

Our volunteer was a seasoned old dairy veterinarian from Wisconsin. He had come to Mongolia to train our young veterinarians. We planned a trip for him to a distant state where he could work with herders and their livestock. The veteran "shuttle-vet" soon learned to tell Mongolian time during his stay in this country expressed as "before lunch" or "after lunch." Herders are never compelled by the need to keep an appointment on time. They come when they can, and it is often a couple of hours after the training is to begin. Patience is a key prerequisite for working with Mongolian herders. This new friend of ours came from a very busy veterinary practice where time was considered money, so he nearly had a heart attack from the stress of waiting for meetings to start. He was accustomed to being overly busy and found it impossible to relax while waiting patiently for the herders to arrive.

In the end, the training was completed, and our team was on its way back to Ulaanbaatar. In spite of the schedule, the older veterinarian had a great time, and came to our home to share his experiences. "Listen," he said, "I want to give you a tip for the next volunteers. Tell them to bring lots of books. I had so much downtime, and I only had one book. I finished it the first day, and after that, all I had was the Bible." What a great book to be marooned with! We pray that this volunteer from Wisconsin came to appreciate the Bible more as he saw God working around him.

Ruminate on the Word

> *How sweet are Your words to my taste, sweeter than honey to my mouth!*
>
> –Psalm 119:103, NIV

The Apostle Paul teaches that in the beginning we are babies in our faith who know only how to drink milk. But in time, we are meant to move on to the solid food of spiritual maturity.

Most Mongolians love to drink horse milk; it is a real treat. In fact, it is the Mongolian equivalent to Coca Cola. Foals are tied side-by-side on a long rope stretched across the ground between two stakes. The mares go out in the morning to graze and later return home to be milked and nurse their foals. The women actually do the milking, while the men hold the foal near the mare to give her the impression that the foal is nursing. I know it sounds dangerous to be underneath a horse trying to fill a bucket with milk, and sometimes it is.

The mare's milk is fermented for twelve days until it becomes slightly alcoholic. The alcohol preserves the milk making it possible to be stored even in warm weather. It tastes a bit like—well, there is really nothing to compare it to.

The only problem with this practice, besides the obvious danger to the herder's wife, is that milking the mare takes part of the milk that would otherwise feed the foal. If the young horses do not get adequate nutrition, they become underdeveloped and can be stunted for the rest of their life. The same can be said of young Christians who desperately need the pure milk of the Word of God, but only hear the gospel without being exposed to the complete teachings of the Bible; they are predisposed to accept false beliefs. This causes them to be stunted in their spiritual growth.

Ruminants, such as cows, have four-compartment stomachs with the last one being more like the simple stomach of non-ruminants. The first stomach, the rumen, is a large tank where cellulose is broken down by micro-organisms and made absorbable. Young ruminants have a bypass around the rumen for the first months of their life. The milk is shunted to the last stomach where it can be immediately prepared for use by the young. As these calves, lambs and kids begin to graze, their feed goes directly into the rumen to be broken down into useful nutrients, and the shunt is no longer needed. Ruminants gather their feed as they graze the lush pastures, then lie down in the shade to regurgitate and re-chew their cud.

When we first come to know Christ, we need the simple teachings of the Bible that allow us to mature to a point where we can handle more complex principles. As we continue to study deeper truths, we must ruminate on the Word. It does not always go down as easily as the shunted milk, so we need to regurgitate it and ruminate on it continually. In a similar manner, when the Holy Spirit breaks down God's Word for us, it becomes a powerful nutrient for our soul. Jesus taught simple truths to the disciples as they walked with Him, before challenging them to learn deeper life principles.

In cattle production, we use creep-feeders for the calves. These allow small calves to go between the bars to access the feed. The calves soon become self-feeders as they eat as much and as often as they want. They go in and out of these feeders and constantly fill themselves with grain. This is exactly what we encourage the V.E.T. Net staff to do. We want to wean them from the spiritual milk and see them begin to eat the solid food of God. Eventually, they will become self-feeders, and mature in their walk so that they can hold the bottle for younger Christians.

It is encouraging to see our V.E.T. Net team engrossed in the Word on their own. There is one huge difference in creep-feeding calves and those who feed themselves on the Word. Ultimately, the calves get too large to enter the feeder. This never happens with Christians. We are never too spiritually mature to stop feeding on God's Field Manual. We are in the trenches, and the enemy surrounds us. However, when we ingest and ruminate on the teachings of Jesus, we incorporate these principles into our life in a way that prepares us for the battle.

It is God's will for us to ravenously eat and digest His Word because it makes us strong and ready to deliver the message of salvation to the nations. In the beginning, V.E.T. Net was a small, ill-defined team. As we grew in number, the need for more structure geared toward sustainability became apparent. If this ministry is going to continue past our time of leadership, the team must be discipled by mature Christians empowered to lead themselves and others into the future. Unless they are feeding on Scripture, they will never be able to take the reins to complete the task. We often talk of sustainability when we think of financial stability. But more important by far is spiritual sustainability.

Too Comfortable

> *Praise be to the God and Father of our Lord Jesus Christ, the Father of compassion and the God of all comfort, who comforts us in all our troubles, so that we can comfort those in any trouble with the comfort we ourselves have received from God.*
>
> –2 Corinthians 1:3–4, NIV

My pen was nearly frozen, and the ink was flowing reluctantly that morning. The Mongolian winter was just around the bend. The worst part of the day was getting up and leaving our warm, cozy sleeping bags.

I love camping in the countryside this time of year. Indeed, fall is my favorite season. The grass is turning brown even as the weeds and shrubs turn brilliantly colorful. Larch trees are like a golden blanket stretched over the shoulders of the stooped mountains. Everything is wonderful—except for the morning icy air with its shocking greeting.

God imprinted our furry friend, the marmot, with genetic wisdom to avoid this early, jolting chill. Marmots are a seasonal gift to this nation. After months of eating mutton, the herders are ready for a change in diet. Then, this fat little rodent bursts onto the scene in the spring with his tasty, greasy meat that tempts the palate of almost every Mongolian. The fur is valuable, and the economy of the herding families is boosted with every crack of rifle fire as the men lay motionless for hours on end just to get a clear shot. The ring of the rifle serves as a warning bell for the wife to begin stoking the dung fire in preparation for the feast.

My grandfather, Clyde Edwards, farmed the red clay hills of Anson County, North Carolina for many years. I remember him enjoying much the same kind of treat when the hounds put a 'possum to tree. He would cage his catch for a couple of weeks and purge the varmint's gruesome eating habits with cornbread and milk. When this rat-like marsupial was too fat to walk, the mouth-watering victuals blessed the black, cast-iron frying pan, and later, our stomachs.

As I walked around the hillsides one day, I saw that the marmots had moved their families underground and pulled the holes in behind them. Most of the 12-inch holes were completely closed to protect these fat balls of fur from the ensuing winter and from morning shivers. Even though these marmots were my close neighbors, they were oblivious to my suffering as I combated a cruel, cold world that took my breath away while they crossed their legs in the warmth of their dens and snored peacefully. Clearly, they did not give my hardships a passing thought.

In 2 Corinthians 1:3-4, Paul is not talking about comfort as in a stuffed sofa, familiar foods, or mattresses that guarantee a peaceful sleep. The Church of Jesus Christ is not a dwelling in which to become complacent. It is indeed a wonderful place of comfort from a world that seems to be spinning totally out of control, but one that cannot confine us within its physical walls. As Jesus' earthly ministry was nearing completion, He essentially said to get out of our holes and go to the ends of the earth to make disciples (see Mathew 28:19). Eventually, as our team became more mature in faith, we began to kick them out of their comfort zones and into the cruel world.

> *One man's faith allows him to eat everything, but another man, whose faith is weak, eats only vegetables. The man who eats everything must not look down on him who does not, and the man who does not eat everything must not condemn the man who does, for God has accepted him.*
>
> --Romans 14:2–3, NIV

I almost forgot. In talking about this mouth-watering, culinary delight, it would be inexcusable not to share the **roasted marmot recipe**. Instructions:

Take one plump (approximately 20 pound) marmot and singe the hair off with a Russian blowtorch. While singeing the hair, have assistants build a dung fire with seasoned yak dung. Place

Ingredients for **Roasted Marmot:**

1. One fat marmot
2. Seven round two-inch stones
3. A Russian blow torch
4. A blazing dung fire
5. No pot needed

the seven round stones in the fire, and heat to red-hot temperatures. Incise the marmot down the midsection, and peal the skin off the varmint. Cut the meat into serving-size pieces before placing it back into the skin. Carefully remove the red-hot stones from the dung and place them in the skin with the meat. Sew the incision back together with a piece of ligament. Next, place the marmot over the fire, and roast until well done. Reopen the incision, and share the delectable morsels with your friends. Remember, it goes well with fermented horse milk.

Get Out of Your Burrow

In all my prayers for all of you, I always pray with joy because of your partnership in the gospel from the first day until now, being confident of this, that he who began a good work in you will carry it on to completion until the day of Christ Jesus.

–Philippians 1:4–6, NIV

What is it like to be in partnership with the Apostle Paul? I have been involved in several partnerships during my career as a veterinary practitioner. All of these were successful because we had the same goals, the same focus and the same values. In order to be in partnership with Paul, we must share the same goals, focus and values with him. Indeed, we must accept the likelihood of risks—stoning, chains, imprisonment, lashes, hunger, shipwreck, snakebite and death. We must be willing to suffer for Christ in unimaginable ways if we are to effectively share the gospel message.

We can't stay in the comfortable hole with our family if we truly want to enjoy a rich, full Christian life. If we want the "good work to be carried to completion," we must crawl from our warm dens and begin to look around for those who are in need of food, clothing, shelter, and even more importantly, Christ. The new church organ can wait. The extension on the building can be postponed, and even the cost of living increases might be put on the back burner. However, reaching out to the hurting and dying in our neighborhoods and those beyond the mountains and oceans must not wait. We cannot know His fullness unless we dare to share Him with others. Christ wants you and me to walk along beside Him. If we are in partnership with Paul, we, too, will be looking for opportunities to share the gospel. What an honor it is to be invited to go along with the eternal God's plans, for surely our reward will be great.

Trust Me

> *Do not take along any gold or silver or copper in your belts; take no bag for the journey, or extra tunic, or sandals or a staff; for the worker is worth his keep.*
>
> – Matthew 10:9–10, NIV

Jesus was the disciples' shepherd. He prepared them and mentored them as they walked together. Finally, He empowered them, and pushed them out of the nest. It must have been a frightening time for the disciples. They had been with Jesus and watched Him perform miracle after miracle. Now they were on their own. He had kicked all of the props out from under them, and they found themselves without a guide. That is, except for the Holy Spirit.

Faith is considerably easier when you have a sizable bank account in reserve. Oh yes, my friend; we can be pridefully inflated with faith when we know there is a cushion to catch our fall. But when we leave the extra tunic and sandals at home and there is no cash in the bag, that is where true faith has its beginning. This is where we truly see God and experience Him personally.

Notice that God provides everything we need just like He provided manna and quail and water for the Israelites in the desert during their exodus from Egypt. As we leave the comfort of our Christian family, we find this is exactly how it is with God. He supplies everything we need when we are about His business. When Jesus sent the disciples out two-by-two, He said to them, *"Don't take a bunch of stuff with you. Travel light"* (Matthew 10:9).

I'm always amazed when we travel with our Mongolian teammates. They take so little when they go on extended trips into the countryside. Westerners, including Frances, carry large suitcases filled with enough stuff for a year's stay, while the Mongols only take a little bag with bare essentials. When we stop for an overnight stay, they often go to a stream to wash out a few things and suspend them on branches or lay them flat on the grass to dry.

Fan the Flames

For this reason I remind you to fan into flame the gift of God.

–2 Timothy 1:6a, NIV

The edelweiss blossom is not really white like snow, but more of a grey-green color that grows in star shapes with more than one flower on each stalk. A single flower is not particularly impressive or attractive. However, when viewed together on the hillsides of the Mongolian mountain passes, they offer another awesome view of God's creative handiwork that is simply breathtaking to behold.

Just a few years ago, Mongolians picked these quarter-size flowers to carefully dry at just the right stage of maturity. No wise herder would be caught dead without a supply of these dried stars in his pocket. In fact, he might well be found very dead if he forgot them. That is because the standard piece of herder equipment in the past was a little flint stone and accompanying steel. An ample supply of dried edelweiss, flint, and steel could always be found in a carefully packed pouch that hung by his side. When dry, the edelweiss was extremely flammable, and when held close to the flint, a spark from striking the steel would start the flower smoldering. After a few strong puffs on the petals, a little flame ignited. Soon, some dry dung gently crumbled on the edelweiss encouraging the flame. Sticks were added to boost the flames into a cozy fire. Cold hands could be warmed and food and tea cooked and brewed, or heated. Before matches were common, only a few years ago, this little packet of equipment and dried edelweiss could spell the difference between life and death, or worse, not having a light for their rolled smokes.

In 1995, we saw the spark that began to smolder in the hearts of many of our Mongolian students and friends. A revolution began in V.E.T. Net that spread across the land like wildfire from a spark escaping the edelweiss. The flame was in the hearts of the staff: teachers, veterinarians, administrators, drivers, cleaners, accountants. It has since turned into a roaring fire. The old religious practices are now being replaced by a relationship with the one True God.

> *Turning around, Jesus saw them following and asked, "What do you want?" They said, "Rabbi" (which means Teacher), "Where are you staying?" "Come," he replied, "and you will see." So they went and saw where he was staying, and spent that day with him. It was about the tenth hour.*
>
> –John 1:38-39, NIV

A couple of John the Baptist's disciples accepted the offer of Jesus. They went home with Him to spend the day together. What a great example and lesson this was for us. Our tiny apartment in Mongolia has been used to see the lives of many students changed for God. It might be considered a slum apartment in our American culture, but the love that radiates from a balanced Christian marriage and family speaks loudly, regardless of size or cost of the home. A Christian home that is filled with hospitality is one of the greatest places in which to influence the lives of others. There is not a better venue for people to see the love of Christ than the home.

We started sending the V.E.T. Net Team into the world. It was obvious the only thing that would make this a lasting work was the maturity of the believers. They were like Jesus' own original disciples—not people we might have chosen. What a blessing to see these young folks growing into roles of responsibility just as the original disciples of Jesus. We stand amazed at the effectiveness of the strategy of Jesus on these lives, and the power of multiplying themselves in their own culture. V.E.T. Net teams are going to places we have never been before—all over Mongolia—taking modern, veterinary drugs, quality education and the message of Christ to remote communities. Yes, the spark that started a fire for God is being blown by the wind of the Spirit all over this country. We will continue to fan the flames with the Word of God in these distant areas and watch with awe as He reaps His harvest in this land of the Khans.

Jesus could have had a mega church. After all, He attracted thousands to hear Him speak and watch Him perform miracles.

It would have been easy for Him to have a huge crowd show up every weekend, but he did something quite different. He chose a small group of men and tied Himself to them. He built into their lives through His teaching and through His example. Jesus could have directly impacted thousands with his ministry, but instead, he influenced the lives of multiple millions through the men he discipled. They are the ones who impacted the world through the power of the Holy Spirit living within them.

Share the Light

> *The light shines in the darkness, but the darkness has not understood it.*
>
> –John 1:5, NIV

The blizzard was fierce, with snow obscuring our windscreen as we made our way into the backcountry of Mongolia. We broke through drift after drift slowly making our way toward a small village. Sometimes we backed out and ran back and forth to pack the snow so that we could make our way. The transmission kept slipping out of reverse, and soon we were only able to move forward. The white bank before us was just too much for our Russian van. We were hopelessly trapped—the blizzard had won the battle. But we had a shovel and lots of help, so we dug and pushed and dug and pushed. Inch by inch, we progressed until the drift was broken only to find that now we were unable to engage any gear. The motor hummed beautifully, but we were stuck in neutral. The transmission was helpless to convert the hum of the engine into motion.

What's this? Perhaps someone to help us! No, it was two men on a motorcycle wanting to borrow a headlight. These two men were on a motorcycle in a blinding blizzard with no windshield! I guess they figured we weren't going anywhere, so we didn't need our headlights. Any other time, I would have laughed, but tonight with five Mongolians, an American veterinarian, and a little girl, I couldn't see the humor. I have been in some tough circumstances, but this time I was certain that if God did not intervene, we would spend a very miserable night; that is if we didn't freeze to death. Well, God did intervene! Our driver and translator were able to patch the transmission, so we blundered on until we came to the remote ger-town. It was 3:00 a.m. when we finally closed our eyes for sleep.

This is the confidence we have in approaching God; that if we ask anything according to his will, he hears us. And if we know that he hears us—whatever we ask—we know that we have what we asked of him.

–1 John 5:14–15, NIV

We can ask for anything—that's anything—absolutely anything in His will, and we have it. If we are where He wants us to be doing what He has planned for us to do, we have that kind of power. You see, it is all about being close to God. If we are walking along by ourselves, asking is a waste of time.

And the gospel must first be preached to all nations.

–Mark 13:10, NIV

As Jesus was talking with His disciples about the *end times,* He made this statement: "Before I return, all the nations of the world will hear the gospel" (Paraphrase Mark 13:10).

As I explained earlier, Mongolia was one of those nations that had not heard the gospel of Jesus Christ. This country was closed to the gospel for centuries, but now, we had been allowed to cross the border through a wide-open door. The challenge was this: What would be the strategy? How would we gain the opportunity to share about the Savior in a loving and caring way?

V.E.T. Net had a project to train veterinarians in the counties in the state of Ovs. We worked with private practitioners in the state capital as well as in rural counties. In addition, we visited most of the counties and those along the northwestern border with Russia. One county had an unusual name—Salt. As we traveled across the county, we were able to see the reason for its name. Along the Russian border was a huge mountain that was almost solid salt. A mine was constantly producing large rock-size pieces of this valuable product. The wife of one of our herder friends gave us a large chunk of salt that now sits in the windowsill of our Mongolian home. When we rub a piece of meat on this rock, it gives the steak added flavor. This salt is shipped all over Mongolia and into other countries. This is exactly how the Christian faith should spread. We must bring a great flavor as we spread across this country—and beyond.

Note:

1. Anderson, L. (1997). *They Smell Like Sheep.* (Howard Publishing, New York, New York) p. 93.

Figure 8.1. "Bolshevik Wonders"—van in the water

Chapter 8

Molding a Team

> *What business is it of mine to judge those outside the church? Are you not to judge those inside? God will judge those outside. "Expel the wicked man from among you."*
>
> –1 Corinthians 5:12–13, NIV

We were about to retest the *Big Bang Theory*, but would soon discover vastly different results than the original evolutionary supposition. Everything was ready for a major countryside trip one Sunday, as we prepared to visit several potential school and veterinary-project sites.

Two vans were scheduled to depart early in the morning, and a third would follow two days later. On Saturday morning, our driver, Dermee, interrupted a meeting we were having with two of our Mongolian teachers. He motioned for me to come immediately to look at a problem with the van. "Ah, just fix it, Dermee," I said nonchalantly. "I'm busy." I noticed that he had a look of panic on his face before I realized this was not just another flat tire or electrical problem; it was a real emergency!

A factory defect in the clutch plate had caused the 20-pound disc to break apart while spinning at a tremendous speed. It flew through the van like a cannon ball scattering shrapnel that ruptured the gas tank before breaking through the side of the van. In the process, the floor of the vehicle was ripped apart as if a giant can opener had been used. Even the transmission, motor and drivetrain were effected. The force was so great that the concrete underneath the van was damaged. Pieces of metal were scattered around like a mini-junkyard, and volatile fuel gushed everywhere. Fortunately, Dermee was the only one in the van at the time. He only had a couple of scratches on his hands. Had this been a few hours later, the van would have been packed with people and supplies. It could have been a major disaster with loss of limb and life. I shudder when I think that Frances would have been sitting over the flying metal and all of the destruction and devastation. The majority of the damage was exactly where she usually sat. God certainly protected her even as He did the rest of us.

Unlike the "Big Bang" scenario, the disparate parts of our vehicle's explosion didn't come together in any kind of orderly fashion to form a Mercedes or Toyota Land Cruiser. Instead, we were left with a Russian van in fragments. This was no outside accident or disaster; the van was destroyed from within.

The Russians may have lost the cold war and exited Mongolia a while ago, but they have continued to impact our work in practical and often frustrating ways. These vehicles that are made in their country are our major means of transportation. The lack of acceptable standards of quality control in the Russian manufacturing plants results in our having to spend hundreds of dollars to get brand-new vans and trucks ready for use. We definitely have a love-hate relationship with these loosely assembled chunks of metal. To say they ride like a wagon is somewhat insulting to the wagon. Still, their redeeming features are that these vehicles are very inexpensive and repairable.

Dermee was a master mechanic, and coupled with our prayers and his skill, he was able to put "Humpty Dumpty" back together again. Thankfully, the repair job had delayed our trip by only a few days before we were able to go on our way—off we went praising God!

Bolshevik Wonders

From Him the whole body, joined and held together by every supporting ligament, grows and builds itself up in love, as each part does its work.

–Ephesians 4:16, NIV

My old friend, our Russian-made vehicle, seemed to work overtime to defeat me many times. He tried to burn me, electrocute me, freeze me, drown me and even push me over a potentially deadly cliff. Yet, I still have a great admiration for him, for without our Russian vehicles, the V.E.T. Net ministry in Mongolia would be virtually impossible.

We are often asked, "Why do you drive these old Russian vans?" The short answer is—we can afford them. They are fixable, and parts are readily available. Besides, these vehicles are common in the countryside and we know that if we ever dared to show up in a Land Cruiser or Land Rover, we would immediately be considered outsiders. True, we've had our share of hair-raising experiences as a result of our association with these lovable, drab-gray vehicles, but they have added color to our experience in Mongolia. However, I must confess that this last trip just about ended my tolerant relationship with them.

We had been in the countryside for 22 days, and the winter weather was turning fierce. Out of necessity, van repairs were often made on cold, windy slopes or near icy streams. Let's see now if I can remember all the break-downs we had on this trip. First, the tailpipe fell off and needed a spot of welding. Then the fuel pump gave out, and when the fuel pump stops, so do we. We should have had an extra pump with us, but should have and reality are often worlds apart in this country. Next, the door on the front passenger's side would not stay closed. This wouldn't have been a problem in the summer, but it happened when it was downright freezing. Next came the brake failure—a much more serious problem. Driving without brakes for almost two days was hair-raising, not to mention extremely dangerous. Finally, we had brakes on three of the four wheels which made for many unscheduled left-hand turns.

The breakdowns were annoying, tiresome, dangerous, but great teachers of patience. However, it was the flat tires that were the most exasperating of all. Interestingly enough, it was not the nails and sharpies on the outside that caused that all too familiar deflating hissing sound. Instead, it was an internal problem. The steel belts would disintegrate and send fragments of metal throughout the inside of the tire. Almost every morning, we awakened to another flat tire or two. We were forced to patch tubes and tires to keep the old boy floating on his cushions of air.

This is so much like missions, and the church in general, for that matter. It is the fragmentation of the little parts within that causes the whole body to screech to a halt. Blame Satan if you will, but it is most likely us. Instead of operating within the unity of the body (see Ephesians 4:15), we focus on self and the trivial issues of life. We fail to keep our eyes on the most significant person in the entire universe—that is, Christ the Creator—the One who holds it all together.

The solution is clear, but often missed. It is a headlong rushing into the arms of Christ with our head, heart and soul having total confidence in Him. He is absolutely reliable and trustworthy. We can have complete confidence in Him, for only He can weld us together into an unbreakable bond sufficient to stand against all odds and emerge victorious in life and death.

The threats to V.E.T. Net have been many over these years, and sometimes they have come from the outside. However, the inside threats to the unity of the organization have been by far the greatest—like the separated clutch plate in the van and the broken steel belts in the tires. Some of the challenges in the organization are unspeakable because of their personal nature, but all made their deep mark on Frances and me and the V.E.T. Net Team. Often the healing and the reestablishment of unity was slow and painful, but Christ was always there. I take a long backward look and see that V.E.T. Net frequently was held by a thread. Jesus never let go. His power protected us and held us fast. He was the glue that made it all work.

Super Glue

> *In him the whole building is joined together and rises to become a holy temple in the Lord. And in him you too are being built together to become a dwelling in which God lives by his Spirit.*
>
> –Ephesians 2:21–22, NIV

We began countryside work in Ik Bulag (Big Spring) by testing the large yak herds for **Brucellosis**. Local herds had an extremely high prevalence of the disease, and mixing the milk of infected and non-infected animals was dangerous because it would mean exposing many in the local population to the disease.

> **Brucellosis** is a serious zoonotic disease that spreads from ruminants to people through ingestion of unpasteurized milk. This disease is called undulate fever due to the flu-like syndrome that comes and goes over many months. Infected people often develop severe arthritis, and this can hasten death in this harsh environment.

It all began when we agreed to an old grandfather's request. Bor said, "My grandchildren need to attend school." He asked , "Can you help us?" He had 14 children and countless grandchildren. Ik Bulag was not an organized village as such, but merely a collection of gers scattered throughout the mountain valley. It was situated far from the end of the main dirt road. A visit to this clan required 21 bridgeless river crossings. Sometimes the river was impassable for our four-wheel drive vans, especially during the rainy season. When that happened, we were forced to hire military trucks with head-high tires to take us across the raging fords.

There was no school near this valley, and as a result, many of the children were growing up illiterate. The year after the grandfather's request, we started a summer school for the herder children using a three-sided, flapping canvas tarp. As you might imagine, the tarp was of little use in the unpredictable winds. Later on, a ger offered us a more substantial classroom.

At the time, we were already working with the school in Ulaan Am, about 20 miles away. So, we agreed to help the community build a small dormitory. The principal and teachers were excited at the possibility of having these very remote herder children from Ik Bulag and other areas attend their school. However, we committed to help with the construction before we understood the challenges of getting materials to the site.

Some of the necessary supplies for the dormitory were purchased in Ulaanbaatar. We were careful to place the crate of glass in the safest location on the truck and pad it with felt. Even so, getting the truck out of the parking lot filled with deep ravines and mud holes caused our truck to sway and bounce. The 50 pieces of glass we had so carefully crated were smashed into fragments. If we could not even get this glass across town, how could we ever get it safely the 300 miles of neck-snapping roads to the construction site? An older man dressed in his traditional del walked to our truck as we shoveled out the broken glass. He rubbed his chin as he looked at our disaster before guardedly giving this advice, "Pour water on the glass." What? Pour water on the glass? The man explained that the water would cause the panes to stick to each other thereby making a stronger, break-resistant mass. What an engineering miracle! We loaded another crate of glass on the truck, soaked it with water as the man suggested, and were soon on the road again. We made the whole trip without the glass breaking.

On the day our construction materials were scheduled to arrive, we patiently sat waiting beside the ancient, army-green truck one-half mile from our destination, Ulaan Am. After traveling roughly 299 miles, the truck refused to budge another inch. Thankfully, its final resting point was close enough for us to deliver the materials safely, even if we had to carry them by yak, and for the last half mile on foot. Finally and fortunately, after a few minor but necessary engine repairs, the old truck was able to sputter its way the last half-mile to the waiting village delivering the glass intact. Once again, we said, "Thank you, Lord."

He is before all things, and in him all things hold together.

– Colossians 1:17, NIV

Like the glass on our truck, our V.E.T. Net team was learning how to stick together glued by the power of the Holy Spirit that dwelled in each person. Many veterinarians came into our office from all over Mongolia. When they walked in the door, they sensed there was something very different about V.E.T. Net. It was the unity within our team that was most noteworthy and absolutely essential. We presented a sweet aroma to those who entered our world.

Family Day

The team began to grow in their understanding of God's transforming power. They wanted to tell their families and friends about how their lives had changed. As a result of much prayer and careful planning, the V.E.T. Net *Family Day* was conceived. Close relatives and friends were invited to an open house at V.E.T. Net. Many had not understood the work of their family member at this unusual organization, so this offered an ideal way to introduce them to our work and mission.

Massive amounts of food were lovingly served as music filled the room. A group performed a drama to prepare them to hear the message of Christ. Afterwards, the guests gathered in small groups with a V.E.T. Net discussion leader acting as facilitator. This proved to be a great success. Our most recent *Family Day* ended with 21 family members and close friends asking Christ to be their Lord and Savior! The changed lives and unity of our team was an irresistible attraction to those who had never witnessed, or felt, the love of Christ.

Building the team over time did not come without its costs. Having a short memory is sometimes a gift that allows us to forget the struggles enough to accentuate the positives. The unity of the team grew stronger and was a healing salve during difficult times bringing us even closer together. A groundswell of concern and care for fellow countrymen began to grow, and the resulting impact on Mongolia has been absolutely amazing.

Oil on Aaron's Beard

All of us who are mature should take such a view of things. And if on some point you think differently, that too God will make clear to you. Only let us live up to what we have already attained.

–Philippians 3:15–16, NIV

In the beginning, all our V.E.T. Net staff members attended the same church. That really simplified life. Then, some of our teammates began to attend other churches because of location, friendships, disagreements or the usual denominational issues. Short-term missionaries coming from many different church denominations may have influenced church choices as well. In the final analysis, we were an interdenominational organization focused on asking individuals a few basic questions: "What have you done with Christ? Is He central to your life, and are you following Him?"

How good and pleasant it is when brothers live together in unity! It is like precious oil poured on the head, running down on the beard, running down on Aaron's beard, down upon the collar of his robes.

–Psalm 133: 1–2, NIV

We work together with other believers of different denominations with the common goal of reaching our world with the love and message of Jesus Christ. There are many areas where we can disagree, yet still be yoked together. Some of these issues have been divisive through the ages. V.E.T. Net is not a church, so its team members are encouraged to attend a church where the Word of God is rightly divided. Because of this, we ask staff and Western short-term missionaries to refrain from bringing denominational or potentially divisive issues to V.E.T. Net. We have a list of common causes of breakdowns in Western churches that we share with our staff and volunteers. This prevents a lot of strife and heartbreak.

Over the years, we have seen many small rural churches planted by the ministry of V.E.T. Net in distant states. Recently, a group conducted surveys on countryside churches in our area and asked this question: What denomination are you associated with? Many left the question blank, but some responded, "We are members of the V.E.T. Net denomination." Of course, we correct this because we do not encourage denominationalism. Others responded that they are part of the Jesus denomination. That is the correct answer.

Figure 9.1. "Panning for Gold"—men gold mining

Chapter 9

The Gold Mine–Shuttle Vets

> *We continued our voyage from Tyre and landed at Ptolemais, where we greeted the brothers and stayed with them for a day. Leaving the next day, we reached Caesarea and stayed at the house of Phillip the evangelist.*
>
> –Acts 21:7–8a, NIV

The Apostle Paul was one of the first short-term missionaries. He visited the early churches he had established and stayed a day, a few months or even a few years. The impact of this itinerant preacher in the places where he ministered was immeasurable. Unlike Paul for whom travel was both difficult and dangerous, today's modern transportation makes it possible to be almost anywhere on earth in a day or two. We are able to function as real-time shuttle diplomats for the King as we strive to spread the word about His grace and mercy to the nations.

It is a known fact that one of the largest gold-ore deposits in the world was hiding for millenniums under the desert sands of the Gobi Desert. It is located in southern Mongolia and northern and northwestern China. Mining companies from Russia, China, Canada, Australia, and the United States first came to explore the vast mineral resources of Mongolia only in the last two decades. What was once thought to be a poor country of semi-nomadic herders turned out to be a nation with immense wealth just waiting to be mined. Today, much of this wealth still goes unclaimed because the government and mining companies have been slow to agree on contracts to extract the ore.

Herders who lived near these mines wanted to supplement their meager existence. Sometimes they left their livestock with family in order to spend weeks sifting through tailings left by mining companies. There were often brawls, fights, stabbings and murders. Such an atmosphere was not a healthy place to pitch a tent no matter how enticing the call to find wealth. But with persistence and a little luck, a herder would occasionally hear the exciting sound of a nugget pinging against the pan.

Nuggets

> *The kingdom of heaven is like treasure hidden in a field. When a man found it, he hid it again, and then in his joy went and sold all he had and bought that field.*
>
> –Matthew 13:44, NIV

In this passage, Jesus speaks of the joyful discovery of the kingdom of God in a way that reminds us of searching for that proverbial pot of gold or winning the lottery. We see a similar scene played out frequently in Mongolia. Some of the poorest people in Mongolia find God and go from spiritual poverty to spiritual wealth in a flash. Oh, they may not have the wealth of this world, but the treasure they uncover is of incalculable value. We watch in gratitude as many mired in squalor and poverty discover a life filled with joy and peace. To see these former paupers worshiping their newly found King and Father is a testimony to the mystery of the gospel. These new believers are like treasure to us as we work to disciple them in the ways of the Lord.

V.E.T. Net unearthed another valuable treasure. It was a large group of potential short-term missionaries eagerly waiting for an assignment from God. Their worth was inestimable to us and to Mongolia.

Dr. Leroy Dorminy was a veterinary practitioner in Ocilla, Georgia. He attended a mission conference in Stockholm, Sweden in 1975 and recorded his experience:

> There were about 15 or 20 of us participating in one small group. We were discussing a particular point in Scripture. In the group was a woman from one of the emerging nations of Africa.
>
> Our discussion leader turned to her and asked, "How can we, Christians of the developed world,

> help you, in the developing countries?"
>
> Quick as a flash came her reply, "Come and teach us your skills, that we may do things for ourselves." [1]

Dr. Dorminy left the conference to return to the U.S. with the nucleus of a vision that led to the incorporation of a new mission organization, *Christian Veterinary Mission*. The doctor was initially rejected by his denomination for short-term missions. They could not envision how a veterinarian could be useful in ministry at home or abroad. However, through foresight, determination and God's direction, he paved the way for veterinarians to serve through long- and short-term Christian mission endeavors throughout the world.

Dr. Dorminy (1923-2016) became the Founder of *Christian Veterinary Mission* in 1979. In the intervening 40 years, he faithfully served to challenge, mobilize, and empower veterinarians in their Christian faith.

Short-term missionaries were called "shuttles" in the early days, and they became an important part of *Christian Veterinary Mission*. This term was derived from the fact that they shuttled back and forth to minister in various countries and within the United States. Frances and I, along with our two boys, were early shuttles. We travelled to Aneth, Utah in the late 70s to work with livestock and to minister to Native Americans on the Navajo Reservation. This life-changing experience was instrumental in setting us on the road to fulltime service in Mongolia. (Unbeknown to us at that time.)

Part of our responsibility in Mongolia was to host one or two shuttles each year. We quickly learned that we were staring at a virtual gold mine! We were limited in funds for the ministry, but we discovered a hidden treasure that was almost unlimited that, like the Mongolian minerals, was virtually going unmined.

Dr. Dorminy wrote related to our mission work in Mongolia:

> Dr. Gerald Mitchum is another veterinarian who eventually wound up in Mongolia working long-term. He and his wife Frances went the following year. (Note: This was after my own first shuttle trip

> to Mongolia in 1994.)
>
> On the shuttle Gerald observed, "There is no extension system at the University [in Mongolia]. This is an area of desperate need for the retraining of the large State-operated service to prepare them for privatization."
>
> It is interesting that he made this observation, because one of Gerald's duties was to organize the shuttle program. He brought in specialists to deal with specific needs [in Mongolia]. No one had ever taken the shuttle program to such heights before. [1]

Shuttles have been an important part of *Christian Veterinary Mission* over the years, and we found a way to utilize them extensively in the V.E.T. Net ministry. In fact, they are one of the foundational pillars of V.E.T. Net. There have been over 1,000 short-term-mission positions filled—one or two people at a time. We rarely have large groups, but occasionally have a few students who come together.

Over time, *Christian Veterinary Mission* was able to establish a large pool of veterinarians who wanted to serve. Even though they were unable to leave their practice for extended periods, they felt called to become directly involved in missions. The infrastructure was in place, and the well-oiled machine, operated by dedicated staff at *Christian Veterinary Mission,* was finally ready to implement this Christian service. All that was needed were opportunities, and in Mongolia the possibilities were limitless.

Secular organizations sometimes question how we can afford to have so many expert professionals come to work with V.E.T. Net. These organizations often pay $10,000 to $20,000 or more for their consultants. They are happy when they find the money to budget for one or two each year. It is difficult for them to understand Christian values and the fact that our shuttles are all volunteers. Happily, for us, our shuttles do not require a salary, and are able to pay their own travel and in-country expenses. These volunteers are frequently exceptional veterinarians in their specific fields of veterinary medicine. We could never afford to pay for their service.

Some long-term missionaries question the usefulness of short-term volunteers, but for us, they are like finding gold nuggets. Practitioners, faculty members, deans, and administrators of veterinary schools, as well as teachers, principals, medical and dental personnel, businessmen, builders, students and countless others have proved to be effective short-term missionaries. The value of their contributions in donated services is impossible to calculate.

Shuttle Number 1

Our very first shuttle was a regulatory veterinarian. Since he dealt with the prevention of infectious diseases in America, he was very cautious about taking unwanted viruses and bacteria back to the United States. Mongolia had several diseases that had been eradicated, or at least controlled in America. Still, U.S. regulatory veterinarians are especially vigilant in preventing foreign diseases from entering the country.

This particular veterinarian arrived at the Mongolian airport in protective gear. He had worn his work clothes and gumboots across the wide Pacific to be fully protected against infectious disease organisms such as foot and mouth, brucellosis, sheep pox, and others. As a volunteer, he was scheduled to teach regulatory medicine at the Mongolian Veterinary School during his time with us. His clothes were fine for a field trip, but unknown to him, the faculty at the university dressed immaculately for their lecture responsibilities. A three-piece suit with tie was the expected dress code because they were very proud of their profession and university.

I didn't want to offend our new arrival, but I knew he could not teach at the university dressed in his coveralls. "Listen," I said, "I have extra clothes that you are welcome to wear, as well as a new pair of shoes." I had bought the shoes in the States expecting that I would not find my size in Mongolia. Most Mongolians are short in height and the length of their feet matches their elevation. These shoes were the most expensive that I had ever bought, but I knew they would last me a long time.

Two weeks passed quickly, and soon it was time for our veterinary shuttle to pack up and return to his home. He was staying in the apartment next door to us and came over with a request: "Do you have any medicine for athlete's foot?" he asked. "I seem to have developed a bad case since I came to Mongolia." "Well," I said, "why don't you just wear my shoes home? It will not be good for your feet, with a fungal infection, to be in those gumboots with no ventilation."

Sadly, I watched my expensive shoes walk out the door. Oh, well; I felt a little guilty anyway for paying so much for a couple of pieces of leather. At least he wouldn't be carrying foot and mouth disease back with him; just his own foot disease and my shoes.

In truth, he had been well received at the university. His dress problems were entirely my fault because I had not properly prepared him before his trip. It was no wonder that he was totally surprised that his protective attire was inappropriate. As a result of our oversight, we developed a more descriptive short-term mission program and literature, and now do a much better job in preparing our volunteers for their time with us.

Our *Shuttle Manual* covers everything anyone would ever need to know about working with V.E.T. Net. I remember when one of our early shuttles came to our apartment after being with us for only three days and asked, "When will my sheets be changed?" Frances was shocked, but politely told him that she would get right on it. To make sure that people are reading the *Shuttle Manual,* we have since added a question and answer section. One of the questions is: "How often will my sheets be changed?" Answer: "They will be changed between every third shuttle." If we don't get a comment from them, we know they didn't read the manual.

Shuttle Number 2

Our second shuttle was another one for the record books. He came from a small-animal practice in Pennsylvania and was on the *Board of Directors for Christian Veterinary Mission.* Like our first shuttle, he was given an opportunity to teach at the Veterinary School. In the beginning, we had only a limited number of opportunities, but that quickly changed over time.

This shuttle arrived well dressed for his assignments with a nice pair of dress shoes. Whew! His responsibility was to work with our congenial head of the surgery department. Pet care was in its infancy in Mongolia. Consequently, small animals did not receive adequate treatment. Dogs were primarily used as guards and were chained to stakes during the day and released only at night. And cats, well let's just say that Mongolians did not like cats. I think this may have stemmed from a religious belief that has caused them to be fearful of cats. We are gratified to see a change, and now cats and dogs are valued pets in the city. In some cases, they are pampered couch potatoes much like our Western pets.

The university surgeon had a difficult case to share with our second shuttle. A dog's leg was badly mangled in an accident, and the veterinarian tried to save it with medical care. Unfortunately, the damage was too extensive, and the leg needed to be amputated. The leg was prepared for surgery so that the operation could begin with the shuttle assisting. The only anesthetic available was a barbiturate that had to be administered intravenously. Barbiturates are reasonably safe when given by an experienced person. A needle was inserted into the vein with the syringe taped to the uninjured leg. The drug was injected until the patient was in surgical anesthesia.

Students crowded around the surgery team shrouded in their white smocks. The excitement was palpable as the scalpel incised the skin in an elliptical arc. The doctors clamped the vessels with hemostats, and the bone was sawed in two well above the injury. The amputation was uneventful, and the closure soon followed. As the skin sutures were being placed, the dog began to awaken, and the request came for a little more barbiturate. Unfortunately, the request to carry out this extra dosage was miscommunicated resulting in an entire syringe full of the anesthetic being pumped into the vein. Even though the surgery was successful, the patient died from the overdose. It was heartbreaking for our volunteer; he had expected a much different outcome. His teaching was excellent and the students and staff were appreciative, but the loss of the pet put a damper on the whole experience.

We all lamented the loss of the dog and tried to encourage our new shuttle friend. We decided to take him to the best restaurant in the city to get his mind off the loss. The Ulaanbaatar Hotel not only had the best restaurant, but also was practically the only one in town. For $3, a diner could order a prime steak. We all enjoyed a relaxing dinner in the expansive hotel ballroom with its extravagant chandeliers. We had milked the moment, but the time had come to leave the hotel and head for home.

We casually strolled through the park in front of the hotel and walked beside the famous statue of Vladimir Lenin on our way to Peace

Avenue, the main street in this capital city. Stalin's statue had already fallen, but Lenin still stood prominently along the main thoroughfare. Later, he, too, would become a casualty of the failed socialist system, but he managed to occupy his pedestal for more than another decade.

We approached the curb, and I held out my hand to indicate that we needed a ride. There were no official cabs at that time, so any one of the scarce cars that passed by was a potential taxi. We never worried about getting into the car of a stranger. Even single women flagged a passing vehicle without fear. The ride might be a wild and a fearful adventure, but the driver usually acted in a gentlemanly manner. There were no women drivers.

The driver in the car in the opposite lane saw that we were looking for a ride, and he made a U-turn in the middle of the four-lane street to pull beside the curb. We opened the rear door. Our translator entered the car followed by Frances. It was the shuttle's turn to slide in next. I was holding the rear door open for him to enter when the two men who had been standing idly by, observing as we entered the car, rushed us. They pinned the shuttle against the door and began to frisk him for valuables. It all happened so fast that we hardly realized what was taking place.

Immediately, the driver of the car jumped from beneath the steering wheel to circle the car and grab the men accosting us. With a police baton and handcuffs in hand, he escorted the thieves to the metal fence surrounding the park in front of the hotel and handcuffed them to the fence. We got into the car and drove off leaving the perplexed scoundrels in our dust—instant justice!

As we drove to our separate apartments, we learned the rest of the story. The driver of our taxi was an off-duty policeman. He recognized the men loitering on the sidewalk and knew they were planning to frisk the naïve Americans. Even though our second shuttle proved to be an excellent, albeit temporary addition to our staff, he only made one trip to Mongolia. Regardless, he had reason to appreciate God's protective mercy and grace on our behalf.

The Good Samaritan

But a Samaritan, as he traveled, came where the man was; and when he saw him, he took pity on him. He went to

> *him and bandaged his wounds, pouring on oil and wine. Then he put the man on his own donkey, brought him to an inn and took care of him. The next day he took out two denarii and gave them to the innkeeper. "Look after him," he said, "and when I return, I will reimburse you for any extra expense you may have."*
>
> –Luke 10:33–35, NIV

It was around the year 2000 when two shuttles came to Mongolia from opposite sides of the U.S.; one from the west coast, and the other from the east. They met at V.E.T. Net while working in different areas of the ministry but living in the same apartment. Our volunteer from the east coast helped us at the small animal hospital. We began to suspect that something was wrong when our team questioned us about his performance at the clinic. It was warm at the office, so he would take off his shirt and crawl up on the table to enjoy a nice nap after lunch. Apparently, this had been his usual routine at his office at home, so he was used to an afternoon siesta.

During one practical surgery lesson given by this shuttle, a dog underwent a routine spay procedure. Some days later, the patient was readmitted with abdominal pain and a lack of appetite. Additional surgery revealed the cause of the problem—gauze sponges had been left in the abdomen. No one realized this had happened until it was too late, and the patient died. It was yet another sad, avoidable case.

The Mongolians truly love the shuttles, so it was unusual for them to criticize or question these short-term workers. I was greatly troubled when the team first approached me about this man's work. When we met to discuss the situation, I gave the new shuttle the opportunity to share his feelings, but he became defensive and hostile. He was convinced that he had discovered an evil empire and was determined to uncover the source. Before coming to Mongolia, he had read about a drug ring along the US Interstate Highway 95 corridor. The pieces appeared to have fallen in place for him. He was certain that I was part of the drug ring, and the V.E.T. Net team-members were slave laborers managing the hideous operation. This was an astounding revelation to me! I was ready to make arrangements for an early departure for him, but he was having none of it. He was fully committed to uncovering and exposing our supposed dastardly operation.

Fortunately, our shuttle from the west coast proved to be an angel in disguise. Although he was a veterinarian, he had experience working with people with similar problems. He exercised an extraordinary gift of compassion and patience and turned out to be a wonderful encouragement to this man as well as to me. He was also instrumental in helping me understand the root of the problem.

It seems that God provided just the right people for the specific moment. We were extremely busy at the time, and I felt this person was a huge distraction. The ministry was vitally important, and I didn't want anything to get in the way of God's work. But here was a man with a need that God had brought across my path. I was forced to examine my own compassion and empathy.

The *Good Samaritan* (see Luke 10:25–37) was likely a very busy man as well, but he stopped to help. When God put someone in his path, he did not detour, but rather dealt with the problem head-on. Regardless of how important the mission, I realized I must always take the time to reach out to a hurting neighbor. What did Jesus say was the second greatest commandment?

And the second is like it: 'Love your neighbor as yourself.'

–Matthew 22:39, NIV

Both of these men have remained firm supporters of V.E.T. Net for many years now. I never dreamed they would consider supporting the ministry after that difficult encounter. Yes; forgiveness is a powerful tool in the arsenal of our Father. I'm glad both these men as well as V.E.T. Net learned to practice it. We now endeavor to be more like the *Good Samaritan* as we work with each unique person that God sends our way. Our desire is to bless the shuttles as they bring joy and encouragement to us and to the ministry. This, too, is a witness to our V.E.T. Net team as we work together.

Makeover

During one of our countryside trips, we awakened to a strange sight. Two young girls on the team, both students, had risen early in the morning to cover their faces with some kind of white muck. Was this a strange ritual, we wondered? When Frances and I confronted our young friends about the masks, they replied, "Oh, this is just mayonnaise. It's good for your complexion."

We recognized two changes in the newly developing country of Mongolia: The first thing we noticed was that Mongolians seemed to love their photographs. Every family had albums, and any time we visited their home, we were invited to look at their photo memories. They always took great pleasure in sharing these with us and seemed especially delighted when we asked questions.

We took many photos during our visits and had them developed when we returned to the city. We made sure our friends received priceless copies on our next visit. Overnight, photo kiosks began to spring up on every corner to develop film. Of course, this was prior to digital photography. We used rolls and rolls of film, but it was well worth the expense.

We were almost always served vodka when we visited Mongolian families. It is the custom to pass the glass around three times to each guest adding a little vodka each time it is passed. Eventually, our hosts learned that we did not drink alcohol, but in the beginning, they were very insistent. Usually after several attempts on their part to insist we partake, they appeared to be satisfied if we simply touched the glass to our lips. Occasionally, however, there were herders who insisted that we empty the glass. We soon discovered a surefire way to distract them. We would grab our camera and say, "Put on your del; let's take a group picture outside the ger!" They would immediately start rummaging for their best clothes because everyone wanted to be in the picture. As they posed in front of their home, the vodka requirement was soon forgotten. We have many treasured Mongolian pictures of such memorable occasions.

The second change we saw develop quickly was the expansion of the cosmetic business. A ravenous appetite for beauty aids in the city accompanied privatization. Brand name products from all over the world poured into Mongolia—American, Japanese, Korean, European. One Swedish company used a pyramid-marketing scheme that became very popular and provided work for a number of young entrepreneurs even as it emptied the pockets of beauty-conscious women and their husbands.

We also saw a change in the shuttle trips as spouses decided to join their veterinary mate. To accommodate them, we gladly find opportunities for teachers, computer experts, doctors, dentists, builders, sportsmen, musicians, artists, housewives, craft teachers and others. The short-term ministry openings were becoming limitless. We learned quickly to never say "No" to anyone's request to join us. It is amazing to witness the number of different gifts and skills that God made available to our work and ministry.

The explosion of cosmetics in the city was slow to reach the countryside. We could never have imagined this becoming important to herder wives who were always so busy with cooking, milking, taking care of kids and kids (young goats) among their various other responsibilities. Yet, it did.

Mary Kay, Anyone?

We happily welcomed Dr. Paul Welch, a small animal veterinarian from Tulsa, Oklahoma, to work in Caring Animal Hospital—our V.E.T. Net model veterinary clinic and training center. A variety of pets were becoming more valuable in the city, so his expertise with exotics was especially useful. He particularly enjoyed several turtle patients in need of his care. Turtles are frequently brought to the clinic with shell injuries necessitating restoration of their mobile home. This is not so unusual as it may seem since our hospital regularly treats cats and dogs, birds and bunnies, turtles and toads, lizards and snakes, guinea pigs and rats, or any other creature that people fall in love with—even baby bears.

When Paul made the decision to join us in Mongolia, he wanted to bring his wife, Sarah, with him. As it turned out, she was a successful executive with the Mary Kay Cosmetic Company. I was thinking, "What in the world would we do with a Mary Kay Cosmetic executive?" I wasn't alone in wondering how the countryside women would receive her. These women had no clue about all the cosmetics designed to beautify. What would they think when a person from Mary Kay invaded their world? Little did we know how effective she would be!

Paul taught wide-eyed V.E.T. Net small animal veterinarians in Ulaanbaatar while Sarah went with a team to one particular rural county. She met the governor's assistant, a woman, to whom she explained her makeup-training program. Excitement boiled over as the assistant listened intently. She was thrilled that the women in her little town would have access to such a beauty-enhancing experience.

The first cosmetic training was scheduled in the local church with members asked to invite non-Christian women as part of an outreach effort. The 30 participants broke into small groups, and each woman received an attractive bag filled with exotic bottles and tubes of makeup with strange applicators. These fragrant gifts brought broad smiles to the women. Sarah made an excellent connection of these gifts to the present that God gave when He sent Jesus to be our Savior. Several of these rural women accepted Christ that day, and through this ministry the little community church began to grow and become more stable. I wonder if Mary Kay ever thought she would be helping to build the church in Mongolia? Surely, she would be pleased, if not tickled pink.

Leg Problem

Later on, the team traveled to another remote site to meet with herder families. As Dorjpagam, the team leader, started to leave the van, she suddenly experienced a knee problem that prevented her from walking. She had worked with V.E.T. Net for many years, and this had never happened before. The other team members went to the herder's ger, and soon the herder's wife came to the van to check on Dorjpagam. The wife was not a believer, but she joined Dorjpagam in prayer for the leg to be healed. Instantly, Dorjpagam was able to stand and walk normally. The herder's wife was so amazed that she prayed to this God and accepted Jesus into her life. Truly, God still uses miracles to help bring people to Jesus.

The woman's husband was a famous horse trainer and was often given alcohol as a gift. Unfortunately, he drank excessively, and his marriage suffered as a result. Praise God that he decided to ask Jesus into his life. Before long, most of his family also claimed Christ as their Savior. Their lives were dramatically changed. The husband turned from alcohol and the couple found healing for their marriage. Such is the power of the gospel.

We do not major on the miraculous in our teaching, but sometimes God decides it is the time to reveal Himself through a miracle. This was the case when the bone-dry spring at Muren Bag was renewed, and it was true with Dorjpagam's healed leg. It is impossible to put God in a box even though His love is sometimes delivered in a box of makeup to open the hearts of women in remote areas. It may not be politically correct to say this, but women like to be women all over the world—even in the outback of Mongolia.[2]

The Tattoo Girl

A young female veterinary student from Australia came to minister with us, and on her way to Mongolia, she stopped in India to work with another mission organization. She had been so busy at school and with her preparation for the trip to India that she had not found time to read the *Shuttle Manual*. We had dinner together at our home the evening she arrived, and quickly noticed something strange about her. The outside weather was comfortably warm, as was our apartment, but she was wearing long sleeves and gloves.

She had waited to read the *Shuttle Manual* until her flight from India to Mongolia—the dress code and rule against exposed tattoos came as a shock to her. V.E.T. Net has a policy requiring shuttles with tattoos to have them covered. It seems she had temporary henna tattoos placed on her arms while in India that went the full length right to the tips of her fingers. There was no possible way to discreetly hide these works of art. They were quite intricate, colorful and artistic. Finally, she confessed and took off her gloves to reveal the tattoos. We all had a good laugh. In a few days, the tattoos began to disappear. Thankfully, they weren't permanent. This delightful young woman did a wonderful job fulfilling her role with V.E.T. Net, and the Team learned to love her. We were all sad when the tattoo girl had to return home.

Dr. Dave

During one especially unusual week, we experienced a roller-coaster ride unlike any we have ever had in our more than 20 years in Mongolia. Nothing like this could have ever been scripted in our wildest thoughts on what it was like to be a missionary.

Our relationships and cooperation with the Mongolian Agricultural University and the Veterinary School continued to grow. We supplied teachers for both veterinary medicine and English programs at the request of the Dean of the School. This, of course, opened doors to share the message of Jesus Christ with students and faculty. We had worked from the beginning of our stay in Mongolia for these opportunities.

Dr. Dave (fictitious name), a gifted veterinarian on faculty at a Michigan college, volunteered to teach for six months at the Mongolian Veterinary School and at *Caring Animal Hospital*. The months ticked away, and finally, one Sunday he was retrieved from the Chinggis Khan International Airport to join Frances and me at our home for the evening meal. He was obviously tired, but that is certainly not unusual for those who travel halfway around the world. We have had a few short-term missionaries with severe jet lag nearly bump their nose on their plates while trying to stay awake long enough to eat. Dave went to his apartment after dinner and battled jet lag throughout the night. The next day he looked totally whipped. We went with Dave to meet the Dean and his assistant at the Veterinary School. They were impressed with his sterling credentials and vast experience and were eager for his help.

Late that Monday afternoon, I received a call from Dave. "I can't do it; I am not your man," were the words I heard on the phone. "I'm going home." I thought it was a jet-lag problem. We met and prayed, and I encouraged him to take a few days before making a decision. "It is not wise to decide something this important when you are depressed and tired," I told him. The next morning, Tuesday, his attitude was no better. Dave was adamant about leaving even if we refused to help him. All of my words hit a brick wall and crumbled at my feet. Of course, we would make arrangements for him to leave, I assured him. On Wednesday, we spent much of the day getting the necessary stamps, letters and ticket changes. That night, he came back to our apartment and spent a considerable amount of time with Frances and me.

"Do you want to hear the rest of the story?" he asked. Certainly, we wanted to hear, and so he began his dire tale. "I don't believe God is all powerful, nor do I believe in the Trinity, and certainly I do not believe that Jesus is the only way to God." "That's interesting," I said, "how in the world did you get here?" Dave continued to share his story of living two lives. He was raised a Catholic and had been on multiple short-term mission trips in hopes of working his way into a right relationship with God. When he saw the unity, sincerity and love of the V.E.T. Net Team that God had put together in Mongolia, the charade was over. He knew he was in the wrong place, and he was headed home. We knew that our promises to the university would be difficult to keep since his departure would leave a huge hole in the entire ministry.

Frances and I continued to pray and share the truth with him. We told him that his god was a puny, little powerless midget. Dave wanted to be the potter and wanted god to be the clay. He wanted to mold god into a tiny little idol that he could control, with eyes that could not see and ears that could not hear. His god was much like the Buddhist gods that adorn the shelves in many *gers* we visit in Mongolia. Before he left our home, we prayed a prayer of hope for his salvation.

Dave came into the office on Thursday morning and asked to talk with me. "Can I do the devotion this morning?" "No Dave, I'm sorry, but unless you have given your life to God through Jesus Christ, I can not allow you to do the devotion." "Well," I read the Bible and wrestled with God until early this morning," he said. "I fell on the Cross in faith, and finally surrendered my life to Him. I want to share my story with the Team."

What followed was one of the most powerful devotions we have ever had. A man in his 60s humbled himself before a group of young believers and opened his heart with humility and sincerity. He shared how he had tried so hard for many years to work his way to God, but Dave finally understood that he could only get there through what Jesus had done for him and not by any of his best personal efforts. The V.E.T. Net staff placed their hands on him and prayed for him as he started his new walk with God. Holding hands with Jesus and fully endowed by the Holy Spirit, he joyfully embraced his new brothers and sisters in Christ. What an experience, and what a story! Praise the Lord!

That would be enough for anybody, but the story did not end there. Dave went home for a short time to make things right with friends and family. He sought help from a local, committed Christian and asked him to disciple him in his newfound faith. Dave then returned to Mongolia to fulfill his obligations with V.E.T. Net and teach at the University. He came back as a new creation in Christ. I can only say, "All honor and glory belong to you, O Lord."

So, What Is a Shuttle?

The value added to the ministry of V.E.T. Net by many volunteers over these years has been a true blessing from God. We often thank Him for the people who have unselfishly given their time and resources to come to Mongolia and join Him in what He is doing through V.E.T. Net. Although their own contributions are considerable, they invariably report that they have gained far more than they left behind—you can read some of the testimonies in the "Testimonies" section in the back of this book. Not all stories are as dramatic as Dave's, but nearly all our volunteers return home with a sense of fulfillment after having spent time in Mongolia. Not only are they influenced personally in dramatic ways, but also their friends, family, church and ministry partners are impacted. Many have a renewed commitment to missions in their own areas, and their churches are often challenged to become more missions oriented. The shuttle concept has blessed V.E.T. Net and Mongolia, and its blessings have extended into other nations and ministries as well. I wrote this little jingle after much reflection on our shuttles:

So, What Is a Shuttle?

What is a shuttle? We've often been asked.
Who can you use and what is their task?
When can they come and where will they go?
What age should they be, and how 'bout the "dough?"

After the multiple vaccinations,
It's time to deal with the reservations,
Then three in the morning is three at night,
After the twenty-four hours of flight.

They step from the plane and front-up to customs,
That smile-less official is sure to bust'em,
But V.E.T. Net arrives in a mighty hurry,
Like the Bible says, "Don't you dare worry."

Frances' table is only a tease.
Tomorrow your stomach will start on it's "quease."
Intestinal soup with a side dish of rectum,
I'm sorry, but you don't get to select'em.

Shuttles have truly been one of the cornerstones of all that has happened at V.E.T. Net. Although we use the name short-term, it is really a misnomer. God does not call people into short-term missions. We are all long-termers in His view, and our location is the only thing that changes. The people who are used by God here are the ones who leave part of their heart with V.E.T. Net when they return to their home. The following is a great example of how God uses these short-term missionaries.

Long-term/Short-term Shuttle Vets

Mongolian horse trainers believed for centuries that withholding water makes the horses lighter, enabling them to run faster. They not only withheld water, but they exercised their horses that wore heavy coats to sweat them and reduce their weight. Before the races, competing horses trotted 20 to 30 kilometers to the starting line. With the withholding of water, sweating and all the excitement and prancing about, the horses were already dehydrated before the beginning of the race. At that time of year, the weather was often hot and dry, adding insult to injury.

The Dean of Sidney Australia Veterinary School came to Mongolia in 1999 to offer his expertise in equine distance racing. He was a famous expert in equine medicine, and as such, was invited to attend the ***Naadam Horse Races***. He worked with the Mongolian Veterinary School and consulted with the equine veterinarian.

> ***Naadam Horse Races***
>
> These are prestigious, long-distance races with horses competing from all over Mongolia. Naadam is one of the major Mongolian holidays and it occurs in July. It is a great family time, and there are exciting competitions in wrestling, archery, and long-distance horse racing.

The Naadam races were a real eye-opener for the Australian visitor. In the distance, a cloud of dust could be seen as the first group of horses neared the home stretch. The large crowd cheered ecstatically as the winner crossed the finished line. Spectators ran to the winner's circle to vie for the opportunity to get sweat from the victor. It was sure to bring good luck.

However, what a horrific sight! The hills and valleys were

strewn with dead and dying horses. One hundred started the race, but only 80 survived. Twenty outstanding horses died while others were left with debilitating lameness issues that ensured they would never race again. It did not require an expert to understand that changes had to be made.

The following year, **Dr. Tom Juergens** attended a *Christian Veterinary Mission* meeting in the States. It was there that he asked **Dr. Kit Flowers**, the Director of CVM, if he could use an old horse doctor in their short-term mission program. "There just happens to be a place in Mongolia where I think you can fit," was the reply. This was the beginning of the long-term/short-term program that endures to this day.

Dr. Kit Flowers and his wife Jan served as *Christian Veterinary Mission* (CVM) field workers in Kenya, East Africa, from 1985-1990. In 1990, Dr. Flowers joined the CVM home office staff, and in 1994, he became the executive director of CVM (www.cvmusa.org)

Dr. Juergens came to Mongolia in the summer of 2000 to join the V.E.T. Net team during the Naadam races. The races were always held at the south edge of Ulaanbaatar, just outside of town. The starting gate was 20-35 kilometers away depending on the age of the horses. Part of the uniqueness of these races is children, boys and girls, ride the horses. There are no professional jockeys.

V.E.T. Net was given a site to set up a ger, a field hospital and a huge army tent for meetings with spectators and horse trainers. Our fence was set, and we were ready for the races when the police came roaring to our site. "You must move your fence and ger a few feet. We are not happy with the placement." So, we took down the fence and started all over again. When the crowds began to gather, we had everything back in place.

Another addition to our site was a large watering tank for horses with a water truck to keep the tank filled with fresh water from the river. The riders came to the tank and allowed their horses to look at the cool water. Unfortunately, these horses stood with forlorn expressions since none of the riders allowed them to drink. The police horses were some of the few to enjoy the water.

The results of the races were similar to those we experienced when we attended our first Naadam. Some horses died, and many had severe injuries. These abused, dehydrated horses were forced to absorb water from the gastrointestinal track and muscles to keep their blood pressure near normal. Severe colic (a life threatening abdominal disease with intense pain) and muscle damage was the result.

Dr. Juergens and **Dr. John Haffner** worked alongside the V.E.T. Net team to save some of the horses. Large volumes of fluids were administered intravenously and by stomach tube. Even with aggressive therapy, however, some of the equine patients still succumbed to the trauma of the event.

Unfortunately, many horsemen did not allow their horses to be treated with modern veterinary therapy. Instead, they chose to seek treatment from a traditional medicine "doctor." The cruelty of some of these practices was outrageous. The faces of these stately animals were sometimes sliced with knives, supposedly to allow more air into the lungs; horses' tongues were cut; knives were stuck in the tendons of the legs, and splenic acupuncture was attempted with blades penetrating the abdomen.

The most exotic treatment was so astoundingly jaw-dropping that we neglected to take a picture. Dr. Juergens and I just watched as the traditional treatment was administered. There was no chance for the patient's recovery, even with the best of care. As the horse lay stretched on his side, the therapist inhaled a large lung-full of smoke from his cigarette and administered it into the horse's anus. I will not give details on the exact method of administration of the smoke except to say that it was surprising. Unfortunately, the poor patient did not respond to the "Marlboro" therapy. This terrible experience gave us a shocking education.

These treatments were terribly cruel, but truthfully, the Mongolians actually love their horses. The lack of good care stemmed from ignorance and their lack of modern education. These tough little animals have always been an important part of their lives for centuries, but we knew we could help them take better care of their horses while still honoring their culture.

On this day, our Vet Net Team busily treated ten horses with modern drugs while an old Mongolian horseman stood beside his bloodied, pitiful horse. He had chosen to have a traditionalist cut his horse on the forehead, carve gashes around the eyes and stick knives in the veins to let the bad blood flow to the ground. Later, he watched his neighbor's ten horses recover while his own horse slumped to the ground and gave in to the harsh world of pain and suffering.

The Naadam Fast Horse Workshop

Drs. Juergens and Haffner have since worked with the V.E.T. Net team to establish *The Naadam Fast Horse Workshop*. They have returned each year for the past 18 years to teach the horsemen how to take better care of their horses. They taught the importance of hydrating horses before races, as well as proper prevention and treatment for various equine problems. Mongolian veterinarians value this training and come long distances to learn from these godly men. The veterinarians use the training as a platform to tell the horsemen the reason they come to Mongolia. Few people have had a key to unlock the hearts of these leather-face horsemen like these two American veterinarians. Now, even the government is cooperating by supplying water for the horses at the races. Things are beginning to change, and the humane treatment of the beloved, wiry little horses is improving.

Following the first hands-on session of *The Naadam Fast Horse Workshop* at our large animal clinic, we gathered inside to share portions of a film on creation translated into the Mongolian language. "Where Did the Horse Come From?" was the title of this part of our program led by Dr. Haffner. Did the Mongolian's graceful and complex animals come from a series of chance mutations over a period of hundreds of millions of years, or did the Creator God speak them into existence? That, of course, sparked a lively discussion in this former atheist country and led to questions of supreme importance to all of us. Where did I come from? Why am I here? Is there really a God, and if there is, does He care about me?

After the meeting and the opportunity to share in small groups, many of these tough countryside veterinarians asked for a Bible to take back to their homes. Some wanted to go to church, and others were genuinely interested in this possibility of a caring, Creator God. Some have accepted Jesus as their Savior.

We often shrivel meekly when confronted by great scientists who have proclaimed theory to be truth. But it is the first question that an atheist must settle. Is there truly a God who is powerful enough to actually have created everything we know in this universe, or did we slide on primordial slime into existence on our own? The biblical book of Genesis becomes pivotal for these veterinarians and horsemen. They have learned that the information we teach about horse medicine is factual. When they compare modern medicine with their folklore and traditional care, the latter goes out the window. Why, then, would we offer a religion that begins with a fairytale? The answer, to be sure, is that Genesis is not a fairytale, but rather part of a complex Book that claims that all Scripture is God-breathed (see 2 Timothy 3:16a, NIV.) The world has been duped by a subtle lie that requires us to throw away every logical thought process with which we are endowed, to blindly accept the fairytale of a godless self-creation.

The following year after this life-changing race, black and white police cars roared back onto the scene. The District Director of Police strode around our treatment site while his pudgy deputy who had torn down our fence the previous year stood scowling at our Team. Suddenly, a broad grin spread across his jowlly face. "Oh, you are the Jesus people who were here last year," the Director said. "We can work together this year." Unlike the year before when we were forced to move our fence, *ger* and tents, the police were now offering to cooperate with us. This was certainly music to our ears.

The ***American Association of Equine Practitioners*** chose V.E.T. Net as one of their international projects. They have now funded the equine workshops for several years while we strive to make these trainings more self-sustaining. The organization is interested in promoting humane treatment of horses around the world. In 2012, Dr. Tom Juergens, after working for years with V.E.T.

> The ***American Association of Equine Practitioners*** is the national organization for equine veterinarians. They present ***The Lavin Cup***, the Equine Welfare Award, given to organizations or individuals that have distinguished themselves by showing compassion through services that improve the welfare of horses. This is a coveted award that has only been given a few times over the years.

Net during the equine events, was named the recipient of the prestigious AAEP's equine welfare award, ***The Lavin Cup***.

The Naadam Fast Horse Workshop became one of our more high-profile endeavours in Mongolia. Government officials were often present along with Mongolian TV crews and photographers from around the world. They all wanted to have their pictures taken in hopes of having their faces appear on the cover of the *National Geographic Magazine*. Our purpose for being at that hot, dusty stadium treating dying horses, however, was to gain an opportunity to proclaim Christ in a culturally sensitive way. Our mission goes far beyond the excitement of the races and the attraction of wealthy and important people.

Drs. Tom Juergens and John Haffner came to Mongolia to share their love of Christ and to tell these rugged horsemen of their Savior and Lord. They used their skills to open the doors into the hearts of these Mongolian horsemen. It was difficult for us to share our deep values when horses were falling like flies from dehydration and exhaustion, and owners were torn by the loss of their animals on which they place great value. We had to show the horsemen that we really cared before we could earn the right to share the Good News of Jesus Christ.

Sometimes we must jump the boundaries of superstition and ignorance before gaining a hearing. Drs. Juergens and Haffner have been able to do that by visiting veterinarians all over this country. They have had a dramatic impact on the spiritual and professional side of the team as they travel together, share meals, devotions, and life experiences with one another. They return to the city each year for the annual V.E.T. Net men's retreat where Dr. Juergens leads a poignant Bible study. They have truly taken up their own cross, and God has multiplied their contributions exponentially. [3,4]

We know that if we want to share effectively and with gentleness, while respecting the reason for this wonderful hope that is in us, we must build a bridge. We call this bridge "relationship building." I fear we often use this expression carelessly and casually, but the truth is, we must enter the Mongolians' world to make an impact. We must be visibly different in the work place, as we travel about and as we play. If Christ is in us, there will be dramatic change that makes those around us declare, "You must be Jesus people. I see a difference in your life, and I want to know what makes you like you are—because I want that, too."

Paul, Sarah, Tom, and Johnny are great examples of what we have dubbed long-term/short-term missionaries. They each came to Mongolia with a heart to serve, but for various reasons, did not initially feel God leading them to be in Mongolia full time. However, they quickly caught the vision of God's work in this country and enthusiastically joined the Team. Although they are not with us throughout the entire year, they continue to be actively involved in the ministry. First and foremost, they pray for us. They also mobilize their church and other people to pray and to establish support for the ministry of V.E.T. Net. This type of service has been vital to our success.

Dr. Charles Stanley describes well the heart of a committed shuttle:

> He has a plan for each one of us. When we make a decision to walk by faith, He will reveal it to us. And that plan always includes service and dedication to Him and to those He brings into our lives. God loves us so that we might love others. He blesses us so that we might bless others. That's what the Christian life is all about. [5]

Frances and I would like to express our deepest appreciation to all of the shuttles who have sacrificially served in Mongolia over the past 23 years. God knows each one of you, and He is the one who will ultimately distribute the crowns as rewards for service to Him.

Notes:

1. Dorminy, A.L. (2003). *Mission Vet*. (Christian Veterinary Mission, Seattle, Washington) Pp. 1–3, 18, 195.

2. Dr. Paul and Sarah Welch live in Tulsa, Oklahoma where he is the director of a private veterinary clinic and Sarah has her office for Mary Kay Cosmetics.

3. Dr. Thomas Juergens is an equine practitioner from Anoka, Minnesota where he was the founder of Anoka Equine Hospital.

4. Dr. John Haffner is on faculty at Middle Tennessee State University in Murfreesboro, Tennessee.

5. Stanley, C.F. (2009). *The Life Principles Bible, NASB,* Ephesians 4:28, loc 95304, (Thomas Nelson Publishers, Nashville, Tennessee), Kindle Book.

Figure 10.1. *"What Is Success?"*—discouraged vet in front of his clinic

Chapter 10

Fulfilled Dream

> *All those gathered here will know that it is not by sword or spear that the Lord saves; for the battle is the Lord's, and he will give all of you into our hands.*
>
> –1 Samuel 17:47, NIV

I remember well an American church we visited over 20 years ago to share our plans to minister in Mongolia. One of the members stood in the service and asked, "What's a veterinarian going to do in missions? Do you plan to share the gospel with horses?" I took offense at the time. Obviously, he was unable to see the possibilities of veterinarians reaching people for Christ through their profession. Years later, we acknowledge that many horses have heard the gospel. While the herder held the reins and heard the Good News for the first time, his horse stood by attentively eavesdropping on the conversation. Reaching out to these semi-nomadic people through their animals has been an effective way to carry the message of Christ to the people.

There are not many ways to reach these remote Mongolian herders with news and information. Their local veterinarian is one of the few who consistently enters their isolated life. When a herder becomes a believer in Christ, the door is opened to take the life-giving gospel to the entire family and to other herders. As the veterinarian routinely returns for animal care, there is an opportunity to continue to build into the lives of the herder families with the Word. In a very real way, the veterinarian becomes their "Paul." The combination of treating the animals and sharing the Good News is precisely the vision of V.E.T. Net.

Land of Genghis Khan

The Great Khan thundered across the steppe with his hordes of leather-armored horsemen during the 12th and 13th centuries.

The merging of legend and the reality of this Mongolian King amazes our generation endowed with modern technology and communications. How this master leader successfully conquered much of the known world on horseback, establishing the largest land empire in the history of the world, is still a mystery for the ages. Yet, there is a different battle being waged in this Empire of the Khans that is not based on land acquisition or military power. It is a war in the spiritual realm; a war for the hearts of the people of this ancient land; a conflict infinitely more important. It is a battle for the souls of men.

The Launch of V.E.T. Net *Continuing Education* (CE)

We had God and all the tools: The V.E.T. Net Team, the *Field Manual*, the shuttles. Now, we needed a plan that was expandable; one that could reach this entire nation for Christ. Our dream was to see countryside veterinarians become followers of Christ and spread the gospel to the uttermost parts of Mongolia. This concept was conceived during my first trip in 1994. I discovered an obvious need for a modern veterinary extension system that could carry information across this country. [1]

We began to develop the framework for the V.E.T. Net *Continuing Education* program—a massive undertaking that would impact this entire nation. How small we felt at the time when confronted with the enormity of this Mongolian Christian challenge. We believed that God was telling us to "Go to the whole nation; He wants everyone to hear the Good News." It was with fear and trembling that we stepped into the unknown with trust in the all-knowing, all-powerful God. We realized that it was not the size of V.E.T. Net that counted; it was the size of God—and He would carry us through the depths and lift us up on wings of eagles.

The Plan

> *May he give you the desire of your heart and make all your plans succeed.*
>
> –Psalm 20:4, NIV

As I visited the lonely countryside veterinary practitioners, I consistently found boredom; they had nothing productive to do. With no challenge in their life, they turned to alcohol. We noticed this as we traveled from one veterinary practice to another. It was always the same—hopelessness. The desperate condition of rural veterinarians led us to develop an extensive, non-government, national continuing-education system. It began quite small, but eventually reached into all 19 rural states and virtually every county.

Veterinary Service Vouchers

We huddled in the bushes beside a tiny, frozen stream to escape the biting, freezing cold as we cooked a warming soup. It was the wind this time of year that made travel so dangerous and difficult. At the same time that springtime azaleas and dogwoods were blossoming in our home state of North Carolina, the Mongolian wind was bringing an icy chill that slashed at our faces painfully. However, neither the wind nor freezing temperatures could extinguish the glow we all felt inside our spirit; it was as warming as our soup. We were returning from two new countryside sites where our team had implemented our very first veterinary-training project.

Veterinarians are often political leaders in their county. We had recently met the current governor and former governor of one of the new sites. Both were veterinarians. It was usual for them to have several technicians working with them in every district of their huge county. The plan was to use veterinary shuttles to train our V.E.T. Net veterinarians. In turn, our team veterinarians trained the countryside veterinarians who then trained their veterinary technicians. Together, we all trained the herders. It was designed to be a cascading training program to improve the skills of each person in the knowledge stream, and at the same time, change the lives for the better of all involved.

At last, everything was in place, and the plan was implemented by launching a *Voucher Program*. One hundred herding families were given the equivalent of vouchers to spend with their rural veterinarian or technician in the project. The herder families received decreasing amounts of vouchers over a three-year period. The rural veterinarians and technicians were trained in modern veterinary skills, and after the specified timeframe, they would be able to develop a viable, production-oriented practice. The herder families involved in the project became examples to surrounding families who learned the value of good veterinary care as they watched their neighbors' animals improve. As a result, some wanted this same service.

The *Voucher Program* worked well on a small scale, but it was too cumbersome for expansion. Our next challenge was to implement another small project to save the yak after a hard winter storm.

Save-the-Yak Project

> *Our barns will be filled with every kind of provision. Our sheep will increase by thousands, by tens of thousands in our fields;*
>
> – Psalm 144:13, NIV

As we drove in the countryside one spring day, we noticed the absence of the pastoral serenity to which we had become accustomed. International news carried the sad saga of the winter of 2000 in rural Mongolia. Death and destruction were evident everywhere. Desperate herdsmen stripped the hides from deteriorating carcasses hoping to salvage something from the disaster, while fat vultures perched on decaying animals appearing to discuss which delicacy to eat next.

Mongolian winters are always difficult, but the winter of 2000 was one to break records. Blowing snow covered any sparse grass left for livestock. Temperatures hovered in the negative range, sometimes reaching -50° F. Many families lost every animal they owned, and herdsmen, long accustomed to a fine horse beneath them, were reduced to foot transportation.

The ultimate sadness of this situation was that much of the devastation was preventable. Fall grazing had reduced the grasses to ground level, and an inadequate amount of hay was stored for winter. Over-grazing had become a common practice as herders counted wealth by the number of their animals. These were costly mistakes. Many yak herds in the mountainous areas of Mongolia were decimated.

Unfortunately, the herders also allowed their yak herds to start the winter with heavy loads of internal and external parasites. Consequently, yak share their feed with parasites in the gastro-intestinal track; lice and ticks destroy their beautiful coats causing the yak to go into the cold months without their winter del to protect them. Parasites amplify the problem of limited feed and greatly exacerbates the effects of severe weather.

As the yak struggled through the winter, a cold air was also blowing across V.E.T. Net. We were down to our last few dollars. The salaries were meager for our young team, but it was enough for them to meet their obligations. Frances and I felt totally responsible for these young folks who had chosen to work at V.E.T. Net instead of pursuing another, more stable career.

A Swiss agency had given us a large supply of medication to treat livestock for parasitic problems. Unfortunately, funds to pay salaries and transportation to get to the countryside were not included. We asked for permission from a Swiss representative to monetize these drugs giving us the money to pay salaries, transport drugs to the countryside, train rural veterinarians and provide a stipend for countryside veterinarians to administer the anti-parasitic medication.

Dr. Flowers suggested we send a proposal to a large development organization. He knew a Christian man who worked in the organization. If awarded the funds, V.E.T. Net would be paid for the drugs donated by the Swiss agency, and the money could be used to implement the project. We submitted the application to fund the *Save-the-Yak* project, and the waiting game began. Time was of the essence, and we believed that to be effective, this project would need to be implemented in November or, at the very latest, December.

The plan was for our team to train rural veterinarians to administer medication to the yak in their areas to treat external and internal parasites. Frances and I waited patiently in our ger in Bat-Ulzi for word the project had been approved. When days turned into weeks, we were forced to return to the city disappointed, wondering how we would break the news to our young team that there would be no more salaries.

Do not be anxious about anything, but in every situation,

by prayer and petition, with thanksgiving, present your requests to God. And the peace of God, which transcends all understanding, will guard your hearts and your minds in Christ Jesus.

–Philippians 4:6–7, NIV

At the end of all hope, the news came: The *Save-the-Yak* project grant was approved and the yak could be saved! V.E.T. Net was snatched from the brink of an early grave by the hand of God. The cogs started to turn, and soon the medicine was on its way to the countryside. Countryside veterinarians received payment from the project grant for each yak treated. It was a glorious time as we watched the yak and V.E.T. Net revived and the rural vets had meaningful work. They had a sense of hope at last.

The *Save-the-Yak* project and other small projects kept us going when we were a small team, but as we grew, we were increasingly challenged to provide salaries, vehicles and office space. God met our needs in miraculous ways. We were frugal and planned as carefully as we could for the coming months, but ultimately, He was our Provider. Often the word "trust" carried us over shaky ground. Although these were lean times physically, they were spiritual cornucopias of God's grace as we waited patiently on Him to meet our needs. The difficult times drew us closer to Him and hardened the glue that held us together as a team.

Continuing-Education-Extension Program

Then Job replied to the Lord: "I know that you can do all things; no plan of yours can be thwarted."

–Job 42:1–2, NIV

The plan to develop a nongovernment, *Continuing-Education-Extension* program began to take shape in 2004 and became the core of our veterinary operation and ministry in Mongolia. The large animal clinic/training center, the small animal hospital/training center, veterinary internships, the *Distance-Master's* program, the large and small animal student clubs and the drug and equipment revolving account were all geared toward the promotion and success of this program.

In hindsight, the month of May 2005 was a landmark period in the work of V.E.T. Net. Over the last few years, we had come to understand the needs of herders, their animals and the hundreds of local veterinarians who served them. Moving from a socialist veterinary system to a private one was not easy. The struggle for veterinarians began when the Mongolian government decided to halt payment of their salaries as federal employees. Suddenly, they were on their own with little useful knowledge, no modern pharmaceuticals or equipment, and a clientele of herders that had no cash to pay for veterinary care. This enormous challenge became an opportunity for V.E.T. Net. No other organization was sufficiently able to muster a robust response to the needs of the remote veterinarians and herders. *Christian Veterinary Mission* and its Mongolian affiliate, V.E.T. Net, were in a remarkable position to make a difference in the lives of the people of rural Mongolia.

In 2003, the Mongolia V.E.T. Net NGO was registered, and almost simultaneously, a key couple arrived from Tulsa, Oklahoma to work with the V.E.T. Net Team. Dr. Mary and Richard Ballenger's arrival was an example of God's perfect timing. They would be crucial to the development of the *Continuing-Education-Extension* program. God knew that and sent them to us.

In the following story, Dr. Batsukh is a *fictitious* Mongolian character. However, the story is based on truth. This encompasses the activities of our V.E.T. Net's *Continuing-Education-Extension* program. Dr. Batshkh represents hundreds of countryside veterinarians who come for our *CE* training.

> It was 2005, and Dr. Batsukh was filled with excitement as he boarded the bus packed with his colleagues. The veterinary practitioners in his state had been invited to spend a week at V.E.T. Net for continuing education. Many questions echoed on the "Mongolian Greyhound" as they traveled on the rough, dirt road. They were too excited to feel the bumps as the old bus rattled along on their ten-hour journey.
>
> Dr. Batsukh couldn't stop chattering: "What do you think they will teach? Will it be the same old regulations we always study? Who will teach us?

Will they give us some new veterinary drugs and equipment? Do you think we will see any animals, or will it all be from a book? Will they teach us something that is practical that I can use in my practice?"

The V.E.T. Net Team veterinarians spent the whole year of 2004 preparing for Dr. Batsukh and his veterinary friends from his state. They had thoughtfully written the curriculum for the week of training. These countryside veterinarians needed basic information that would be useful to them in their own practices that would help the herders improve their livestock. Everything was directed towards just that kind of training—practical, useful and interesting.

Shock was the best word to describe the reaction as the countryside veterinarians entered the V.E.T. Net training facility. "Where are the old experienced teachers?" Dr. Batsukh thought to himself. "All I see is a bunch of wet behind the ears young whippersnappers. What could they possibly teach me? I've been doing this veterinary job for 25 years."

Little did Dr. Batsukh know that the young V.E.T. Net veterinarians had been studying the material in the curriculum all year. They were full of knowledge, having been taught day after day by Western advisors and practical veterinary shuttles. They had traveled together with many of these shuttles and had hands-on experience. They were primed and ready to deliver the lessons in their heart language with a bang.

The day started with some milk-tea and cookies—just the kind they were accustomed to eating. They were starting to feel more at home already. The kindness, respect and hospitality of the Team soon overcame the anxious feelings of the group as they moved into the lecture room.

A young veterinarian, Tserendorj, stepped to the podium and began his talk with the aid of a well-prepared PowerPoint presentation. He began the lesson with a short video on common equine lameness and continued with his presentation of diagnosis and treatment. "This is amazing teaching," thought Dr. Batsukh, "This kid really knows his stuff." Ganzo then taught on parasite control, and Naranwuu presented a useful talk on hoof disease. "These are just the kind of problems I see every day," Batsukh exclaimed to his neighbor sitting next to him. "And this book they have prepared is going to be a great reference when I return home—my first veterinary book in the Mongolian language."

The lunch that was served was not some strange city food, just good downhome Mongolian cuisine. They ate hardily and talked of all the things they had learned in the morning session. The day was filled with new and exciting information.

On Wednesday, our guests were loaded into the bus to travel to a herder site not far from Ulaanbaatar. V.E.T. Net had arranged for a local herder to provide animals for a practical exercise. This kind of hands-on training was totally alien to the students. They had never experienced this before in Veterinary School or at conferences.

After the evening meal, the fun began—no more information to be stuffed into their brimming heads. They enjoyed singing beautiful Mongolian folk songs that were etched on their hearts. They loved the music, and some volunteered solos they had sung since their childhood when they belted out their songs from horseback. Then there were riotous games with prizes for the winners. "I've never had so much fun," said Dr. Batsukh, "and nobody is even drinking vodka."

Later in the week during the evening sessions,

they heard about Jesus. "This was strange talk for a veterinary meeting," Dr. Batsukh mumbled. But, by that time we were friends, and it was easy to talk about our values, and why we wanted to help them have a better life. "Would you like a Bible, Dr. Batsukh?" Nuda asked him. The teachers and other team members joined together in small groups at the appointed ministry time to discuss the little "What is Success?" booklet.

The week ended all too soon with a banquet and entertainment. Prizes were awarded to the best students and everyone received a certificate that would soon find itself hanging prominently in their practices. They were very proud of all they had learned. Speeches of appreciation were given. The countryside veterinarians presented V.E.T. Net with a beautiful hand painted picture of the mountains in their state. The participants were loaded down with new drugs and equipment to test in their practices. They all boarded the bus with smiles on their faces. They had a lot to talk about on the trip home.

Some weeks later a Russian van drove into Dr. Batsukh's small town. It was his new friends from V.E.T. Net, and they were there to help him put into practice all that he had learned at the meeting. Now, it was his turn to be hospitable, and he didn't spare the horses. His wife had their ger filled with aromas of great smelling horsemeat that bubbled on the stove. Dr. Batsukh was already making plans for his trip back to V.E.T. Net next year—he couldn't wait.

This *Continuing-Education-Extension* program is designed to educate countryside animal doctors in the disciplines of veterinary medicine to help them improve animal production and animal health in their work area. Each year, they study new practical topics that dramatically expand their knowledge and skills. Our Team veterinarians are the best trained and most qualified practicing veterinarians in Mongolia. They are admired and respected by their colleagues and countryside veterinarians.

One young female veterinarian who attended church with a team member on a Sunday, heard the gospel, and received Christ as her personal Savior. She went back to her remote area with the potential to reach many for Jesus. Others visited a V.E.T. Net family asking for Bibles. All the Christian literature we made available was quickly taken.

Another female veterinarian pulled me over to the side one day and said, "I am so impressed with the maturity and knowledge of these young people. I have four daughters, and I want each of them to marry a V.E.T. Net veterinarian." What a wonderful complement! We might run out of single men, but the thought was most encouraging.

V.E.T. Net's Finances

While Dr. Mary, our long-term veterinarian, was busy organizing training for the *Continuing-Education-Extension* program, Richard, Dr. Mary's husband, was using his gifts as a businessman and negotiator to secure funds through organizations who had access to USDA funds.

Interestingly, the American taxpayers did not pay for the *Continuing-Education-Extension* program, since it was funded through surplus agricultural products. At that time, surplus wheat was monetized by the United States through large development organizations like Mercy Corps and World Vision. The equation was simple: The U.S. had surplus wheat, and Mongolia had a deficit. The wheat was sold to Mongolia, and the income from the wheat went to the development of the country. Richard applied for a portion of this money, and V.E.T. Net was awarded funds for our programs.

These large and complicated projects required accurate and timely reporting. God sent an American engineer, Leon Heisey, to assist Richard with project reporting. Leon had the right skills and temperament to prepare the required reports and teach the Mongolians how to handle the process in the future.

Leon's wife, Heather Heisey, a veterinarian, became the director of V.E.T. Net's newly established *Distance-Master's* program for Mongolian graduate veterinarians. V.E.T. Net and the Mongolian

Agriculture University signed memorandums of understanding with five American universities: Middle Tennessee State University, Mississippi State University, North Dakota State University, Oklahoma State University, and Virginia Polytechnic Institute.

Modern, practical veterinary training is provided for graduate veterinarians through computerized training prepared by faculty and others working with these five universities. V.E.T. Net facilitates the training and cooperates with the faculty and staff of the Mongolian Veterinary Institute, Mongolian Research Institute and the Mongolian Central Diagnostic Laboratory on research projects. This is affordable, modern education that allows students to study in their own country. It is amazing to see how God brought all of this together.

Veterinary Drug and Equipment Revolving Account

For many years, corrupt companies abused herders by selling them poor quality medicine for their animals before V.E.T. Net began to register and bring quality medicine into Mongolia. As one veterinarian said, "Training without good drugs is like a gun without bullets." As a result, the herders began to call our long-acting penicillin "Jesus white medicine" while they dubbed oxytetracycline the "Jesus brown medicine." Now, veterinarians and herders associate V.E.T. Net with high-quality veterinary drugs—and Jesus. To be sure, our work and our faith should never be separated.

We knew there was a desperate need for high-quality, economical veterinary drugs and equipment, and we also knew that someday the funds to run V.E.T. Net would be depleted. Most of the large funders in the early stages of this program eventually disappeared. It seemed a natural step for V.E.T. Net to bring good veterinary medicine and supplies into the country and become a distributor of these products each time the team visited the local veterinary practices. We realized this plan could be the answer to long-term financial sustainability for all our programs. So, every time we wrote a proposal for a project, we included requests for funds to purchase veterinary drugs and equipment.

The sale of drugs is connected to our training of veterinarians and herders. It is not only important that they use quality products, but also that they know how to use them properly. Equally important is the understanding that meat and milk products must not be consumed until sufficient time is allowed for medication to leave the animal's system.

V.E.T. Net sends teams to the countryside with a veterinarian, a businessperson, a teacher, often a shuttle and a driver with a truck full of our quality veterinary products. Typically, a V.E.T. Net veterinarian has already contacted the local veterinarian in the county so that his herder clients can be assembled and prepared for the arrival of our team. The team joins the local veterinarian to train the herders on methods for improving their animal production and simple business principals as well as instruction on such character qualities as honesty, truthfulness, and loyalty.

Herders are delighted to have access to good medicine for their animals. Their animals are more productive, their families have better lives and they have safe meat and milk products. Additionally, the local veterinarian gets a share of the profit from the sales of the medicine and equipment that helps to sustain his practice while providing good services for his herder clients. V.E.T. Net markets veterinary drugs at a fair wholesale price and develops an expanded market. Everybody wins, and the gospel is carried throughout Mongolia.

Over the years that we had large secular funders, we developed a *Revolving-Drug-and-Equipment* Account. This became an important asset with a potential for sustaining the ministry for years to come. Some of these drug products were given to remote veterinarians for their herders. As they saw results, veterinarians began to purchase their products from V.E.T. Net. The funds remained in the revolving account allowing it to grow larger every year. Richard Ballenger was key in the development of the drug and equipment distribution system, and now the V.E.T. Net team is learning to manage this asset effectively and efficiently. At the current time, we have distributors in most of the states throughout the country.

As we continue the ministry in Mongolia, it is quite apparent that sustainability involves far more than financial security for projects. True sustainability demands that we encourage believers who are willing to multiply their efforts to make disciples as God's Word commands. Spiritual sustainability is crucial to any Christ-centered organization.

Model-Herder Program

In 2007, we conceived a plan to develop and organize the *Model-Herder* program. This involved using existing herding sites to demonstrate the effectiveness of good animal care to surrounding herders.

The *Model-Herder* program proved to be an idea that revolutionized our work in Mongolia. The veterinarians of the past were poorly equipped to help their clients. It was easy to understand why herders did not want to throw good money after worthless care. The result was a general lack of trust between herders and their veterinarian. V.E.T. Net viewed the *Model-Herder* program as a way to re-establish good relationships between client and provider.

The concept of the *Model-Herder* program was to furnish modern veterinary service and products, and to provide a preventive health-care program for all the animals—cattle, yak, sheep, goats, horses and camels. It would allow the model herders to see what good quality animal care could do for their herds and flocks. This built credibility for veterinarians and strengthened relationships with their herders. We have had over 700 of these demonstration farms, and the results have been most extraordinary.

Model herders have healthier animals; the animals are more productive, and survivability has been significantly increased during the severe winter storms that frequently impact Mongolia. From the spiritual perspective, it doesn't take much imagination to see the potential for the *Model-Herder* program to reach across a nation of herders with the gospel of Jesus Christ. Neighbors notice and start to talk and ask, "What is going on with your animals? They are fat and have beautiful hair coats and aren't dying off like mine during the winter storms. What are you doing differently?"

Countryside CE Trips

From the east I summon a bird of prey; from a far-off land, a man to fulfill my purpose. What I have said, that will I bring about; what I have planned, that will I do.

–Isaiah 46:11, NIV

The creek was beginning to freeze, but it wasn't solid enough to keep our van from breaking through the ice and send it crashing against the far bank. The front wheel finally came to a rest, but it was pointing at an ugly angle. The diagnosis was a broken front axle. Not many challenges bring our vans to a halt for more than a few hours, but this was a *coup de grâce,* unusual even for this machine.

How could God let this happen to our V.E.T. Net Team? We were eagerly doing His work, and now here we were completely and absolutely stopped. To make matters worse, there were two veterinary shuttles with the team on this trip. We so wanted to take full advantage of their teaching skills.

However, all was not lost as we first thought. Tserendorj caught a motorcycle ride to the next town, and our friend, the local veterinarian, returned with his jeep to save the day. He hauled all of the supplies and people to his home while the driver stayed with the van until it could be moved to the watchful care of a herder family nearby.

This seemed disastrous at first, but God had a plan, and it was vastly better than the team's plan. Living in this same little county seat of Ondor Ulaan was an old lady who had become a Christian some years before. Unfortunately, there were no other believers in this little village. Her eyesight was failing, and she was unable to read her Bible. She had been praying for some time that God would bring other believers to fellowship with her and teach her more about her God. It seemed this old lady was responsible for our broken axle.

During our four-day breakdown, many people in Ondor Ulaan heard of Jesus. Some even asked Him to be their Savior. The veterinarian's wife was counted among those who made a choice for Christ, and he was also very interested. It all began with the prayers of one elderly woman. Soon it turned into a village revival because the Holy Spirit had already been working there long before our arrival. In the end, the prayer of this one elderly lady living in a remote mountain village proved to be far more powerful than our vehicle or our plan. As pastor and author Dr. Charles Stanley writes: "We stand tallest and strongest on our knees." [2]

Through the work of V.E.T. Net and the *Continuing-Education* (CE) program, tremendous changes have taken place in the countryside. Veterinarians are now able to make a reasonable living practicing what they have been trained to do. Many are now quite prosperous, while their herder clients also enjoy improved livelihoods. Families are able to afford a better way of life, children are educated, and the whole area has benefited from healthier, more productive animals.

What Is Success?

As these veterinarians' lives improved, we worried that they would begin to worship the god of materialism. This nation began to change with the new mining wealth. The gap between the haves and have-nots is growing even wider. V.E.T. Net has an unbelievable opportunity to reach the nation for Christ though, and see it influenced for good before the effects of materialism spread from their newly found wealth. Because of this concern, our outreach to them intensified with the use of a small booklet we produced to use with the gospel message, *"What is Success?"* (by Gerald Mitchum, illustrated by Tamir Dugermaa, and translated by Undraa Dugermaa).

What is Success?

> In 1999, Bayarbat was a veterinarian in Gobi Altai. Times were hard for him, but the government payments allowed him to eke out a living. He was devastated when he heard the news that his practice would be privatized. He was able to buy the practice, but he found himself in a desperate situation. The herders that he served were not accustomed to paying for veterinary care. They also did not have cash to pay for services. To compound the problem, Bayarbat knew very little modern medicine, and he had no quality veterinary drugs on his shelves.
>
> An organization, owned and operated by a team of young, caring Mongolian people was established. Their veterinarians are trained by western veterinarians in modern, practical veterinary medicine. Quality, modern veterinary drugs and equipment from foreign countries are available

through this organization.

Bayarbat attended *Continuing-Education* training by this organization. He saw all of the young staff and thought, "What do these young people have to teach me?" However, he was amazed at the maturity and knowledge of the veterinarians as well as the integrity and strong moral principles that he saw in the staff. "I want my children to grow up to be like them," he shared with other participants. When he returned to his county, he took equipment and drugs that were given to him as a gift by the organization, and some other needed supplies. He is aware that the organization always has a consistent supply of necessary medicines and equipment.

Now Bayarbat had all of the tools he needed to have a successful practice. He had new knowledge that helped his herders to prosper with improved production of their animals; he used the best drugs available to him. He began to make a good living for his family through his own profession and every year he went for more training. Later, the organization would send a small team to his practice to help him implement what he had learned.

Over the years Bayarbat's practice flourished. He became the wealthiest man in his county. He drove a black Land Cruiser, built a new office, and lived with his family in a beautiful house just on the edge of the county center. Life was truly good.

Although the medicines were quality, there was one problem. Each of them had an expiration date. This is also true for people—we are all born with an "expiration date" and must someday stand before God and be judged. Although the organization had helped him professionally, they had failed to help him find the most important thing. Now, Bayabat was very ill and his "expiration day" had come. All of his wealth did not seem very important.

> There is a similar story in the Bible in Luke 16:19–31. It is about a rich man and a poor man. The rich man had everything on this earth but when his "expiration date" came, he was eternally separated from God. The poor man died and went to live with God forever. The rich man pleaded with God to send the poor man to go and warn his brothers—but it was too late.
>
> We love each of you and so does God. We will always work with you regardless of your religion, but we feel we must warn you about the coming judgment. We will never try to force anyone to believe as we do—that is your decision. But we do want to tell you how you can know this God who loves you and wants to spend eternity with you. We do not want you to be like Bayarbat and think, "They helped me become a prosperous veterinarian, but they neglected to tell me the most important news. I was successful in everything except that which was most important—my relationship with the creator God."

The booklet was given out and the gospel story was shared; the veterinarians were given an opportunity to accept Christ as their Savior. Today, there are many countryside veterinarians who have a personal relationship with Jesus. These men and women are true believers in Jesus Christ as a result of the outreach through the V.E.T. Net *Continuing-Education* program.

Recently, one of these veterinarians attended a leadership conference. Near the end, she approached a member of our staff and asked for 50 of the *Good Shepherd* booklets (by Gerald Mitchum, illustrated by Tamir Dugermaa, and translated by Undraa Dugermaa) told in the language of herders. She said, "I need these little booklets to share with my herder clients. I treat their animals, and often I stay with the families in their ger. I want to share the message of Christ with all of my herder families."

This is the fulfillment of a vision for us. There is nobody else likely to go to these places. This veterinarian realizes she has a virgin field to reach with the gospel message. She is the only person on earth with such a unique opportunity. V.E.T. Net can reach a few of these herder families, but it is the remote local practitioner like this woman who has the wide-open door. These families trust her because she visits them every year and sometimes several times a year. Helping these veterinarians come to a saving knowledge of Christ, discipling and enabling them is a strategy with the potential to yield a bountiful harvest. It is the strategy of V.E.T. Net that God has developed through the V.E.T. Net *Continuing-Education* program. What a wonderful method our Father has given us! That is, to help solve the livestock dilemma and at the same time, share Jesus with the people of this land of herders who love their animals and only want the best care for them.

Animal Hospital/Training Centers

We decided to supplement the V.E.T. Net *Continuing-Education* program by building small and large-animal clinics strategically located. The small-animal practice was named *Caring Animal Hospital and Training Center.* Long-term missionaries, Drs. Clay Ashely and Karen Smirmaul, were involved in developing the pet practice.

Dr. Jeff Duke was one of our early shuttles to work at the Small Animal Hospital. He made a significant impact on the practice through training, discipleship and the provision of supplies and equipment. Dr. Ed Neufeld is a Canadian veterinarian who also has had a dramatic influence on the Small Animal Hospital. While his wife, Anne, taught English, Dr. Ed instructed the team and interns at the Hospital. He was also involved in developing and teaching in the *Distance Master's* program.

Caring Animal Hospital/Training Center offers practical training for CE attendees and veterinary students, as well as our V.E.T. Net staff veterinarians. Small animal clubs continue to offer students the opportunity to see Christ through the staff of the hospital. There are other long-term/short-term shuttles that continue to actively support the ministry in many ways:

Dr. Justin Woolsey, his wife Helen and their children Caleb and Caroline, have now joined the V.E.T. Net staff. Dr. Justin is the advisor to *Caring Animal Hospital/Training Center,* and as such, is leading the clinic to new heights. The practice is being computerized and will serve as a model to other clinics. A new x-ray machine has also been donated. Our clinic serves as a center for other developing practices. *Caring Animal Hospital* is becoming a referral practice for start-up clinics.

It is not an easy responsibility to homeschool two young children in this country. The winters are long, and the kids are house bound for months on end. Helen's compassionate personality and the family's love of hospitality have become key to their ministry here. The whole family is involved in outreach to the veterinary students who come for veterinary training, English, and Bible study either at the V.E.T. Net office or in their apartment. Justin and Helen are continually discipling the clinic staff.

Our *Large Animal Hospital/Training Center* is located about 15 miles south of Ulaanbaatar. It is a work in progress. One of our buildings doubles as a training facility and as housing for Dr. Andrew and Chris Spence and their family from New Zealand. Andrew came as a shuttle, and some years later contacted me with an interest in returning long-term. Recall that I previously said, "Never, ever say no." Even so, I admit that I had second and third thoughts about this tribe. You see, Andrew and Chris have nine children—that's right, nine children—and they wanted to bring eight of them to Mongolia. How could a family of ten people possibly live in one of these confining apartments?

"Well, we will build a house," I thought, "and it will later become the large animal training center." This would be another one of those commitments like building the dormitory in Ulaan Am. "You can't possibly get materials for this, and winter will come before the building is closed in," we were told. However, we had already committed, and the family was on its way. God expected us to keep our commitments. Trusting God may sometimes seem risky, but it always pays enormous dividends in the end.

This project would have been impossible for us, but it wasn't for God. The walls went up; the septic tank and well went in, and the family moved in late November. The building doubles for a house for the Spences and as a large animal training center. They have been a wonderful blessing to V.E.T. Net as they model a godly family. To date, the *Large Animal Hospital* is still being developed. We also have plans for a small dairy to be used as a training center for the expanding dairy industry in Mongolia. Andrew was a mixed practitioner in New Zealand, with experience in dairy practice. He also helps at the small animal practice when needed. Chris and the family are envolved with the outreach to rural areas.

Dr. Hillary Mincher and her husband Michael joined V.E.T. Net in 2016. Dr. Hillary is presently working on plans for the *Large Animal Clinic* expansion and leads the charge for the internship program. Without these national interns, the future of V.E.T. Net would be in jeopardy. Some of these young veterinarians will accept Christ and eventually become part of the V.E.T. Net staff. Michael is serving as a Christian counselor for the staff. They are both committed to reaching Mongolia for Christ, and their impact at V.E.T. Net has already been enormous. They are active in discipling the V.E.T. Net staff as they challenge all of us to new highs in our relationship with God.

Both the large animal and the small-animal hospitals are used as part of our internship program. Countryside veterinarians and recent graduates of the Vet School spend several months working with the V.E.T. Net team veterinarians. They learn new skills and have the opportunity to be involved in devotions and the V.E.T. Net culture.

Notes:

1. Dorminy, A.L. (2003). *Mission Vet*. (Christian Veterinary Mission, Seattle, Washington) Pp. 195.

2. Stanley, C.F. (2009). *The Life Principles Bible, NASB*, Life Principle 6, loc 2196. (Thomas Nelson Publishers, Nashville, Tennessee), Kindle Book.

Figure 11.1. Drawing: "Classroom in Ger"—teacher in countryside

Chapter 11

Claim-a-County for Christ

> *People were also bringing babies to Jesus for him to place his hands on them. When the disciples saw this, they rebuked them. But Jesus called the children to him and said, "Let the little children come to me, and do not hinder them, for the kingdom of God belongs to such as these. Truly I tell you, anyone who will not receive the kingdom of God like a little child will never enter it."*
>
> –Luke 18:15-17, NIV

It was 1996, and I was working with countryside veterinarians, herders and their livestock. This was Frances' first trip to visit a village school. She wrote down her thoughts as she spent time in the small countryside school and dormitory:

> I am remaining with Tserennadmid and her three young boys while Gerald works with Erdeneochir and the animals. Tserennadmid is the principal of the local elementary school. About 200 students, 8 to 13 years of age, attend school with 10 teachers. Some students live with relatives or friends since they are from so far away. A total of 60 students live in the dark, cold dormitory with 5 to 8 children housed in each room. I see no TV, no radio, no extra clothes and no toys

Tserennadmid and her husband, **Erdeneochir**, were our first countryside friends. We spent many nights and had many meals in their ger. It is from them that we learned how to survive and flourish in remote Mongolia. Unfortunately, during those early years, our dear friends did not choose to follow our God. (See endnote update.)

or games—only a bed for each child with a small roll of covers. It is difficult for these students of herding families who live in the distant surrounding area to be separated from their families. Yesterday, we gave a ride to a 17 year-old herder who had come to get his little sister to take her 17 kilometers to their home for the weekend. The principal and teachers are trying to discourage this practice because school continues through Saturday.

A small building beside the dormitory serves as the shower room. Every other Sunday, dorm workers heat water for the children to "get a wash." Two outhouses located further away are made of slabs of wood with slats on the ground and no doors. Temperatures are below freezing now. I'm wondering how they will survive these conditions when temperatures hover around -30 to -40 degrees Fahrenheit.

Children in Mongolia begin school at eight years of age. Most of these children do not know their Mongolian alphabet. They cannot even write their name, and they have limited access to pen and paper in the ger and at school. When they see the concrete school buildings with windows, primitive as they are, many are amazed. These are the first they have seen since gers have no windows. Everything is strange and new to them. They are not accustomed to sitting on a chair and writing on a table. What is a telephone? What is a television? What is a blackboard? The teacher even has to explain the few pictures she displays on the walls.

Tserennadmid wants so much for these young ones to have the best education possible, but it is difficult to hire qualified, modern teachers and entice them to come to such a remote area. Thankfully, one new teacher has moved here with her family this year. Her bonus for doing so is free coal and meat for the winter.

> Only four grades are taught in this school. There is no middle or high school. What happens when a child finishes here? That is a big concern. Some children will live with friends or relatives to continue their studies in a city school, but many will return to the family ger, and their education is effectively ended. By law, children must go to school until they are 16 years old.

Even if teachers had funds to buy the necessary materials, they were almost non-existent in this country in the beginning. Gifts of school supplies from American churches enabled us to help these children who had so little. As I look back, one of our most rewarding ministries in the early days was helping these little dormitory schools to keep operating.

Requests by governors and school administrators were usually overwhelming—new buildings, heating systems, gymnasiums. We tried to meet many of these, but soon found they were too great for our limited budget. We found individuals and organizations to fund specific projects like the solar system for Jaragalant and the dormitory building in Ulaan Am, but all too often we were only able to help with smaller projects such as painting dormitories and school buildings, decorating classrooms, starting libraries and replacing broken glass. The long distances to these villages was a major challenge for us as it consumed the lion's share of our funds. Not only that, but travel was difficult.

Living on the Edge

One day we were on our way to survey the needs of a countryside school when it became apparent that darkness would soon overtake us before we reached our destination. It was early spring and too cold and windy to pitch the tent. My two Mongolian assistants stayed in a small-town hotel with our short-term Australian mate while I volunteered to sleep in the van with my driver, Dermee. I was hesitant to leave him alone in the vehicle with valuable cargo on the roof rack because drivers were sometimes arrested without cause, or vehicles were stripped of valuables.

These were scenarios I wanted to avoid, so we chose to drive out of town to a quiet place at the base of a small mountain where we found ourselves fighting off the cold and wind during the night. The next morning, with temperatures hovering below zero and the breeze picking up, we hurriedly dressed and heated coffee. When it came time to leave, I held my breath as I waited to see if the van's temperamental motor would catch so we could head back into town.

Why we took the shortcut back to town will never be clear to me. After all, the route to our camp had been so easy and gentle. However, to save 30 seconds, we took the road less travelled and slipped over the edge of the mountain down the steep slope. Unfortunately, we took a wrong turn, and the trail dropped away leaving us teetering on the edge of a canyon. I quickly realized we needed to lighten the load, so ever so gently, I slid out the door and closed it carefully behind me. Dermee put the transmission into reverse and tried to ease the van from the cliff. I watched as gravel scattered under the tires. The situation worsened leaving the van hanging almost in midair. I agreed to stand watch as Dermee quickly headed into town on foot to get help.

As I waited for Dermee to return, the wind continued to cut through my -50 degree-tested arctic coat. What a relief to finally see an old blue Russian truck crawling up the steep hill. Apparently, this was the only running vehicle in town. The driver was an engineer, but after only a glance, he was not about to hook his truck to what seemed to him a disaster waiting to happen. If his truck was connected and our van tumbled over the edge, he would be charged in the accident and would lose his only means of transportation. However, this driver was wise in the ways of angles and gravitational force. "We must have another vehicle to prevent the van from slipping over the edge as it is pulled away from this precipice," he exclaimed! He drove off with Dermee and my translator who had also arrived to help.

The minutes stretched into hours as the search for more help continued. The men finally located a tractor that could be started in these frigid temperatures. What a sight as the machine led the way up the hill with our friend in the blue truck following behind! A large diameter cable was soon threaded through the windows and around the top of the van. I could envision the collapse of the roof as the tractor began to pull, but through an amazing orchestration of crude machinery, the two giants began to dance, and our van slid to safety. One small window next to the driver's side of the back seat was broken almost as if to remind us that God had been there. I can't explain the lack of scratches on the paint from that frayed steel cable sliding over the roof and inside the van. Once the window was replaced, no one would have guessed that our old friend, the van, had looked retirement in the face and laughed as it rolled along on the security of flat land.

First Responders

Our original team of teachers who began their work in 2000-2001 included Undraa, Nara, and Nuda. We were working in a relatively small area around Jaragalant, Bat-Ulzi, Ulaan Am and Ik Bulag. These were mountain villages a long day's trip from Ulaanbaatar. Bat-Ulzi became the center of our activity, so Frances and I had a ger that was placed in the local veterinarian's yard. Our motorcycle gave us freedom to visit surrounding sites when our driver was away on other errands. All of these sites were within a 50 to 60-mile radius from Bat-Ulzi.

Our fledgling V.E.T. Net team was small and uncertain as Undraa, Nara and Nuda took a giant step of faith and committed to work with us even though we had little to offer in the way of security or future. They were willing to trust God and proved to be genuine pioneers. All three continue to work at V.E.T. Net to this day.

God's Strategic Plan

> *I thank my God every time I remember you. In all my prayers for all of you, I always pray with joy because of your partnership in the gospel from the first day until now.*
>
> –Philippians 1:3–5, NIV

We soon reached our limit with the small group of teachers and scant financial resources. We needed a plan that would multiply the community development ministry into multiple remote counties where the gospel had not been heard and churches were absent. A 50 to 60-mile radius was manageable—but the whole country? Did we say we wanted a God-size work? Well, we got it!

Claim-a-County for Christ rolled out of heaven like a breath of fresh air from the very mouth of God. It was to become a major part of V.E.T. Net to enable the team to reach right into the uttermost parts of this vast country. This major program would not only touch the lives of many rural Mongolians, but would also impact Western churches and short-term missionaries.

Before long, the concept of *Claim-a-County for Christ* began to take shape. We needed players, prayers, and payers if this was going to work. In fact, we wanted many partnerships in the gospel—not just donors. We were looking for real commitment from people and churches willing to become active participants in the ministry. Sure, they needed to be willing to invest in the ministry financially, but for some, that was the easy part.

Our prayers were answered, and a chain reaction was set off that has since touched the lives of untold thousands in Mongolia and many in the churches of our partners. *Claim-a-County for Christ* is at its best when our partners do the following: pray for us consistently; come as short-term missionaries and get personally involved; and help with the financial needs. They build relationships with our Mongolian team and people in the villages and motivate their own churches to greater involvement in missions.

How It Works

Churches, individuals and foundations in the United States as well as other countries, partner with V.E.T. Net to claim a specific county in which to invest. V.E.T. Net provides the national team—mostly teachers—to select counties in which to implement the community-development project based primarily on education needs. The heart of the project is the assistance we provide to the community to improve their schools. Working with the local schools insures that improvements will continue long after we have advanced to other counties. We work in each county for three years before moving on to adjacent counties. After all, just look at what Jesus accomplished in His three years of ministry!

During the first year that we work in a particular county, the V.E.T. Net teacher responsible for that state meets in the spring with the county governor to explain *Claim-a-County for Christ*. They decide on curriculum and discuss scheduling. Usually the officials have already heard of V.E.T. Net and are aware of the benefits our organization brings to their areas. They are always told that we are Christians. We never hide this. However, we are careful not to take advantage of our position and do not proselytize in the classroom setting.

The first year is spent concentrating on quality teaching and building strong relationships with government staff, school principals, teachers, children and families. We are watched carefully and know that the villagers are thinking, "What will these strange people do in our community?" They soon find out, because in addition to working with the schools, our ministry expands into other areas as we see real needs among government officials, medical personnel and small business entrepreneurs.

During the second and third years, we continue teaching and training. This is when we have the greatest opportunities to share our faith. Most of these small villages have no church, or if they do, it usually consists of a struggling handful of people. We have been gratified to watch as locals slowly begin to accept Christ, and where needed, allow us to help establish a small church. We don't go into a county as church planters, but that is exactly what happens. It is a natural, spontaneous outcome. It is truly amazing to see.

Little groups of believers blossom from the most unlikely places. These are areas where few Christians go, so the impact on whole communities is dramatic. This opens up a whole new and exciting challenge for us as we look for ways to help these little churches grow in their knowledge of the Word and in their walk with Christ.

V.E.T. Net has claimed over 120 counties with our partners in the three-year program, and we are presently active in 28 counties. Our vision is to continue to roll across this entire country of 332 counties with the *Claim-a-County for Christ* program. We have accomplished much in reaching remote counties, but there is more work to be done.

While we have not been totally surprised by the positive influence on the Mongolian communities, the impact on our partners has been both amazing and remarkable. Often short-term volunteers see their lives drastically changed when they give of themselves to join in this ministry. They are personally transformed as they take this renewed spirit back to their local churches. This produces a snowball effect: The Mongolian community is changed, the short-term missionary is changed and the supporting church is changed. For these partners, the concept of missions is no longer vague or distant. These short-term missionaries are able to clearly articulate the outcome of their investment. It is no longer just about giving money. Instead it has become real and personal. They have lived it and now it is their mission.

In May of 2000, Frances and I attended a ***Campus Crusade for Christ*** Sunday meeting hoping to recruit additional teachers for our community outreach. We met with the director who introduced us to a young man named Aggii. Soon Aggii was invited to join our little team where he soon shared his heartbreaking story. The following is a summary of Aggii's story.

> The ***Campus Crusade for Christ*** organization (now called "***Cru***") in Mongolia focuses on sharing the Good News and discipling Ulaanbaatar teachers who accept Jesus as their Savior. The purpose of the organization is to fulfill the great commission in the power of the Holy Spirit by winning people to faith in Jesus Christ, building them up in their faith and sending them out to win and equip others. Campus Crusade also equips believers to evangelize and disciple others.

Aggii had been living in Moscow where he attended military school. He returned to Mongolia as a young officer after his four years of training with great potential for a military career. Stiff-backed and wearing his smart uniform, Aggii stepped off the train in Ulaanbaatar into a crumbling world. He quickly discovered that the Soviet Union was rapidly disintegrating. He was shipped to the Chinese-Mongolian border as an officer to guard against the feared and much-hated Chinese. The long, desolate border was virtually impossible to control, and word was increasingly whispered of the teetering Soviet Bear. The cracks widened, and history ultimately swallowed one of the great military giants of all time. As the Berlin wall tumbled on the other side of the empire, it had a domino effect that traveled thousands of miles to the east into Mongolia.

Leaving the career he loved, Aggii returned to Ulaanbaatar with his beautiful young wife to enroll at the teacher university. After graduation, he managed to find work in one of the city schools. A little girl was born blessing this couple in the midst of a world of shortages and confusion. Bread lines and empty stomachs were all too common as the former communist government attempted to move toward a democracy and a free enterprise system. Later, twin boys and a fourth son were born.

Aggii found a life of order amidst the chaos and rubble left by 70 years of godless socialism, atheism and decadence from Soviet occupation. This order came in the person of a simple Carpenter from Galilee—the One who claimed to be the very Son of God offering a life with assurance of eternal stability. But what of the cost in this world where everything seemed to be spiraling out of control? No charge you say? Yes! This life of peace and security comes without cost! Free indeed is the offer of inviting Christ into your heart. However, for the Mongolians who chose to follow Him, now that was a different story. They often paid a high price indeed for the privilege of walking with Him through the glass-littered streets of the towns and cities and riding the roadless steppe of the wide Mongolian countryside.

There is a very sad note to Aggii's saga. The apartment was no longer welcoming when Aggii came home. There was no wife to greet him at the door and no laughing children to climb into his lap. His wife's parents had demanded she leave this crazy husband who chose to follow a "foreign god." They were certain that such a wayward husband would offend Buddha. The whole family would surely suffer their god's retribution. What a disappointment this promising, young military officer had become to the entire family. Periodically, Aggii and his wife and children would reunite only to go through more turmoil.

After awhile, his wife drifted even further away from him. Although she claimed to have accepted Christ earlier, her life no longer reflected her words. She became very interested in wealth and accepted a good job making an excellent salary. She took her daughter and twin boys leaving Aggii with his fourth child. Eventually, she reverted to her family's religion of Buddhism/ Shamanism.

"Aggii," she said, "if you will renounce your Christ and follow Shamanism, I will return to you, and we will live together again." Aggii loved his wife and children. This was a devastating time in his life. However, he could not turn from Christ to worship Satan regardless of the cost in this life. To this day, he continues to work as a teacher with V.E.T. Net, and as a result, has impacted the lives of thousands of people.

Aggii had been crucified with Christ (see Galatians 2:20) and was reborn with a glowing testimony. Now, he lived to share the wonderful news of Jesus in a world where the light of Christ needed to shine to illuminate this blessed mystery. "We must plow the soil and plant the seed in a fertile spot," he thought as he began to help his fellow Mongolians recover from the devastation of the fallen Soviet Empire. "They've never heard of Jesus. They must see Him in us."

A small group of believers in the remote herding settlement, Ulaan Am, grew from Aggii's ministry. He soon became a true circuit-riding evangelist/teacher as he traveled over many barren miles on horseback to visit herder families in the outlying areas where he shared the precious gospel message. He spoke freely of the One who died for them, the One who could bring order and peace to a life pained by foiled careers and broken marriages.

This scene continues to be repeated in village after village where the name of Jesus is unknown. By helping the poor herding families with their livestock and tiny schools, the love of Jesus is lived out every day by the V.E.T. Net team of young Christian professionals banding together to reach their beloved homeland with Christ. Most of us do not know what it is to suffer for Christ in the way that Aggii does. Sadly, it is common in Mongolia for people who follow Christ to be ostracized by their family and friends. Yet, it is a price they are willing to pay.

Dorjpagam (goes by the name "Pagma") was another one of our early teachers. She was raised in the countryside by strict Buddhist parents. It was logical for her to follow her parent's religion. Dorjpagam returned to her home town of Khujirt following completion of her teaching degree. After teaching for 11 years, she decided to return to the teacher's university to earn a Master's degree. It was there that she met some Christian students through Campus Crusade for Christ. Dorjpagam quickly recognized that she had discovered Truth and made a commitment to follow Jesus.

She returned to Khujirt after completing her degree but found that she missed her church and Christian friends. She had heard about V.E.T. Net through Aggii at Campus Crusade and immediately applied for a summer teaching position. After two years as a summer teacher, she was invited to join V.E.T. Net as a full-time staff member. Her husband was living in Ulaanbaatar because there was no work in the countryside, so it was an easy decision for Dorjpagam to join the V.E.T. Net staff. She began her work in October 2003, and excelled in every part of the ministry. Soon, she became a state coordinator, and in 2008, was appointed to be the national director of our education ministry.

Her husband, Davasuren, encouraged Dorjpagam to continue attending the Christian meetings because he had seen such a positive change in her life. Soon, he declared Jesus to be his Savior as well. He even donated their own large and valuable Buddhist painting to the Buddhist Temple. They no longer had any use for it. The young children accompanied their mother on summer mission trips and accepted Christ at an early age. They quickly became effective missionaries to their countryside playmates.

This might be an unremarkable story except for the fact that God chose this family to play a major role in reaching all of Mongolia with the gospel. Think of it! This woman from a Buddhist family and rural background was now in a position of authority and influence. Dorjpagam is humble, prayerful and compassionate, but when she talks to God in prayer, things begin to happen. [See Testimonial of Dorjpagam (goes by "Pagma") in the back of the book in the section "Testimonials of Mongolian Nationals"]

High-Flyer Lands in Mongolia

There was no usual danger—no flooding river this time—just ice-cold, clear water. The problem this time was that the van was stuck solid in the middle of the Orkhon River with no help in sight. I can still see **Morris Harper** tiptoeing among the rocks as he navigated the river with a cooler on his shoulder and trousers rolled above his knees exposing white legs to sunlight. How did this high-flying real-estate investor from Texas get into such a predicament in the backcountry of Mongolia?

It all began in the Seattle airport where we had a few minutes before catching the next flight back to Mongolia after our earlier stay in the States. Morris was with Dr. Kit Flowers, the Director of

Christian Veterinary Mission, who was waiting to meet us. "Morris is interested in a short-term mission trip," Dr. Flowers informed us, "but we are having trouble placing him." I guess the demand for real-estate investors wasn't high for mission projects.

Just as God has always used all kinds of people in Mongolia, we knew there would be something for this man, especially if God was directing him our way. God doesn't call us into futility. This was true of Morris because he never seemed out of place in any situation. He was smart, confident and full of probing questions. "Do you want me," this straight-talking Texan barked, "or do you just want my money?" "We want both," was my candid response.

The truly interesting thing about Morris is that although he lives in the world of high finance, he can get right down on the level of the Mongolian small-business shop owner. He has become a consistent and valuable part of the *Claim-a-County for Christ* program by offering business training for aspiring mini-entrepreneurs in remote villages. It doesn't matter if you are talking millions of dollars or merely a few hundred; Morris figures the principles are the same. Bible and business have become his trademarks in Mongolia over the past 18 years as he travels to share his knowledge and expertise with the people of this country.

Morris and his wife, Nancy, have claimed multiple counties in which to invest and involve their church and Sunday school class directly in the ministry. He has brought numerous short-term missionaries with him on subsequent trips to encourage their involvement in V.E.T. Net. Morris and Nancy are truly players, prayers and payers, and prime examples of short-term missionaries who shuttle back-and-forth between their home in the States and their chosen mission field.

I digressed, so let me take you back to the river and our stuck vehicle. In the end, I walked several miles with the driver to the nearest village in search of help. Fortunately, we were able to return with a truck to pull us to the other side of the river. Even this didn't dampen Morris' spirit. He was still smiling as he rolled down his pant legs ready to set off for our next divine appointment.

Al Dorminy is another person involved in real estate who has impacted the ministry in Mongolia. Al is the nephew of **Dr. Leroy Dorminy**, founder of CVM. When we have had real estate and business questions Al and Morris have been valuable. Al has worked with the financial department helping them with accounting training. God knows our needs long before they occur, and He provides people to fill these slots to make the ministry seamless.

As we begin to look at owning our own office building, it is amazing that God has brought Al and Morris to V.E.T. Net. Without them, this venture would be virtually impossible. But, of course, God knew all along.

Gold Mine Number 2

Resources had to be stretched, and if we were to go nationwide, God would need to multiply the bread and the fishes like He did in the biblical story. (See Mark 8:1–10.)

Our first gold mine, the idea of using shuttle vets, was described in Chapter 9. It produced valuable short-term missionaries from Western countries. Our second gold mine also involved short-term missionaries, but of a different kind. Many public school teachers in the city of Ulaanbaatar have become followers of Christ. They teach during the school year, but are free for the summer. V.E.T. Net began to recruit these Christian teachers for the *Claim-a-County for Christ* summer programs.

First, we employed a handful; then 30; then 40, and eventually 100 of these committed teachers were hired. This has given them an opportunity to be short-term missionaries in the summer while maintaining a steady position with the public school system during the school year. It is an economical way to keep our costs down, and at the same time, have qualified and committed Christian teachers for the project. V.E.T. Net pays them a small salary in the summer and provides food and lodging. In turn, they have the opportunity to live in the countryside away from the noise and pollution of the city in a place where they can become real missionaries. In the process, they grow in their faith as they are taught and discipled by the V.E.T Net Team. Some will go on to become full-time V.E.T. Net teachers.

Amaraa and Altai, for instance, were hired as summer teachers to work in our most distant community—a two-day trip away.

They are parents of Bayraa, one of our small-animal veterinarians who led them to Christ. Young in their faith, but with a zeal that was not to be denied, they ventured into a village expecting results even though there were no Christians. After a month of teaching the children and trying to reach out to the adults, they grew discouraged and impatient.

Amaraa and Altai prayed and talked together. Amaraa decided to fast for three days until God gave them direction for reaching these people with the message of this Jesus who had dramatically changed their own lives. In a short time, parents of the children began to show interest in studying the Bible. The committed couple persevered, and soon two older men began to lead a vibrant little group that worshipped and studied the Bible together. Just a few years ago we never would have dreamed that people in their 50s and 60s and even older would take this radical step of following Jesus Christ and winning others to Him out in the countryside.

Claim-a-County for Christ/Veterinary CE Dovetailed

> *Two are better than one, because they have a good return for their work: If one falls down, his friend can help him up. But pity the man who falls and has no one to help him up!*
>
> –Ecclesiastes 4:9-10, NIV

One of the problems with these small emerging churches is the lack of middle and upper class members. They are generally comprised of the very poor and often jobless people. V.E.T. Net is helping to bridge this gap through animal care, and hope is flowing into these herder communities.

The V.E.T. Net *Veterinary-Continuing-Education* program and the *Claim-a-County for Christ* program are now working hand-in-hand. For many years they were separate programs that went their own ways. Today, we send out teams of veterinarians and teachers together. As a result, they are even more effective than they were before. Teachers already have established relationships in the counties with the governor and other leaders in the community. The governor can be instrumental in congregating herders for training. Working with the local veterinarian, the governor has tremendous influence on the herders, and when he invites them to come, they come!

Many have come to Christ through this ministry—herders, veterinarians, teachers, principals, and other community leaders. The combined ministries of the veterinarians and educators make it possible for these leaders to be open with us. Our good works certainly do not save us or anyone else, but it is a part of what faith in Jesus is about. If our lives are transformed, we cannot help but live differently as we reach out to those in need. This caring attitude, when put into practice, is a real expression of the faith within us and causes others to want to know what empowers us. Our veterinary teams are working with the education program to bring training to the herders. One of the county governors called us; he was ecstatic about our herder training. In his remote village, we had been able to share the gospel with the community leaders. In their eyes, because of our community service, we have earned the right to be heard.

Tales of Triumph and Defeat

Russian motorcycles were, unfortunately, similar to Russian vans and trucks—they always broke down.

Morning is such a wonderful time in the desert. The incessant wind no longer blows sand in our eyes and mouth, and the cool of the breaking morn refreshes and renews us for another run at the day. It was on just such a day that we sat under the lonely desert trees and finished our coffee while continuing our study of 1 Samuel.

Two herders, an old man and a younger driver, came toward us on their motorcycle from some distance away. They had animals nearby and had come to greet their temporary neighbors hoping to find another drink of vodka. We left our study of the prophet Samuel and turned to John in his Gospel. We began to tell the two herders of this God who, unlike Buddha, loved them. We explained that He is alive and could bring order and meaning to their lives. They listened intently but declined our offer of a Bible. "We would waste it and probably use it for cigarette paper, tissue, or fire-making material." At least they were honest.

Their departure was unique and most interesting. The younger man mounted the cycle and was given a push by our team to start the motor. The clutch was broken, and the motorcycle could only be stopped if the engine was turned off. The old man missed his leap, and the driver circled in vain as he tried to pick up his friend. Around and around in circles of blue smoke went the two of them with the old man huffing and puffing as he tried to catch his speeding, young friend. If there was ever a picture of a life without purpose, this was it. The motorcycle kept going 'round and 'round with the poor old man trying to catch it. Solomon put it this way:

> *I have seen all of the things that are done under the sun; all of them are meaningless, a chasing after the wind.*
>
> –Ecclesiastes 1:14, NIV

It is critical that we understand exactly whom we represent when we go out into the world. People are caught in the circle of life—always searching. Yes, there are many parts of the Word where we can find disagreement, but we must have the basics firmly anchored in our heart. We must be prepared to help people who try to "catch the motorcycle" so that we can get them headed on the right road. They do not need lessons on denominations. Instead, they need to find the hope within us. That hope is Jesus. Our Team brings many stories back to us from their countryside trips. Again and again they include tales of someone chasing after the wind—stories of drunkards, prostitutes, wife-beaters, child abusers who have tried to find happiness in life and have fallen deeply into pits of hopelessness and addictive habits. Let me tell you a story of one man who "caught the motorcycle," and his life was forever changed:

During the time when the communist regime was in place, everyone feared the police because they had almost unlimited power. Mongolians were afraid to go to them even with serious problems. This fear still persists today.

Orchirhyag was a policeman in Ulaanbaatar. He was angry, rude, profane and abusive to his wife. After they divorced, he moved to Delgersokt, a desert town in Middle Gobi. Unfortunately, he took his problems with him.

While working as a policeman in the small county seat, he

arrested a young man for rustling livestock. He beat the poor boy unmercifully, frightening him into a state of absolute terror. Later, Ochirhyag met our V.E.T. Net Team and attended their devotions. This man with a stone heart began to understand God's love through the life of these young teammates, and he eventually trusted in Jesus for His salvation and gave his life to Christ.

Some people are slow learners it seems. The same young thief was caught once again with another herder's sheep. Knowing what was coming, he shrank into submission awaiting another severe beating. This time, however, it was a caring policeman who apprehended him. Unlike before, Orchirhyag was now gentle and kind to the young man. The light of Christ shone through his new life. The young man was so surprised at this total change of character in the feared policeman that he simply cried and said, "Now you are like my brother." Orchirhyag soon gained the respect and admiration of his whole community. Today, he is trusted throughout the entire county as he models the servant life of Christ.

That's what it is like to catch the wind—to catch the motorcycle. We go from circling incessantly, to finding a path that is straight and true. We are seeing lives transformed in Mongolia because this team genuinely reflects the overflowing love of Christ. It is impossible to contain it. The results are highly infectious and life-changing. Mongolia is so vast, so empty, and yet we are privileged to watch a little shower of rain as it brings life shooting up from the ground. This is a great picture of the life that flows from the person who hears and responds to the greatest story of all—the story of Christ Jesus. This is the picture of Orchirhyag.

Hongora was a teenager in Munkhhan County, Sukhbaatar. Her face was deformed. It is because she was so different that she was teased and taunted by her classmates. Her teachers also treated her with contempt and withheld from her the love and care they gave the other children. She was a very sad person with little hope in her life. That is until V.E.T. Net summer teachers began to wrap Hongora with love and compassion. They bathed her from head to toe and dressed her in clean clothes. As they spent precious time with this lonely girl, she began to respond to the love shown by these dedicated teachers. Her self-esteem improved dramatically, and she became a better student. Now, she is participating in sports and is gaining acceptance by her peers.

Hongora lives with her grandmother. Her grandmother was a devout Buddhist with shelves lined with Buddhist books and literature. One of her relatives is a Christian from a nearby town. He is a driver and has become a good friend of our Team. One day, he walked into this woman's house and was astounded to see a Bible sitting in front of her other books. "What has happened?" he asked. "I have shared my faith with this woman many times, and she never showed any openness. She was totally committed to her Buddhist beliefs and would never listen to me. Now she is reading the Bible and has become a Christian."

What happened? Well, somebody showed Christian love to this young Hongora after the students and teachers mistreated her for years. When her grandmother saw this love, she caught her very first glimpse of Christ. It is the love of Christ that changes the world by changing people's hearts, and the way people are exposed to His love is through us.

The Bible continues to come to life at V.E.T. Net. For that reason, and many others, I love living here. Oh, I don't mean Mongolia, although we are happy here as well. I mean in His hands where dependence is essential and where we come to expect Him to provide. That is the place to be!

> *Always be prepared to give an answer to everyone who asks you to give the reason for the hope that you have. But do this with gentleness and respect.*
>
> –1 Peter 3:15, NIV

Notes:

1. In December, 2016, we received a phone call from **Tserennadmid**. We had not seen her in many years and were so pleased to hear from her. We invited her to our office. It was exciting to introduce her to all of our V.E.T. Net staff—many had never met her. We enjoyed reminiscing and hearing family news. Unfortunately, **Erdeneochir** was having some health problems and was unable to come. We were unaware that some of our teachers had invited Tserennadmid to our January *Shepherd's Conference*. Normally this is reserved for Christians, but in her case, they made an exception. During the meeting, she had the opportunity to hear many stories of how the lives of participants had been changed through their relationship with God. Before the week was over, she accepted Christ, and on Thursday, she stood before the whole group to tell her story. It was a heart-wrenching but joyful time as she shared how it had taken over 20 years for her to come to the Christian God. She was anxious to get back to her home to tell her ailing husband her own *Good News*.

2. *Campus Crusade for Christ International* (Cru)- www.cru.org.

Figure 12.1. "Ger Church"—church in countryside

Chapter 12

Watering-with-the-Word (WWW)

> *He replied, "Because you have so little faith. Truly I tell you, if you have faith as small as a mustard seed, you can say to this mountain, 'Move from here to there,' and it will move. Nothing will be impossible for you."*
>
> –Matthew 17:20, NIV

On the other side of the mountain lies a place of intense darkness—a place where, for hundreds of years, Satan has owned the real estate. His presence continues to penetrate the surrounding countryside as alcohol deadens the minds of the men and makes them easy captives of demonic forces. The most striking building in this village is the decorative Buddhist temple. It houses 11 of its lamas at the expense of poor herders who come from many miles to pay for prayers asking a god who is deaf to meet their needs.

It was April, and we found ourselves caught in the grasp of winter's last throes. Snow still covered the landscape, and the glare from the reflection brought squinted eyes to our wearied faces. We plowed through drift after drift as we approached the imposing mountain which blocked our way to town. Winding up the serpentine road, the whine of the van was the only sound in this desolate area. At last, the four-wheel drive could take us no further. The incline was too steep, and the snow had become icy from the overnight freeze.

It was a helpless feeling to have come hundreds of miles only to be stopped by the last mountain. We had seen the miraculous hand of God intervene time after time, but praying for this mountain to be moved was all too literal and, frankly, unbelievable. It was not a prayer for some spiritual change that could only be judged by subjective methods; it was a very real, physical roadblock of gigantic proportions. It loomed too high, too steep, too dangerous and too icy.

Dermee kept a roll of canvas tied to the top of our van, and because the night was so cold, he used it to cover the vehicle. He called it the van's sleeping bag. The following day we spread the same canvas on the road in front of the van to get better traction. This allowed us to inch our way to the top while sometimes sliding back surrendering some of the priceless real estate that we had gained. Again, the canvas was pulled to the front. This "cotton road" made it possible to continue moving onward and upward. Hours later, we passed the Buddhist/Shamanist rock pile that marks the crest of nearly every significant hill in Mongolia. We crested the top and coasted down to the tiny village. Once there, we would be able to complete work on the dormitory situated beside the school housing the classrooms of four grades.

> Mongolia is a land of **harsh weather**. Winters are long with thermometers often frequenting the negative numbers. Herders cut blocks of ice from frozen rivers to melt over the fire for their water supply. Oil becomes sludge, and moisture in grease freezes axles and differentials solid. Fires are built under vehicles from wood or dung to thaw frozen parts.

Stoves were installed and dormitory rooms refurbished in the building that had been unusable for three years. Many herding families had moved with their livestock in search of new pastures. This meant that their children could not attend school consistently. Now, however, children would be able to attend school and live in a cozy dormitory room.

A Mongolian V.E.T. Net teacher teamed with a local teacher to work with pre-school children using modern education methods. She modeled Christ in a community that had never seen Him. This earned her the opportunity to tell of His wondrous love and plan to reach down to each of them.

The height of the mountain is unimportant to God—though it may give us some pause for concern. Does He want us on the other side? That is the only question we must answer. Thank you, God, for flattening the mountain—for removing all obstacles that stand between me and where you want me to be.

Don't Forget Us

> *Some time later Paul said to Barnabas, "Let us go back and visit the believers in all the towns where we preached the word of the Lord and see how they are doing."*
>
> –Acts 15:36, NIV

The churches that have been planted as the result of the ministry of our dedicated staff may not resemble your church or mine. But they are faithful little groups of believers meeting together at the feet of Jesus in fellowship and prayer. The mountain we find the most difficult to climb is the one that prevents us from staying in contact with all these Christian groups. The challenge is almost overwhelming. As we spread out across the country in an effort to disciple new believers, we are challenged by great distances and the lack of leadership in the churches.

The number of these remote churches continues to increase in the areas where we have *Claim-a-County for Christ* and veterinary programs. The Apostle Paul was confronted with the same kinds of challenges before the early churches began to expand from his missionary trips.

> *So when we could stand it no longer, we thought it best to be left by ourselves in Athens. We sent Timothy, who is our brother and co-worker in God's service in spreading the gospel of Christ, to strengthen and encourage you in your faith, so that no one would be unsettled by these trials. For you know quite well that we are destined for them.*
>
> –1 Thessalonians 3:1–3, NIV

Paul continues in verse 5:

> *For this reason, when I could stand it no longer, I sent to find out about your faith. I was afraid that in some way the tempter had tempted you and that our labors might have been in vain.*

I can feel Paul's pain as he longed to encourage the church at Thessalonica that he founded on his second missionary journey. As the number of churches increased, he was not able to nurture all at the same time. He only stayed in Thessalonica a few weeks, but he left a piece of his heart with the brothers and sisters there. He needed a strategy to build Christian maturity into this church. Timothy, his beloved son in the faith, was his arm to make that possible.

We also needed a group of Mongolian Timothys to serve as itinerate pastors for the baby churches that sprang from the darkness. Not only did we need these church-building pastors, but we needed a good reason for being in the community in order to be accepted. We searched for God's clear direction in how to achieve the impossible and overcome incredibly difficult odds. One particular challenge was that of shamanism which is flourishing even as Buddhism is on the increase. Thanks be to God, though, the curtain of spiritual darkness is being lifted in many of these forsaken areas. The light of Christ is peaking brightly through the clouds to illuminate the land.

Watering-with-the-Word in Action

With the completion of each *Claim-a-County for Christ* program initiative, we know there continues to be an enormous need and hunger for spiritual support and a connection with other Christians. Countryside believers feel isolated. When friendships are formed, we become an important part of the community, and when we leave, there is a noticeable void.

Watering-with-the-Word is the follow-up project to *Claim-a-County for Christ.* We have enlisted special teams to return to communities with Bibles and other Christian literature, to listen to their many needs and prayer requests, to share in their church services, and to fellowship with them. Once again, we are family.

Rock Eagle

> *Even youths grow tired and weary, and young men stumble and fall; but those who hope in the LORD will*

renew their strength. They will soar on wings like eagles; they will run and not grow weary, they will walk and not be faint.

–Isaiah 40:30–31, NIV

The bus was packed with passengers as it returned at night from Sukhbaatar, a state in eastern Mongolia. About 45 people were on board swaying and rocking with the gentle rhythm of the road as they returned to the capital city. Many were asleep in the darkened seats. The muffled roar of the motor offered a kind of hypnotic music as it harmonized with the hum of the giant tires. In a matter of seconds, however, the peaceful trip erupted into unspeakable horror. Swerving between the roadside ditches, the driver completely lost control. The giant metal-box vehicle rolled, tumbled and slid to an abrupt stop. Nothing was left but twisted wreckage and shattered glass. Moaning survivors struggled to get away from the carnage.

Onboard this Sukhbaatar Special were two missionaries returning from the small town of Munkhaan. One was an older Mongolian Christian, Chuluunburgid (Rock Eagle), who had gone there to visit the village where he was raised. With him was Zorgo, a man of 55 years. Together, they had spent four days in the village with a V.E.T. Net team before they left to return to Ulaanbaatar.

In the moments after the accident, Rock Eagle groped for his friend in the darkness between the bodies of the other victims. With his left ear missing and a gaping hole in the side of his head, Rock Eagle made his way out of the vehicle and continued to search for his friend. As he circled the bus he saw a still, crumpled figure lying on the ground. It was his close friend and fellow partner in the gospel. His lifeless body had been violently thrown from the careening vehicle.

When *Claim-a-County for Christ* first began work in Munkhaan County, only one Christian family lived there. They moved closer to family members who could help take care of the children. Their departure left the community totally void of Christians. However, through V.E.T. Net's ministry, a number of adults became believers in Christ. Thirty to forty children also accepted Him. This group of believers wanted to start a church, but they did not have a leader, so V.E.T. Net teachers continued to visit this group through *Watering-with-the-Word* to help fulfill the needs of life skills, Bible study, family training, and encouragement. They were consistently asking God to provide a fulltime leader.

One day, Rock Eagle unexpectedly came to our office to tell us that God had called him to return to his homeland to pastor the church in Munkhaan. At the time, the congregation did not have an adequate place to meet, and Rock Eagle wanted V.E.T. Net to help. Even though disfigured by his earlier accident, he still wanted to serve. He had an extra-large heart and a love for the people in this tiny village that more than made up for his appearance. V.E.T. Net gladly contributed a ger to the First Church of Munkhaan to help out. It was an honor, indeed, to assist these believers to build God's kingdom.

Pastor Rock Eagle found a way to support his growing ministry by repairing motorcycles that came into the country from China. He even built a motorcycle from spare parts to use when he visited herder families to share the gospel message. Eventually, Rock Eagle moved to an adjacent county to grow another church started by V.E.T. Net, but he left a new church leader in his place to continue to pastor the church in Munkhaan. *Watering-with-the-Word* now works closely with both churches.

Rock Eagle—what a great name for a pastor. Jesus proclaimed to Peter:

> *And I tell you that you are Peter, and on this rock I will build my church, and the gates of Hades will not overcome it.*
>
> –Matthew 16:18, NIV

Shepherd My Sheep

> *When they had finished eating, Jesus said to Simon Peter, "Simon son of John, do you love me more than these?" "Yes, Lord, "you know that I love you." Jesus said, "Feed my lambs." Again Jesus said, "Simon son of John, do you love me?" He answered, "Yes, Lord, you know*

that I love you." Jesus said, "Take care of my sheep." The third time he said to him, "Simon son of John, do you love me?" Peter was hurt because Jesus asked him the third time, "Do you love me?" He said, "Lord, you know all things; you know that I love you." Jesus said, "Feed my sheep."

–John 21:15-17, NIV

"Tend My Sheep" is a command straight from the mouth of our Lord. Jesus put it differently when He said, *"Therefore go and make disciples of all Nations."* (See Matthew 28:19a.) When we are a disciple of Jesus, we become a part of His plan to change the whole world.

What a brilliant strategy to bring the love of God to all people! As we disciple a handful of V.E.T. Net staff, they disciple other staff. Then, they in turn, disciple students at the Veterinary School, and on it goes. As countryside church leaders are discipled, the process releases a fountain-of-truth spilling out across the nation of Mongolia and even beyond. In a very real sense, discipleship is the true fountain of youth.

> We are constantly looking for **aids to help disciple** countryside people. *Theological Education by Extension,*[1] *Mentor Link,* [2] and *Audio-Bibles* [3] are very useful tools for the V.E.T. Net discipleship program.

Yes, this is God's plan to reach the entire world, and it is one that gives me great joy! My heart leaps as I witness the effects of this strategy in the lives of so many—not because we are capable, but simply because we are obedient to Christ.

The *Shepherd's Conference*

Our first *Shepherd's Conference* proved to be one of the most rewarding weeks in the history of V.E.T. Net. It was a source of great encouragement and joy for the whole team. As the first day's activities began, the building was filled with excitement.

This program began years ago when we made a commitment

to reach the whole country for Christ. A number of missionaries worked in the cities, but few had an open door to participate in rural outreach. God put us in the extraordinary position of possessing the key to every community and every ger in this land of Mongolian herder families.

In 2008, about 60 leaders of these little groups came to Ulaanbaatar for a week of Bible study, leadership training, prayer, worship and fellowship together. These *Shepherd's Conferences* are now annual events and are spectacular—not in the way of the world, but in the way of the Spirit. This was the beginning of the expansion of *Watering-with-the-Word.* One-hundred-forty shepherds attended our *Shepherd's Conference* in 2017. It has become a major part of *Watering-with-the-Word* over time, and it continues to spiritually impact the small communities throughout Mongolia.

Our Mongolian staff members often open their homes to these countryside friends, and provide for their needs while they are in Ulaanbaatar. Sometimes our Western staff gets in on the hospitality as well, as explained below.

Dr. Hillary and Michael Mincher from western Tennessee joined our staff shortly before the 2017 *Shepherd's Conference.* Their Mongolian language was almost non-existent at the time, but they still wanted to host two men who had come for the meeting. Needless to say, these men spoke no English and had never been in a modern apartment. It is very difficult for the countryside people to stay as clean as city dwellers, so Hillary offered them a bath while she washed their clothes in the washing machine. All was proceeding well until Hillary put the steam iron into action. When the men saw that, they were totally convinced she was burning the only clothes they had. It took some time for them to calm down.

After a week of caring for these men and communicating through sign language, they became dear friends. During the following summer, Michael and Hillary had the opportunity to visit with one of the men's family in their countryside home where they received royal treatment in return for their earlier hospitality.

As we look back through time at the sea of the dear faces of our countryside leaders all crowned with dark hair and Mongol features, we cannot help but wonder why God chose them to be born in this land. Whatever His reason, He brought them out of alcoholism, abuse, defeat, abortion, lying, cheating and bribery to walk in the light of truth, peace and purpose. He has fashioned them into a beautiful mosaic for Christ. Only the Spirit of the Living God could make such a thing possible.

Each face tells a story of victorious delivery from the consequences of sin such as a man from a broken family who became an itinerate missionary to his own rural people. He travels now on his motorbike with a small bag of food to help people he meets along the way with their needs before telling them about Jesus. This man loves to come to the V.E.T. Net *Shepherd's Conference* in January because it allows him to plan his outreach for the rest of the year. "I learn great Bible principles," he says, "make new friends, return to my home, and travel and share my new gleanings with those God brings into my path." Prior to coming to the *Shepherd's Conference,* he traveled to seven counties in his state to encourage developing churches. Now he wants to go to the Gobi Desert with the message of Christ and later to the Inner Mongolia (China) region to witness to the Mongolian-speaking Chinese.

One face in particular that stands out from the crowd is the daughter of a former Buddhist lama. The lama, a very elderly woman, turned to Christ through the ministry of the V.E.T. Net teachers. Since then, she has led most of her children to Christ. Although she was too old to make the trip to the *Conference,* she sent her daughter to learn more about their Savior. Yet another face is that of a veterinarian from the South Gobi who currently has 50 children coming to her Sunday School class to hear Bible stories and to learn about Christ, the hope of the world.

The numerous stories written on the "faces" of those healed from alcoholism have become commonplace, but their transformation is still as dramatic as any cancer cure. The hopelessness of addiction is being replaced by a life of rich meaning as families are restored to wholeness in Christ in a way that allows them to nurture their children in a loving environment.

I reminisce about a five year-old girl, Nanda, who came to our *Claim-a-County for Christ* summer school ministry in the desert state of East Gobi. She was so consistent in attending her kindergarten classes that her absence one day caused the V.E.T. Net teachers to become very concerned. She returned the following day to share her sordid tale with the teachers. It was the account of something that no small child should ever have to endure. She told them of her father, Munkhtuur, who was an alcoholic and became violent when drinking. He would chase Nanda and her mother with a knife and beat them. Nanda and her mother, Gerlee, would often have to flee from their house and hide in the cold or go to a friend to escape this raging man.

The teachers met with Nanda and her mother and told them about the God who loved them. Both of them readily gave their lives to Christ, and an amazing series of events followed. Every morning, Nanda came to school early to meet with her teachers and to pray for her father. She also prayed for the little sister that she had always wanted.

We know that prayer changes things, but the results in this case were especially dramatic. Our teachers met with the father and shared the Good News with him. He was desperate for help and turned to the Savior. At first, he had trouble giving up alcohol, but over time he drank less and less. Finally, he completely stopped drinking. This man's story is one that is being repeated across Mongolia as V.E.T. Net reaches out with God's truth.

When V.E.T. Net first began working in Khatanbulag, there were no Christians in the county. Eventually, though, a small group of people came to know Christ, and a church was born. Gerlee and Munktuul, along with Nanda, are now active in the little church in their small village. In January we had the youngest participant at our *Shepherd's Conference*—less than one-year old. You guessed it. Nanda now has a little sister, and her mom and dad brought her along for the experience. If you are ever tempted to think prayer doesn't work, just ask Nanda.

The rural people who come to Christ not only have their lives changed, but they also become missionaries to their own counties. Selenge and Batahuu are a great picture of the power of God lived out through the Christian life and its impact on others. Here is the remarkable story that Selenge and Batahuu shared at the *Shepherd's Conference:*

> "Life was so difficult—I was always crying. I was often sick and my husband was an alcoholic drinking heavily much of the time. He was without work. There were gold mines near where we lived, and we would pan enough gold from the tailings of the mine to buy bread and feed the alcohol addiction of my husband, Batahuu. This was six years ago. Then, I met Jesus and there was this unexplainable joy. I was so happy even though we were still very poor and living a difficult life. Batahuu became quite jealous—he thought I had found another man. One day he sneaked into our little church group thinking he would catch me with this new lover, only to find that he did not exist.
>
> He did, however, find someone else; He found the "Man" God, Jesus Christ, and his life was turned upside down. He stopped drinking and became a good husband. Before, I was so stubborn and disrespectful of him. Now, I, too, am changing more and more and becoming submissive to my husband. We have two children and both of them have accepted Jesus Christ as their Lord and Savior.
>
> Now, Batahuu is a missionary to the Gobi Desert. He rides his motorcycle about 1400 kilometers in the summer sharing his faith with herders in ten of these huge desert counties. The herders love to hear about this Jesus. They beg Batahuu to come back each year, and these poorest of the poor say— 'please come back and tell us more about Jesus, and we will buy the gas for your motorcycle.' Now, Batahuu is the leader of our little church and I direct the children's ministries."

These V.E.T. Net programs have worked together to bring the gospel of Jesus Christ to the people in this county in the Mongolian countryside. They are continuing to work in a powerful way as people come to Christ. God is being glorified, and V.E.T. Net staff are being blessed by having the opportunity to help build His Kingdom.

Notes:

1. *Theological Education by Extension* (TEE)-This is a discipleship program now translated in the Mongolian language. Students of TEE are trained and must pass tests to become trainers. Several of the V.E.T. Net staff have become trainers and now, many of our countryside leaders are trainers. They return to their counties and lead a small group of young Christians through TEE books. www.seaninternational.com/tee.html

2. MentorLink–*Days with Jesus* is a series of parables taken from the *Campus Crusade for Christ "Jesus Film."* Jesus becomes the teacher through smart phones and computers and His parables can be presented to rural Christians by their leaders. www.mentorlink.org

3. Audio-Bibles—The entire Bible in the Mongolian Language is put into small electronic devices that can be used as a player/radio. Along with the Bible, there are testimonies by Mongolian Christians as well as praise songs. These are given to rural Mongolians who have problems reading.

Figure 13.1. *"Gift-of-Love"*—widow getting sheep

Chapter 13

Gift-of-Love

> *Command them to do good, to be rich in good deeds, and to be generous and willing to share.*
>
> –1 Timothy 6:18, NIV

Sharing the gospel is essential in our efforts to help our neighbors. But just who are our neighbors? Well, Jesus answered that question in the Gospels. In this global society, our neighbor can easily be across the world from us. Committed followers of Jesus know that He has called us to share the message of salvation with our world. However, of late, I am struck by the number of times God says in His Word that we are to provide for the downcast, the orphan, the widow and the poor. (See Deuteronomy 24:19–21.) Often, these people are unable to help themselves, at least in the beginning.

In the book, *Generous Justice-How God's Grace Makes Us Just,* pastor/author Timothy Keller, states:

> The Biblical writers introduce God as a Father of the fatherless, defender of widows (Psalm 68:4–5). This is one of the main things He does in the world. He identifies with the powerless, He takes up their cause.
>
> You see, we must help these struggling souls with their physical needs because we have God's love living inside of us. We cannot use this as just a way to create opportunity to share our beliefs—we must help them physically, because God would and did and will continue to. He is our Father and we want to please Him—and, then, we share the message of His Son out of love for them, expressing the love of God who lives in us.[1]

The ultimate irony is that becoming a Christian only requires a simple childlike faith. The maturing of that faith multiplies the changes in our heart and releases a desire to help those in need both spiritually and physically. Giving does not originate from a heart of need, but from a heart filled with overflowing love. Where does that love abound from, if not from the God who is its definition? Oh yes, we may help our family and friends, but help for those who cannot return a favor—that is another matter.

In Mongolia, Buddhist shrines and idols are still being built across this nation. They are gaudy chunks of concrete that disfigure the beautiful hillsides. The lamas sing their chants and rub their beads—but helping others does not seem to be their concern. Instead, they charge these poor desperate followers to give their child a name or give the best date for a wedding or funeral. A list of charges for various services available is posted in Buddhist temples. However, the outpouring of Christian love to the poor is challenging the lamas and causing them to be a bit more charitable.

During our almost 25 years in Mongolia, V.E.T. Net has helped many of the poor herders achieve a better lifestyle making it possible for their children to pursue education—many even go to university. However, we have seen countless desperate Mongolians going without enough food in the villages. Our team has become increasingly aware of the numerous widows who have no way of earning a living because job opportunities are limited. To add to their burden, some are left to care for their children or grandchildren. Other families struggle because the husband has serious health issues.

Many of these truly needy people do not have anywhere to turn. While it is not always easy to identify true needs in western countries, this is not the case in Mongolian rural villages. It is only because our teams work with the rural people that we are aware of the great need.

Gift-of-Love in Action

> *He who is kind to the poor lends to the Lord, and he will reward him for what he has done.*
>
> –Proverbs 19:17, NIV

The *Gift-of-Love* Program is an amazing program that actually does lend to the Lord. *Gift-of-Love,* implemented in 2017, is the new V.E.T. Net program that God laid on our hearts. The Bible is filled with admonitions to help the poor. It is obvious this was always on Jesus' heart. He fed them, healed them, expelled demons from them and showed them the path to eternal life.

> ***Gift-of-Love*** is a unique concept that exponentially multiplies donations. Every $100 that we receive provides $100 worth of food for a poor family. This same $100 provides the herder with $100 worth of medicine. In turn, the countryside veterinarian also receives $100 dollars in value for the medication he provides; and V.E.T. Net receives $100 for providing the medication. Only God can make this kind of multiplication possible.

This program is unique in that it is not simply a gift to the poor, which would be good in itself, but it is also a gift that helps the herder who provides the sheep as well as helps the remote veterinarian. By the same token, it helps stabilize the V.E.T. Net organization. It is a bit complicated, but here is how it works:

Herders need quality drugs from their veterinarians, but are often strapped for cash. As a result, their animals go untreated and suffer from parasitism and other diseases. These animals begin the harsh winter thin and with scraggly hair coats. Many will die in the severe spring storms. Rural veterinarians want to help the herders, but they can only extend so much credit because they, too, must have cash to replace depleted inventories of medications. So, the herder trades one or more sheep with his veterinarian for medication supplies. The sheep received by the veterinarian are given to needy people identified by V.E.T. Net, the local governor, church leaders, teachers or other community leaders. V.E.T. Net then re-supplies the medications to the rural veterinarian.

This is an incredible process that allows Western donors to give food directly to the neediest people while helping the herder and the rural veterinarian, and it also helps bring sustainability to V.E.T. Net. In the process, the church and V.E.T. Net become more relevant to the community and have expanded opportunities to share the gospel.

Because we already have the infrastructure in place, one-hundred percent of the gifts we receive go directly to buy food for the poor. Even though there are some administrative expenses associated with sending money to Mongolia, the funds that V.E.T. Net receives go dollar-for-dollar to feed the poor. [2] Now, we are not only encouraging the church spiritually, we are teaching the joy of giving. One jubilant, poor older man who received his sheep gift, insisted on helping with the delivery of sheep to other poor families. Giving becomes contagious as people see the happiness brought to eager, needy families. [2]

What has surprised us most, I think, is how this program impacts the entire community. The status of Christians is elevated in the same villages where they were previously marginalized. Although the community wants to assist its poor people, it doesn't have the means to do so. This is where the *Gift-of-Love* can help. The village people see the contrast between the lamas' practice of always taking from the poor and the love displayed by our giving program. One sad, elderly widow said, "We are always promised things, but nothing ever happens." She was amazed to see the sheep arrive and someone doing exactly what they said they would do. The people are overwhelmed with our Christian charity, and now smiles grace the faces that were molded in discouragement and outright despair.

The *Gift-of-Love* program gives the *Watering-with-the-Word* teams a good reason to return to communities. To help meet the extra requirements of the *Gift-of-Love* program, two mature V.E.T. Net couples are assigned to visit the counties. They are now discipling young Christians, growing church leaders, building relationships throughout the community and meeting with those who receive sheep. Their presence is openly welcomed by local authorities.

Our teachers and accountants have the task of recording all the activities of the *Gift-of-Love* program. They record the location, herder, the local veterinarian, the recipient, our local representative, the donor and identify every sheep. This allows us to show each donor exactly where every dollar given is invested. This program glorifies God through its impeccable integrity and positive results.

Once, a bitter old man was chosen as one of the recipients of sheep from the *Gift-of-Love* program. He was not a Christian. In fact, he was decidedly anti-Christian. Shoe boxes with gifts for children came to his county from *Samaritan's Purse Ministry,* and in them, he found the desiccator packets that had been packed with some of the gift products. Because he was convinced the boxes contained poison that was being used to harm the children, he reported it to the authorities.

When he was offered the gift of sheep through the *Gift-of-Love* program, he said, "I want you to know that I am not a Christian." We told him that the gifts were not only for Christians; they were for any family or individual who was having a difficult time and needed help with their winter food. We added that we did not discriminate between atheists, Muslims, Buddhists or Christians. After all, isn't that what Jesus did? Well, this man hasn't become a believer yet, but his attitude toward Christians has definitely changed, and his heart has softened. Living as Christ taught us, in full view of these hardened souls, is the best way to reach them.

Kherlenchemig is a great example, of which we would all do well to follow. She is one of the leaders of a tiny church started in Munkhan county in the state of Sukhbaatar. She sees the *Gift-of-Love* program as the way to serve God while really helping her people and growing the church. After the sheep are distributed to those in need, Kherlenchemig visits the families who received them. Her desire is to share the real gift of love with them—Jesus Christ. This has become an effective strategy with two of the families accepting the Lord. They now come to her church. Kherlenchemig also meets with four of the families for Bible study. Preaching to people is not always the best way to deliver a sermon. Living a life of integrity and compassion speaks much louder. Kherlenchemig is doing just that and making a difference in her desperate little community.

This *Gift-of-Love* program is touching the lives of Mongolians in many rural counties. We expect it to spread even more as friends around the world join us with their financial contributions. We are committed to continue to disciple, encourage, and support these fledging communities of believers. One national couple that will take on this itinerate ministry through the expansion of *Watering-with-the-Word* is Amaraa and Altai. They have been with V.E.T. Net many years, and are determined to reach the nation of Mongolia with the gospel.

Amaraa and Altai have an interesting story. Altai was raised in a family of 13 children. Their grandfather was an important Buddhist monk, and Altai was following in his footsteps by serving as an assistant and learning the chants and rituals. She became a teacher in the rural school where she grew up and married the Russian-language teacher. Altai's first husband went on to become a spy for the government and died early from chronic alcoholism. Altai was left with two daughters from her first husband.

After some time, Altai married Amaraa, another teacher in her school, but their life was very difficult. They went to the gold rush, but found this venture to be extremely dangerous. Before long, they had nothing but the clothes on their backs and were forced to gather and eat pine nuts in the forest to survive. Eventually, they moved to Ulaanbaatar where they sold shish kebobs and hardboiled eggs at the market. Life was becoming increasingly grim.

Altai's oldest daughter, Bayraa, had the opportunity to attend the Mongolian veterinary school. While a student, she decided to go to V.E.T. Net classes to learn English. She joined the small animal club and soon came to know our Savior. Altai was furious with her for doing so, and scolded her for leaving their traditions. "You can have your Jesus, but don't try to influence our family," Altai told Bayraa.

Bayraa was different now. When Altai and Amaraa had one of their frequent arguments, Bayraa withdrew and sought solitude from the conflict. Eventually, Altai and Amaraa separated, and the family became more dysfunctional. When Bayraa became a veterinarian at V.E.T. Net, she and the team began to pray for her family. Altai heard the Good News and knew she had found truth. She accepted Christ and soon Amaraa followed. Their marriage was restored. They faced the difficult decision of parting with their past by destroying the family idols and Buddhist books. However, it wasn't until after they were baptized that they finally destroyed the family heirlooms and made a clean break with the past. They prayed, "Jesus, you must take care of us now."

After graduation, Bayraa became an important part of the ministry of V.E.T. Net as she exhibited her compassionate personality and gift of evangelism. The New Testament speaks of whole families coming to Christ. That is exactly what happened with Bayraa's family. She led them one by one to the foot of the cross. Her mother and stepfather, her brother and sister and many of her extended family became believers in Christ. Now, her mother, stepfather, as well as her sister, Chuka, work with V.E.T. Net.

Altai and Amaraa are traveling the eastern part of Mongolia administering the *Gift-of-Love* program and discipling the new believers in small churches. They know the countryside life; they understand the darkness of Buddhism and Shamanism, and they understand the perils of alcoholism and how to love these people. They also understand the importance of family and solid marriages, and they often teach on these topics. They live to share their faith and help others grow in their relationship with the Lord.

Muggii and Nuda are another mature Christian couple who have worked at V.E.T. Net for many years. You met teacher Nuda and veterinarian Muggii earlier in the book. They are working in the western part of Mongolia as itinerate ministers. I believe we will see thousands come to know Christ as a result of the sacrifices these two couples are making to see their country turn to Christ.

Nuda called one of the governors where we planned to implement the *Gift-of-Love* program. She asked if he had poor people in his community. His reply was that he did not know. He said, "I never think about the poor; but I should." In a couple of days, he called back to say that he had investigated and found that there were several very poor families in his village. Creating an awareness of the problems of the poor in these rural areas is as important as the program itself.

In a Nutshell

This is a summary of what is happening in just one county as a result of the various programs of V.E.T. Net:

> To put faces on this, the entire story of V.E.T. Net can be captured in the life of Gungaa and his wife, Chimegee. Gungaa has been a part of the *V.E.T. Net Continuing-Education* since 2005. Each year, he has learned more and more useful information to improve his practice and eventually help his herder clients become more productive. At first, he joined in the evening ministry time, but never responded to the messages or the gospel. He was like the veterinarian in the little booklet *What is Success?* He became successful in his practice, but missed the

most important thing in his life—knowing Jesus.

In 2016, *Claim-a-County for Christ* was implemented in Gungaa's county. He told his wife that she should meet the V.E.T. Net teachers because they were really nice people. She went to visit the teachers and found more than she expected. She met God and came to know Him personally through His Son. Soon, Gungaa also decided to follow Jesus, and in 2018, he came to the *Shepherd's Conference*.

Yaroo County in Zaphon Province is one of the most remote places of our work. There is no church in Yaroo, so Gungaa and Chimegee plan to join with another couple to start the First Church of Yaroo. *Watering-with-the-Word* plans to work directly with them as they take on this challenge in the dominantly Buddhist county.

Gungaa's bother-in-law is the country governor. He is excited about what the *Gift-of-Love* program will do for his county. Consequently, he is supportive of the V.E.T. Net work. We pray that he, too, will come to know our Savior. This couple's son is a fourth-year veterinary student. He recently came to our office to meet us. He is very interested in our *Internship Program,* where he will have the opportunity to work with the V.E.T. Net staff and learn more about our faith.

If you would like to be part of this amazing opportunity to feed the poor and help herders and their veterinarians, you can send financial contributions through www.cvmusa.org for the *Gift-of-Love* program. Please see the section, "Website of Christian Veterinary Mission," at the end of the book, for details. These can also be mailed to *Christian Veterinary Mission*, 19303 Fremont Ave. N, Seattle, Washington 98133. Detailed feedback-reports will be sent to you to keep you informed of how your *Gift-of-Love* contributions are being used.

Notes:

1. Keller, Timothy (2010). *Generous Justice/How God's Grace Makes Us Just.* (Penguin Group (U.S.A.) Inc., New York, New York) Pp. 6.

2. There are administrative and transfer fees related to donations that come to V.E.T. Net. These fees vary depending on what country they come from. However, 100% of the donations that V.E.T. Net receives for the *Gift-of-Love* program go to buy sheep (food) for the poor.

Figure 14.1. "Mongolian Bankhar Dog"—classic dog

Chapter 14

A Wolf in Sheep's Clothing

> *But there were also false prophets among the people, just as there will be false teachers among you. They will secretly introduce destructive heresies, even denying the sovereign Lord who bought them—bringing swift destruction on themselves.*
>
> –2 Peter 2:1, NIV

A full moon climbed over the mountains, and seven wolves moved across the bleak field with eyes reflecting from the truck headlights. From the safety of our truck, we were free to enjoy these magnificent animals wearing their beautiful winter coats. After moving along our track for some time, they moved away and disappeared into the darkness. This experience reminded me that we must be vigilant to protect the young churches from the spiritual attack of wolves in sheep's clothing.

Early one morning, I awoke in a herder's ger to sad and pitiful news. During the night, a pack of wolves attacked the sheep and goats of a nearby herder, maiming or killing almost 100 of them. Nothing is as devastating to a herder as the sight of the useless slaughter and destruction of his stock.

Although wolves are nearly extinct and currently protected in America, the opposite is true in Mongolia. They flourish and pose a constant problem for herders. Somehow, they manage to evade guns, poison and traps in their effort to prey off the young and weak animals—sometimes killing them in a frenzy. Because these cunning, sly wolves strike when least expected, herders and their dedicated dogs have to keep a constant vigil. The herders depend on their livestock for the continuation of their livelihood.

Cunning and sly teachers have also invaded Mongolia by creating their own message that adds to or deletes biblical truth. Sometimes, their message is one of distortion as they bend the

Scripture to fit their twisted doctrine. Sadly, their message often sounds sweet to the ears of their listeners as they bring gifts to attract vulnerable, immature Christians. A vivid picture of false teachers is recorded in Ephesians 4:12–14. It provides a warning about false doctrines:

> *For the equipping of the saints for the work of ministry, for the edifying of the body of Christ, till we all come to the unity of the faith and of the knowledge of the Son of God, to a perfect man, to the measure of the stature of the fullness of Christ; that we should no longer be children, tossed to and from and carried about with every wind of doctrine by the trickery of men, in the cunning craftiness of deceitful plotting,*
>
> –Ephesians 4:12–14, NKJV

In many ways, the small churches in Mongolia are like weak lambs. Their members have recently become believers and are easily misled by every wind of doctrine. They have grown up in a world devoid of biblical teaching such as the Old Testament stories on which many of us were weaned. The faith of these young believers is at high risk in the face of false teaching.

When the apostle Paul travelled on his missionary journeys, he often started at the synagogues in the cities he visited where he met with Jews who were steeped in Scripture, the Old Testament. They had memorized much of its content and were intimately familiar with the God of Abraham, Isaac and Jacob. However, in Mongolia there is a blank slate. Mongolians must start from the ground floor, and until they grow in their understanding of the Bible and God's nature and purposes, they are particularly defenseless against false doctrines.

A *Claim-a-County for Christ* team once ministered in a small mountain community where people were hungry for the gospel. The seeds fell on good soil (see Matthew 13:8), and by fall, 35 believers were meeting regularly. The small church grew and was anxious to share its faith. They invited friends and neighbors to join them to hear about their wonderful Savior who loved them and wanted their friendship. However, something terrible happened to this vibrant group of new believers while enjoying fellowship with each other and their newly found God.

A group of foreigners came to this community from another country and culture. "Come and follow us and join our church," they said. They taught divisive doctrines and baptized these new Christians into their church. "Listen," they said, "do not talk to people from V.E.T. Net unless you get permission from us." The results were predictable. The group of young Christians splintered into fragments; some followed Paul, some followed Apollos and some followed Cephas. (See 1 Corinthians 1:12.) Our job was to bring these new Christians back into biblical faith through teaching from the Bible. The book of Jude expresses this clearly:

> *Dear friends, although I was very eager to write to you about the salvation we share, I felt I had to write and urge you to contend for the faith that was once for all entrusted to the saints,*
>
> –Jude 3, NIV

Paraphrasing this passage, it might have read, "I wanted to write you a nice little encouraging letter about how wonderful our salvation is, but there are some awful things happening in the church, and I need instead to send you a warning."

A V.E.T. Net team made a special trip just to help this struggling group of spiritual babies. They were encouraged and strengthened in their faith as they studied Scripture, church unity and the dangers of false doctrine. After much discussion, study and prayer, divisions were healed, and our team returned to Ulaanbaatar. Not long after that, our phone rang, and we heard an excited voice: "We are united again!" What a sweet word to hear—*united*. How pleasing it is to God when we meet together as one at Jesus' feet.

The Mongolian Bankhar Dog

We drove into a serene valley deep in the mountains where the Taatz River was only a trickle. There, I spent my first night in a ger since moving to Mongolia. About midnight, a greasy meal of mutton was served just before bedtime. As the honored guest, I was allowed to crawl into one of three beds. Old men were snoring, and the floor was littered with children dreaming in an unknown tongue—unknown to me that is. I was the first American many of these people had ever seen, and because of the Russian propaganda about Americans, I was considered fearsome indeed.

During the night, my stomach began to feel queasy. I wanted to go outside, but I feared I might walk on sleeping bodies while searching for the darkened door. In addition, there was another, more foreboding reason to be careful. Giant, vicious watchdogs roamed the grounds. These watchdogs kept the wolves and other predators at bay to protect helpless flocks of sheep and goats. I wasn't sure how they felt about Americans either—I stayed in bed and prayed!

The Bankhar dog is native to Mongolia and China and other surrounding countries. A drawing of the Mongolian Bankhar dog is on the facing page of the start of this Chapter 14. These loyal protectors are massive in size and fearless in their duties. They are proud animals with bushy tails that curl over their backs. They have great boxy heads and feet that are bigger than my fist. In the past, these purebreds were a beautiful sight as we drove across the steppe. However, something happened, and now we seldom see these regal animals. It was an insidious invasion that crept in, and because it came so quietly, no one knew it was happening. The Russians and Westerners brought their cherished pets along when they came to Mongolia. Eventually, some escaped to the countryside and mixed with the native dogs. The results were a mongrel mixture that reflected traces of the canine breeds across the world.

Today, it is common to see mongrels in the countryside as a result of crossbreeding. The Bankhar pure breed has been corrupted, and only a few of these beautiful dogs are left. Today, there is a project to reestablish the breed, and V.E.T. Net is helping by providing veterinary care for these dogs.

Some Mongolians believed that, like man, the Bankhar had a soul and that people could be reincarnated as these dogs. They even believed that dogs could be reincarnated as humans. As a result, when Bankhars died, their tails were amputated prior to burial to ensure that those reincarnated as people were not reborn with an embarrassing tail.

Not long ago, we passed a group of gers shrouded in a winter shawl. Prancing across the valley was one of these magnificent Mongolian dogs, the Bankhar. What a delight to see this pure, uncorrupted and stately animal. And, what a joy it is to see a community of believers soaked in the Word of God and uncorrupted in devotion to Him and His principles. Just as V.E.T. Net is committed to ending the continuous destruction of the breed, we are also determined to protect our organization and those we serve from the devastating effects of false teaching.

God requires purity in our work and team relationships, our personal integrity and in our values. He will not have the faith mongrelized. God will not accept a watered-down, lukewarm following that winks at the world while spouting religious jargon in an attempt to pacify Him. Our God will not accept a double-standard that blends the world with the Word. Fighting for the purity of the Gospel is not a popular battle.

False Teachers

> *Dear friends, do not believe every spirit, but test the spirits to see whether they are from God, because many false prophets have gone out into the world. This is how you can recognize the Spirit of God: Every spirit that acknowledges that Jesus Christ has come in the flesh is from God,*
>
> –1 John 4:1–2, NIV

A controlling foreign pastor came into one of our communities in eastern Mongolia. Sometimes she brought her foreign friends to the church, but they refused to include the Mongolians in their fellowship. When our V.ET. Net team arrived, the innocent believers in the Mongolian church were sad and discouraged. It would be an understatement to say that they happily welcomed our team and allowed us to help them through this trying time.

We know that the struggles will accelerate as we continue to meet darkness with God's light. We must stand on the Word and be uncompromising in our commitment to follow Him. We desire unity, and to ensure it, we do not tolerate false teaching. As we fellowship with all true followers of the one and only God through

Jesus Christ, we need His wisdom to saturate this nation with the truth.

Looking for God in the Circumstances

> *I tell you the truth, the Son can do nothing by himself; he can do only what he sees his Father doing, because whatever the Father does the Son also does.*
>
> –John 5:19b, NIV

If Jesus could do nothing without the Father, it is obvious that we should not even try on our own. It is apparent to us that God has often gone before us. He may break the truck's axles, as he did while our team was in Ondor Ulaan, but we must look for Him in the circumstances. What often seems like an inconvenience in sharing the wonderful news about Jesus Christ with the villagers, may turn out to be a blessing.

Sambuu was one of the first women to accept Christ in Ondor Ulaan. She was an enthusiastic evangelist, and soon her five young daughters and her mother came to know Christ—at least all claimed to be Christians. Two of the daughters moved to Ulaanbaatar to attend school. Sambuu was divorced from her husband and realized that she could not afford to pay college tuition for these girls. She moved to the city where she met a famous musician from her village. He offered to pay the tuition for these daughters.

Unfortunately, his assistance came at a heavy price. The generous man also shared his religion with Sambuu. He was involved in a Korean cult called World Mission Society Church of God. The church that was founded in 1964 worships the "mother god." Sambuu and her whole family were swept into a cult that misinterprets verses from the Bible to fit the church narrative. There are other false religions that permeate this culture in Mongolia. Another Korean cult, the "Moonies," is here as are the Jehovah's Witnesses, Mormons, and a host of others. As predicted again and again in the Bible, false teachers will abound. When we first came to Mongolia, we did not dream that a host of others would flood the country bringing their gods with them.

Our team was able to reach out to Sambuu and her family to encourage them to come back into the sheepfold. I wish I could tell you that they have returned, but sadly, that is not the case. Our work against the enemy continues. We are the Body of Christ, and we are concerned that we could be diluted, much like the Mongol dog. Not only are we concerned about hiring non-Christian Mongolians, but we constantly screen our short-term volunteers who, although having a desire to serve, may have a different agenda. When we remain undefiled, can you imagine how that pleases God? It is our deepest desire that the whole V.E.T. Net team will seek Him only and fight to preserve the integrity of all that He has entrusted us with—in Mongolia.

Guard the Good Deposit

Guard the good deposit that was entrusted to you—guard it with the help of the Holy Spirit who lives in us.

–2 Timothy 1:14, NIV

Frances and I have seen our gifts and responsibilities change considerably over many years in Mongolia. Now, our most important ministry is guarding the "good deposit" through the strength of the Holy Spirit. We often face temptation to water down our biblical faith by becoming more inclusive and broadening our acceptance of others. Our methodology may be somewhat homegrown, but our experience with God and faith in Him are unshakable. He continues to show us that He is all that He claims and that His claims are all that we need. It is experience and biblical faith, not armchair theology, that gives us total confidence that He will catch us every time we fall.

A Dog Named Angel

My older brother was a periodontist for many years and decided to take early retirement to enjoy his farm near Snow Camp, North Carolina. Ken thought he was retiring to the easy life, at least one with no complaints from patients in pain. He decided to get into the Beagle business, something that has proved to be far less than an easy life. In the southern part of the United States, many Beagles are not kept as pets, but as rabbit dogs. It has become a religion for those who follow these gifted little hounds that can be bought by the inch—13 to 15 inches at the shoulders, depending on personal taste. Ken built a fence around 40 acres of his farm to keep the rabbits and Beagles in and the predators out.

Beagles are amazing little animals, and for those in the cult, having a champion is the peak of the pinnacle. Ken has now raised and trained his own champ. Let me introduce you to Angel—her registered name is too long for this chapter.

This dog is absolutely brilliant. First of all, she can tell you when a rabbit has been down a trail. She has olfactory capabilities that humans are unable to even imagine. Not only can she acknowledge that Peter Cottontail has passed by the area, but she can also identify what time he traveled and in which direction he was going—all this with just her keen sense of smell. Being able to tell the direction a rabbit is traveling is of utmost importance to these Beagle fanciers. Angel is adept at moving in the right direction to follow close behind the disappearing puff of white. Her wagging tail is a flag that signals the course of the hunt.

Some rabbits in Mongolia have quite a different look than those back home. While walking in the larch forest one day, I startled a rabbit from his cozy bed on a cold day. I saw only a streak of grey. What an astonishing sight—pasted on the back end of this bunny was a black tail.

The rural Mongolian churches do not look any more like Western churches than our American cottontails resemble these black-tail rabbits. No padded pews; no meeting on Sunday at eleven; no lengthy lectures from an elevated podium; no robed choirs. These countryside Mongolians move from place to place, and one of the real challenges is to find a way for the church to meet consistently to grow and not backtrack. We need to build a spiritual fence around these small churches to keep out the predators in the land of the black-tail rabbit. It is our responsibility to disciple and pray for them unwaveringly as we ask the Holy Spirit to protect them from evil and from all wolves in sheep's clothing.

I really do admire Angel because she is always moving in the right direction without any back-tracking. That is the way for us to live—constantly moving closer to Christ without wavering or letting the distance between us grow. We want this for ourselves, and we want it for our friends across this country. We want to keep sharpening each other so that when our race is finished God will say, *"Well done my good and faithful servant."* (See Matthew 25:21a.)

The Black Death

One of the problems that occurs each summer is the disease we call "the plague." The Mongolian juicy-fat marmot roasting on the fire is irresistible, but it does not always come without risk to the family. Marmot fleas carry a micro-organism that causes the dreaded Black Death—the same disease that wiped out much of Europe during the 1300's.

Today, we have antibiotics which are effective against this plague. Even very old drugs are efficacious against this dreaded disease. However, in remote Mongolia, these medications are sometimes not available, and many people have succumbed to the disease even in these times of modern medicine.

False teaching is a destructive disease that enters the church and can be deadly when untreated. There is a serious risk to the church when it is allowed to go unchecked. Not only are churches exposed to obvious cults and false religions, they are often unprotected from teachings that are not biblical and promises that go unfulfilled. When Christianity first came to Mongolia, many young people heard the misdirected message of guaranteed prosperity for all followers of Christ. Times were extraordinarily difficult, and they were grasping for ways to improve their lives. Unfortunately, some of these new believers were disappointed when their difficult lives did not immediately improve. Some became disillusioned and were driven to jump from tall buildings to their death. These tragic incidences led to outrage by those opposed to Christianity—"this foreign religion."

One of the early Christian women leaders in Mongolia rightly began to teach against the notion that everything was going to get better once you become a Christian. "In fact," she said, "things are going to get worse for you. Following Jesus is not going to be easy; it will be more difficult. Your family might turn against you and your friends might leave you. Don't choose to believe in Jesus because you think your life will be easy."

False teachers are an ever-present danger to the church and will become more prevalent in the end times:

> *But, dear friends, remember what the apostles of our Lord Jesus Christ foretold. They said to you, "In the last times there will be scoffers who will follow their own ungodly desires." These are the men who divide you, who follow mere natural instincts and do not have the Spirit.*
>
> –Jude 17–19, NIV

God Looks at Every Person

We keep statistics for our organization on the number of people who hear the gospel and the number who respond positively to Christ. Although it is reasonable to have reports and to be accountable to those in authority, Jesus looks more at the individual than he does at the numbers. He is concerned about every single person. It is that one lost sheep He pursues relentlessly. Although we may not become prosperous and have perfect health, the peace that comes when we give our life to Jesus surpasses all understanding. (See Philippians 4:7)

Otgonchimeg is not a number. She is a real person who has suffered the loss of her husband and dealt with a sister involved in Satan worship. Listen to Otgonchimeg's story of how Jesus Christ changed her broken life to a victorious one:

> My name is Otgonchimeg. I lived with my husband, Enkhbayar, and two children. He first heard about God through the V.E.T. Net summer teacher program in 2007 and then received Jesus in his heart as his Savior. The summer teachers gathered at my house and had Bible study. At that time, I did not want to listen about God, so I left my ger and came back after they finished their study time. Later my husband was sick with lung cancer, but he still went to Ulaanbaatar for the *Shepherd's Conference* in January.

Even though he was sick, he was so happy and excited with the training when he came back. He shared with me what he learned through the V.E.T. Net training and about this wonderful God. He died in 2009. After my husband's death, V.E.T. Net people did not break relationship with my family. When they came to my village, they stayed in my house and continued to share the Good News. I became a believer in Jesus. They invited me many times to participate in the January *Shepherd's Conference,* but I avoided them and had many excuses.

> My sister became a shaman. She said, "Your life is going to get worse so come and live with me." She always called me to move there. Since that time, I always had bad nightmares; I was worried; I suffered with insomnia. In the autumn, the V.E.T. Net team came and stayed in my house. I shared with them what was happening in my life. They explained to me what it means to be a shaman. They counseled me to put my suffering into God's hand and pray for peace. They all prayed for me to conquer fear and chase away the Devil's spirit in Jesus' name. Then my fear disappeared, and I slept peacefully. One-day, sister Altai (V.E.T. Net coordinator), called me and invited me to the *Shepherd's Conference*. This time I understood that God really loves me and calls me now, so I agreed to come for the training. Now I am going to obey God, stand firm before Him and visit families to share the Good News. The important thing is to have inner healing, to show God's love and to lead people in the right way to God. I know that I can do it through His strength.

The next story—that involves Otgonjargal—is so amazing, it walks right off the pages of the New Testament. It is a reminder of the opposing forces in the world, both good and evil, that are doing battle for the souls of men and women. This story took place in the province of Middle Gobi in a county named Caihan Owoo (Nice Idol) in 2009. There, a young married woman began to befriend our teachers as they worked in the *Claim-a-County for Christ* program. It was the second year of the program, and we were beginning to reach out with the gospel. The young woman was attracted to our training and our lifestyle that she saw as honest, open, and positive. These attributes are unique in a land of fear, deception and suspicion.

At the time, she worked as a cook at the public school where we were based. She became good friends with our two female summer teachers who established a close relationship with her and began to invite her to the morning devotion and Bible study. After only two weeks, she said, "I want to receive Jesus Christ as my Savior." She was invited to the evening study to hear more about the Good News where she prayed to receive Christ. Some weeks later, she was baptized, but then something snapped. It was like a demon had captured her mind. She could not speak and began to act in a detached manner.

In Caihan Owoo, everyone was talking about this woman. The entire town was upset and believed that V.E.T. Net had caused this awful problem. Even government officials were complaining and starting to point fingers. The community blamed everything on Agaii, the *Claim-a-County for Christ* coordinator. Agaii told them, "This is not from our Jesus." However, the principal asked him to stop all training. The threat of a lawsuit was hanging over our heads.

Our team left and returned a few months later to find the situation had worsened. The whole community seemed to be waiting for what they thought would be her imminent death. Our teachers found this young woman neglected and alone. As they entered her ger, the stench shoved them back. She was lying in her own filth still unable to speak. Two of our V.E.T. Net women teachers washed her hair and body and cleaned the ger. The other team members returned, and as a group, *prayed intensely for her*. Suddenly, she was completely transformed. She began to talk and act normal. The curse was broken.

The power of Satan is very real, but we can say unequivocally that through the power of prayer, God snatched this woman from the jaws of death and made her whole. At our remote leadership training, there sat Otgonjargal, her face aglow, with Nasalmaa, her friend who was discipling her. Our V.E.T. Net staff were astonished as they saw her face shining brightly. She was now truly a new creation—active in her church and community and sharing her story with her neighbors. Everyone in the community knew of this woman's previous plight, and her miraculous change prompted many to listen to the story of her salvation.

Shamanism is a frightening demonic religion in Mongolia.

People fear shamen and know they have strong powers. Shamanism is often mixed with Buddhism, and together they are a strong force intent on enslaving people across this land. Otgonchimeg and Otgonjargal both had encounters with the forces of evil and found that greater is the power of our God than is that of Satan and his followers. Mark tells the story of a young boy controlled by a demon:

> *When Jesus saw that a crowd was running to the scene, he rebuked the impure spirit. "You deaf and mute spirit," he said, "I command you, come out of him and never enter him again." The spirit shrieked, convulsed him violently and came out. The boy looked so much like a corpse that many said, "He's dead." But Jesus took him by the hand and lifted him to his feet, and he stood up. After Jesus had gone indoors, his disciples asked him privately, "Why couldn't we drive it out?" He replied, "This kind can come out only by prayer.*
>
> –Mark 9:25–29, NIV

We know the power of prayer, and we are dependent on it as we work in some very dark areas where Satan has had a stronghold for many years. Idols abound in this country, and there is nothing at all nice about them. Demonic control is far more visible here than in the Western world. It is real. We must keep up a constant guard against the powers of evil and look to God to protect us.

The University of Shamanism

Dornod is the eastern-most providence of Mongolia with a long finger sticking far out into China. We commonly see grass damaged from overgrazing as we travel across this country, but in Dornod we were tenting in lush grass up to the horses' bellies. It was rainy, and the soaked tents made for unpleasant camping. In addition, the mosquitoes were flourishing. "Where is the insect repellent?" asked Frances. "I didn't bring it," I sheepishly replied. I added, "We've never had a problem before."

We stopped for lunch, but the buzzing of these insect vampires made eating impossible. Our driver had this problem before and knew the perfect solution. He built a dung fire, and when it was burning brightly, he covered it with more dung to maximize the smoke. It worked; we were able to eat our meager meal, rather quickly, I might add, in the protective covering of the dung smoke.

Moving on, we passed a beautiful green valley with multiple gers and small buildings decorated with colorful pieces of streaming cloth. "What is this place?" we asked the local veterinarian who was traveling with us. His reply was stunning. "This is the school where they teach people to be shamans." This beautiful place was the University of Shamanism—literally, the School of Satan.

As we continued our trip, we approached two vehicles parked by the roadside with the driver waving his hands for help. We stopped for our driver to inspect the disabled van and for the chatting men to make the necessary repairs. Frances jumped from our van to stretch her weary legs. She watched as a host of people exited both vehicles. Two of the younger women from the two other vans boldly approached her, so Frances engaged them in conversation. One woman was very excited to talk with a native-English speaker and to use her English to explain the reason for their trip. "I am a shaman, and my family and friends are going with me to the University of Shamanism. I am graduating to the next level of Shamanism, which is a great honor." Frances replied, "Have you ever heard about Jesus?" She froze momentarily with a wolfish look in her fearful eyes. At the name of Jesus, this woman ran for her vehicle, and we did not see her again!

A prayer uttered in the name of Jesus is a force with which the shaman cannot contend. We are comforted and impowered by the words written by John:

> *You, dear children, are from God and have overcome them, because the one who is in you is greater than the one who is in the world.*
>
> –1 John 4:4, NIV

Praise God; we serve a God who is able to shut the mouth of Satan and his followers. God is greater than any obstacle we might come up against, including Satan. Jesus is our offensive and defensive weapon, and we can call on Him in prayer at any time.

Figure 15.1. "The Black Horse Case"—black Mongolian horse

Chapter 15

God's Absolute Provision

For I am convinced that neither death nor life, neither angels nor demons, neither the present nor the future, nor any powers, neither height nor depth, nor anything else in all creation, will be able to separate us from the love of God that is in Christ Jesus our Lord.

– Romans 8:38–39, NIV

In May, 2016, five members of V.E.T. Net were returning in our van to Ulaanbaatar from a countryside trip when they were forced off the road by a large truck. The van rolled over three or four times. Because these Russian vehicles do not have seat belts, this type of accident usually results in fatalities, a fact confirmed by the investigating officer. Although the team members did sustain serious injuries, they were able to return to work after recovering. We know without question that God protected them just as He continues to watch over His ministry in Mongolia.

Angry Mountain

As the work of V.E.T. Net spread rapidly, we found ourselves more and more in the Gobi Desert. It is an awesome, but lonely place. Herders live miles apart and an isolated family may not see another soul for days. The absence of traffic on the desolate, sandy roads means that we can drive all day and pass only a rare car.

It was usually a challenge to find a place to set up our camp. There was so much emptiness that finding a rock for a little protection was nearly impossible. However, at the end of one of our long and tiring trips, we managed to find a small, treeless rocky mountain. We noticed that sand had drifted into a slight depression, so we took advantage of it and pitched our tents. Through the afternoon haze, we could just make out some scattered gers off in the far distance. We all agreed that this would be a quiet place to rest our aching bones.

The first motorcycle came with two men and a small boy. They seemed peaceful enough as they accepted our offer of cookies and drink. After learning that we only intended to have a night's rest, they went on their way. Once people learn that we work with their local veterinarian and schools, we are often shown good will.

Some time later, a second man came, and he too, was friendly. This time, however, we were given a warning, "You are on 'Angry Mountain.' We worship this pile of stone and sand."

Frances and I were settling into our tent when yet a third motorcycle pulled up. This man had a gun and threatened to shoot us if we did any damage to the revered mountain. He said, "I will shoot you if you do any damage to this mountain. We worship this mountain, and it has great power." A circling eagle, no doubt protecting her two baby eaglets nearby, seemed to be keeping watch on us as well. We knew better than to leave anything behind us other than our footprints as we tred lightly on the forlorn desert hump.

This was a sad encounter. We were not as frightened of the gun as we were heartbroken for the local people who were wasting their lives paying homage to lifeless stones. How we longed for them to know the God who created the very place they worshiped. We wanted them to know our God of love and mercy—not a god of fear and anger.

There are risks in working here, but not following God is the greatest of them all. We know that it is Mongolia's time to hear the gospel, and we must not detour from the path He has laid before us. Our V.E.T. Net team must stay strong—one in Him. Our unity and prayers for each other must be unwavering.

As we watch the unfolding work that God is doing here, we can see His fingerprint on everything. His creativity did not end with the completion of the universe. He continues to astound us daily by doing the unexpected. This country can become a Christian nation. We've seen old men who nursed the vodka bottle all of their lives be transformed into church leaders filled with the Spirit of God. Old women say, "I want this Jesus in my life." Children are completely open to the stories from the Bible they never heard before. These young people are often the first to respond to Christ without reservation. Churches are being birthed, and even though they are small in number, they have astounding power. Idols are removed from their honored positions in the houses of believers when people see them for the powerless trinkets they are. We believe that we may very well see the removal of the "high places" in the future as angry mountains are replaced by the Church of the Living God. With God's protection, we advance as a united team committed to reaching every lonely corner of this land.

Covered in Darkness

> *But I trust in you, O Lord; I say, "You are my God." My times are in your hands; deliver me from my enemies and from those who pursue me.*
>
> –Psalm 31:14–15, NIV

Dark moments have sometimes cast shadows along V.E.T. Net's path threatening to ruin us at every turn. Instead, they have helped to shape and strengthen our team. The Master Potter continues to mold us with His expert touch. He may have to apply a little super glue occasionally to us, His fragile children, but He continues to form us into vessels worthy to fulfill His purposes.

One of our darkest times in Mongolia turned into a learning experience for the future work of V.E.T. Net. God sent us a Swiss friend to help us develop a yak-research-project proposal for the Danish Government. Yak were often treated as small cows, and we were interested in learning if there were significate differences in their response to certain vaccines. We were particularly interested in the vaccine for brucellosis, a common bacterial infection among the Mongolian livestock at Ik Bulag and other areas.

Our intention was to partner with a department of the Agriculture University, but as the proposal was nearing completion and readied for submission, greed began to surface. Partners disagreed over how funds would be allocated, and it quickly became apparent that we were unequally yoked. We were threatened with extradition, but God was not finished with us in Mongolia. We praise God that He protected us from the powerful influences trying to expel us from the country. The project was not implemented.

V.E.T. Net has always respected the authority of the Mongolian government, and are grateful for the relationship we enjoy with them. We provided many training sessions for government employees, and cooperate in every way possible. However, we know that it is best to work with the government instead of working directly under it. Bureaucracy is the same here as it is in other countries. It is ineffective, cumbersome, and often it is difficult to achieve maximum efficiency in such an environment. Each lesson learned has served as the foundation for the design of all our projects and programs. God has molded us for His work through what may seem, at the time, to be very painful experiences.

The Black Horse Case

> *How great is your goodness, which You have stored up for those who fear You, which you bestow in the sight of men on those who take refuge in you. In the shelter of your presence you hide them from the intrigues of men; in your dwelling you keep them safe from accusing tongues.*
>
> –Psalm 31:19–20, NIV

While we were preparing to become an independent organization, a horse owner sued us for malpractice. This became known as the "Black Horse Case." It paralyzed us from doing much of our work. Of course, the man's claims were ridiculous, but the trials that ensued were very real.

The horseman claimed that the three liters of fluids our V.E.T. Net team administered to treat his horse for dehydration related to the *Nadaam Horse Race,* had settled in his horse's lower legs causing lameness. In truth, giving an adult horse 25 liters or more of intravenous fluids is commonplace. The three liters were just a drop-in-the-bucket. We had world experts who were willing to testify on our behalf, but they were not respected in this country. Faculty members from the Mongolian Veterinary School were called to give expert testimony for the plaintiff. We lost the early trials, but because we were not willing to admit guilt to such a frivolous charge, we appealed the case to the higher courts. Eventually, the case worked its way up to the Mongolian Supreme Court where it was declared that the plaintiff did not have adequate evidence. The case was sent to the lowest court where we started all over again.

In a new trial, V.E.T. Net was vindicated, and the case was dismissed for lack of evidence. The Black Horse Case that lasted for two years could have been devastating to the ministry. Instead, it only made us stronger as a team as we committed the problem to the Lord through prayer and complete dependence on His sovereign grace.

Throughout all of our years here, we have watched God miraculously reach across this immense nation to nomadic herders with His life-changing message of salvation. He has, indeed, protected His mission just as He has protected us every step of the way.

Breathe Normally

Our Mongolian Airliner 727 was cruising on our flight from Beijing to Ulaanbaatar. Dinner had been served and we were settled in for another hour of what was typically tiring travel. We were just over halfway through the two-hour flight when, suddenly, passengers reached for their ears. The aircraft had lost cabin pressure causing excruciating pain to the inner ear. Oxygen masks dropped, and we all fumbled to get our mask in place. "Breathe normally," we had been told in the safety demonstrations. We were rapidly losing altitude. Breathe normally? What in the world were they talking about?

What occupies our mind when we are confronted with the possibility of having only moments to live? Is it how much wealth we have been able to accumulate in our lifetime? Is it the size of our home, or the brand of our car? As we were dealing with this frightening turn of events, there was, no doubt, a singular thought that ran through the minds of passengers and crew members alike. "Is this the end of my life?" At such a terrifying time, a personal relationship with Christ is the only thing that really counts and the only thing that can bring comfort. We wondered how many were praying for God to save them.

When the emergency was over, the passengers began to laugh and joke and take pictures of the oxygen masks still dangling from the ceiling. God seemed to be quickly forgotten as life returned to normal once again. How difficult it is to live a life of expectancy—to keep God at the forefront of our minds and hearts. There are so many things that get in the way of a close walk with Him regardless of where we are.

Life in Mongolia has given us many opportunities to ponder deep questions. We left the comfort of America to live in a wild and distant land where unusual circumstances are the norm. For us, God's existence and sovereignty cannot be questioned; we have seen Him orchestrate miracle after miracle. Still, we struggle with the same problems that plague Christians around the world. How can we draw closer to our heavenly Father? How can we live for Him every day in a way that allows us to step easily from this world into the next? Jesus has been our constant companion, and nothing, absolutely nothing, can get in the way of His plan. We know that He is always ready to comfort and protect us through the Black Horse Cases and airplane-emergency cases of life.

Buddhist Prophecy

We made our way up the east shore of Lake Khovsgol, the largest lake in Mongolia. During the winter, when it is frozen several feet deep, oil tanker trucks use it as a highway to haul fuel from Russia into Mongolia. For now, though, the weather was warm. It was a time of heavy rainfall in the mountainous area.

As we wound our way around the mountain on a dirt track, we approached a raging river racing down the hills to flow into the deep blue waters of the lake. We expected our driver, Boldoo, to approach the edge of the torrential river and assess our chances before crossing. Instead, we were shocked as he plunged the vehicle ahead to surge into the mighty floodwaters. The vehicle stalled and water began to pour into the van soaking sleeping bags, camping equipment, feet, and legs. The Mongolians on our team were not swimmers. We could see the fear that filled their eyes as the gravel began to wash away from underneath the tires leaving the old Russian van tilting dangerously downstream.

Our salvation came in the person of the driver of an ancient truck that was carrying a load of Mongolian workers. Unlike our vehicle, the truck had wheels large enough to ford the river. The passengers in the truck urged the driver to keep going through the dangerous river, but the man refused to leave a fellow driver in such a precarious predicament. He helped us attach a cable from our van to his truck so that he could tow us to safety on the other side. Safely on the other side, we began to dry equipment and prepared to spend a miserable night shivering around a crackling fire.

We learned later that Boldoo had met with the Buddhist lama for spiritual advice before we left on our trip. The lama had a special prophecy for Boldoo. "You will die by drowning." Obviously, being a good Buddhist, Boldoo felt compelled to speed up the fulfillment of the morbid prophecy. He might drown in his ever-present alcohol bottle sometime in the future, but on this day, at least, God put that time on hold, and we were, thankfully, all spared.

Over the years, V.E.T. Net has come face to face with destructive forces from funding organizations that threatened the life of this ministry. We have been bent like our tent poles, but have sprung back each time stronger than ever before. Although we may be unsure of the future, we are stronger than ever in His strength, and even when our plans for the future look uncertain, our faith remains unshaken. Glory to God in the highest!

Figure 16.1. "Empty Saddle"—groom with riderless horse for bride

Chapter 16

The End

> *Now, brothers and sisters, about times and dates we do not need to write to you, for you know very well that the day of the Lord will come like a thief in the night.*
>
> –1 Thessalonians 5: 1–2, NIV

I see a beautiful picture of the return of Christ lived out through the marriage events of couples living in the remote countryside.

The horses are readied for a long trip as four young men—the bridegroom and his friends—prepare to mount for the overnight ride. Families gather around the horsemen wishing them a safe and speedy journey. The men are dressed in new traditional dels. The horses restlessly paw at the ground as they prepare for their long trip. There is something unusual about this entourage. In addition to the horses to be ridden by the bridegroom and his friends, there is another horse. This one is saddled, but there is no rider. It is intended for the bride on the return trip. The bridegroom's mother casts the traditional milk into the air to insure that the gods will sanction a good trip.

About 20 miles away, the bride waits patiently and expectantly. She does not know the day or the hour that her future husband will come, so she must be ready with her clothes packed for the trip. She keeps peeking out the door at the trail that she knows will bring her beloved.

> *Do not let your heart be troubled. You believe in God; believe also in me. My Father's house has many rooms; if that were not so, would I have told you that I am going there to prepare a place for you?*
>
> –John 14:1–2, NIV

Long after midnight, the bridegroom arrives to steal away his bride. Although she has been waiting in anticipation, she is still surprised when the moment finally comes. The bridegroom whisks her off her feet and places her on the horse with the empty saddle. He carries her back to his homeland where a brand new ger waits in preparation for the couple. This is vividly symbolic of what will transpire when Jesus returns to gather His bride, the Church, to live with Him for all eternity.

Walking on Air

> *For the Lord himself will come down from heaven, with a loud command, with the voice of the archangel and with the trumpet call of God, and the dead in Christ will rise first. After that, we who are still alive and are left will be caught up together with them in the clouds to meet the Lord in the air. And so we will be with the Lord forever. Therefore encourage one another with these words.*
>
> –1 Thessalonians 4:16–18, NIV

How many wordsmiths have tried to capture the image of a cloud on paper? Not a few, I think. Sometimes, I stand in the desert of Mongolia with something of an unobstructed view, I turn full circle to see the earth surrounded by floating balls of cotton. I could try to touch them, but they are not really there. From where I stand, they cover the sky with their mystical mist that has only form, but little substance. High overhead, there are yet other clouds that are flying by—just wispy things of white-horse-tail hair painting on the canvas we call sky. And in the distance, they take on darkness and threaten to attract the attention of all around with thundering sounds and lightening flashing to the ground.

I think of the Son of God who created such a panoramic sight. Deep inside, I have the assurance that He will one day walk on these same clouds. When He does, He will bid us come from the four winds, from one end of the heavens to the other. Mongolia, it seems, is one of the far corners where His clarion call has been heard. Many have responded and will stand in the presence of the One with the appearance of jasper and carnelian and a rainbow resembling emerald encircling His throne. Flashes of lightening, rumblings and peals of thunder will reverberate. (See Revelation

4:3.) Together with you and me, and all those who have gone before, trusting in the Messiah, will give constant praise, worship and exaltation to the King of kings.

> *Then will appear the sign of the Son of Man in heaven. And then all the peoples of the earth will mourn when they see the Son of Man coming on the clouds of heaven, with power and great glory. And he will send his angels with a loud trumpet call, and they will gather his elect from the four winds, from one end of the heavens to the other.*
>
> –Matthew 24:30–31, NIV

Yes, just a very few years ago, most Mongolians had not had the opportunity to hear the gospel. They were trapped in a world that excluded religious freedom. Today, there are tens of thousands who have heard and responded to the call of Christ. When Christ comes to gather His elect, there will be a host of heaven-bound, del-clad Mongols gazing at the clouds and caught up with the Savior.

The Rabbit Ears Are Getting Shorter

Tall grass that once waved in the breeze and sustained the vast Mongolian herds was now severely overgrazed.

"Do you think that the weather has changed and the lack of rain and too many animals have caused severe overgrazing?" I asked the herder couple. "That is exactly right," they responded. "The weather has changed drastically over the past few years, and now we have too many animals for the damaged grasslands to support." This conversation opened the door to talk of eternal things and how clinging to God through Jesus Christ is the only sure thing we have to hold on to.

"Is America experiencing the same climate changes?" they asked. "Indeed, it is a worldwide problem," I told them. "Our Bible teaches that this earth is going to wear out and be replaced someday by a new heaven and a new earth, and Jesus will be the King over all." "You know," they said, "the old people used to say the same thing." "The rabbit ears are getting shorter," they would say, "and the world is wearing out."

I suspect that a very long time ago, just before the angels appeared to the shepherds in Bethlehem, shepherds were talking about the coming Messiah, the Savior. "I know we have been waiting for thousands of years," they might have said, "but one day Messiah is going to come." Perhaps they, too, had heard talk of this before among those who thought they were just fairy tales.

When an angel of the Lord appeared to the shepherds out in the fields of Bethlehem and the glory of the Lord shown around them, the angel announced the birth of the Savior, wrapped in cloths and lying in a manger. A great company of the heavenly host appeared with the angel, praising God. Then, the angels left and returned to heaven. (See Luke 2:8–15.) The shepherds are thinking, "He is here! The Messiah has come!"

Now, over 2,000 years later, we find ourselves watching the skies once again for the return of the Savior. Jesus told us to watch for the signs. (See Matthew 24: 32–35.) "The rabbit ears are getting shorter." The skeptics say, "It's been thousands of years, and this is just a fable. This is like the tales of the Red Sea crossing, Jonah in the whale and other Old Testament stories." But we know these are not fables. It will surely happen quickly, in the blink of an eye, when Jesus suddenly appears in the sky in all His glory to claim His own. Then, it will be too late for a change of heart. Those who doubted Him will fall to the ground in fear, their fate will already be sealed.

Now is the time for Mongolians to hear the Good News, and God is making it possible for us to share it with them. Sometimes we wonder why God waited so long to reveal Himself to these precious people. Why were they closed away for hundreds of years while many of us in the West were exposed to the gospel through churches and multiple media? I cannot answer this question, but I do know this: God is helping us push against the forces of the evil one and his false religions in this country so that all may know of His grace through Jesus Christ.

The Mongolian Herder lives a nomadic lifestyle. The harsh conditions include howling desert winds that sandblast their faces and extreme cold that sometimes stays -30° degrees F for a month at a time. When the grass is low, and the animals search further from the ger to survive, the family is forced to pack up and leave to find new grassy areas. They can only take the minimal necessities that a yak or camel can carry or pull to the next grazing site. There is no garage filled with surplus furniture—no toy box with discarded toys. They can move easily and quickly. That too is the way for the Christian to live. We should always be in a state of expectation, whether it is to go where He sends us, or to meet Him in the clouds upon His arrival.

Get Your Head Out of the Bucket

> *For my thoughts are not your thoughts, neither are your ways my ways, declares the Lord.*
>
> –Isaiah 55:8, NIV

Moving to Mongolia started us on an exhilarating adventure that can only be found while following God and trying to keep up with Him. Through a number of events, we were on track to move to Mongolia and be part of God's plan to reach every person with the gospel of His son, Christ Jesus. Of course, I had my own plan for that too. But I was soon to learn that my plans and God's plan did not always mesh.

It had been a long day of driving across the endless steppe of the wide Mongolian countryside. The roadless terrain invited us to make our own way following tracks created by migrating herders. In the distance were grazing cashmere goats with wooly, fat-tail sheep sprinkled in the flock. Some 200 yards away stood a helpless goat, unable to find her way back to the protection of the group. She was easy pray for the lurking wolves that infested the hills and ravines.

This poor goat stood helpless with her head stuck in a bucket. Some herder had undoubtedly discarded the rusted container, and the inquisitive goat had stuck her head inside to check for possible feed. Unfortunately, her horns were wedged in the bucket, making it impossible to withdraw her head.

I have kept the photo I took of this pitiful goat and have used it countless times in various talks. You see, I was very much like that goat when we first moved to Mongolia. My vision extended about as far as the bottom of the bucket. Fortunately, God began to remove the bucket from my head, much like we did for the helpless goat. As He did, a whole new world opened to me, and I began to see through His eyes. He had in mind a vast work that would lead to innumerable Mongolians claiming Christ as their Savior.

God would not force us to join Him in this monumental venture, but He would extend this opportunity if we were willing to step out in faith. He wanted me to expand my vision to see what He had planned. He also made it clear to Frances and me that we could never reach these isolated Mongolian herders for Christ by ourselves. If we were to be effective, we would need our new friends, the Mongolians, to reach their own people. We, on the other hand, would be the tools that He would use to create opportunities for them to share:

> *You did not choose me, but I chose you and appointed you so that you might go and bear fruit—fruit that will last—and so that whatever you ask in my name the Father will give you.*
>
> –John 15:16, NIV

Indeed, the rabbit ears are shortening, and we are nearing the end. God is giving this nation of Mongolia a chance to hear the Good News before His return. We must persevere, and we too must be ready. May He find us faithful, watching the sky even as we keep our hands firmly fixed to the plow doing the work God has called us to do.

Epilogue

> *I thank my God every time I remember you. In all my prayers for all of you, I always pray with joy because of your partnership in the gospel from the first day until now, being confident of this, that he who began a good work in you will carry it on to completion until the day of Christ Jesus.*
>
> –Philippians 1:3–6, NIV

As I bring this book to an end, I want to close with some of my favorite Bible verses—**Philippians 1:3-6.** Indeed, a good work has begun in Mongolia. In fact, it started in the little church that we were attending in Southern Pines, North Carolina 25-years ago. It was nurtured by the prayers of that handful of Christians along with others who would join in the effort to reach an unreached people with the gospel. The chorus grew with each short-term missionary that joined in the ministry and eventually there was a loud crescendo petitioning God to save the people of the nation of Mongolia.

And now we have the promise that *He will carry the work that He has started on to completion until the day of Christ Jesus.* As the way of all flesh, age is rapidly digging his sharpened fingernails into me. I realized long ago that it would not be me who would carry this work to completion, but it would be God working though a host of nationals committed to reaching their own nation with the life-saving message of Christ. We see that happening.

In fact, as I recount the many events that have taken place over these last 25 years, I have come to a startling realization. If I had to do this over again, I could not possibly do it. This work has been empowered by an outside influence—God! I actually shutter when I think of the many times we were held by His hand in very difficult situations. The strength was in God and certainly not in me. It was a supernatural wind that blew across this ministry and this nation and held Satan at bay. May we continue to lift up prayers for this country and the ministries of V.E.T. Net until the empty saddle is filled by the Church (see the story at the start of Chapter 16).

Prayer is vital to all that is done in V.E.T. Net. **The following are the recorded prayer requests given to me by the V.E.T. Net Mongolian staff integrated with my own prayer requests;** these reflect the heartbeat of the team. We depend on God. Please lift these prayer requests up to the Throne of Grace of our Father in heaven.

1. *Veterinary-Continuing-Education* Program

Rural veterinarians continue to come to the V.E.T. Net office for training. The focus of this program is to increase the professionalism among these rural vets, to help them commit their lives to Christ, and to disciple them so that the herders with whom they associate might also come to Christ.

Pray for:

a. Unity among all veterinarians
b. Spiritual-growth for all veterinarians
c. God's wisdom in planning for the future training of all Mongolian veterinarians and herders
d. God's financial provision for all veterinary needs in order that we may effectively train all veterinarians and herders in Mongolia

2. *Claim-a-County-for-Christ* Program

The *Claim-a-County-for-Christ* (CAC) program continues to sweep across the nation. It is the vision of the Mongolian teachers that they will continue to claim counties until the Gospel has been shared in every village. They are well along with this challenge, having now worked in 11 of the 19 rural provinces.

Pray for:

a. Implementation of the program in Umnugobi, Gobialtai, Tuv, Khovd, Uvs, and Baynulgii Provinces. Please pray for supporters of the program in these provinces.
b. Implementation of a small project to provide character training for the school dormitory teachers. Please pray for

wisdom and finances to support this project.

c. Training for English teachers (both the rural and CAC summer school teachers) to help them learn to teach English more effectively. Pray for suitable people to help with the training and funds to run the program.

3. *Watering-with-the-Word* Program (*WWW*)

The number of small churches continues to increase as we complete the three-year discipleship program in these remote villages. The challenge is to return to these people and help them to grow in understanding their new-found God. This is the road to a sustainable church in the nation.

Pray for:

a. Discipleship training for local believers and preparation of a discipleship training book to help with this
b. The annual Shepherd's Conference
c. The 112 *WWW* counties—for more staff and funds to work in these counties. We also need wisdom to determine how best to encourage, support, and establish home churches in those counties.
d. Nuda and Muugii's prayer requests:
    1. Full time WWW staff
    2. Tsahir, Tuvshiruuleh, Tariat, Murun, Khangai, and Chuluut's County church leaders to grow in their faith and be filled with God's power, wisdom, and knowledge
    3. Spiritual growth for the home-group believers in Khotont County
    4. Teacher Tsetsegsaihan—who worked with V.E.T. Net—wants to start a home group with her husband in Erdenemandal County
    5. Ways in which we can support, encourage, and assist the local-county church leaders that require help for various reasons (health, etc.)
e. Nuda and Muugii's family's increased reliance on God,

their desire to know Him more deeply, and that through His power they will continue to serve the Lord

f. Please pray for family members' health and protection.

g. Amraa and Altai's prayer requests:

    1. Full time WWW staff
    2. Strong leaders for the home groups and churches in WWW counties
    3. Amraa and Altai's family's health and their children's protection
    4. Local church leaders who have difficult lives. We want to provide life-skill training so that they can provide for their families and better reach out to local people.
    5. Local county believers' protection from temptation and addiction and that they would be faithful to God

4. *Gift-of-Love* Program

It is our hope that perhaps thousands of poor widows and handicapped people will be fed physically and spiritually.

Pray for:

a. Government leaders, veterinarians, herders, local churches, and V.E.T. Net workers to catch Christ's vision of helping the poor and the downcast

b. God's Kingdom to be expanded through this project

c. Funds to cover the costs of operating the project, as all donations to the project go to providing animals to poor families

5. *Large Animal Clinic/Training Center & Internship* Program

The expansion of the large animal training facility is a work-in-progress. The importance of this part of the ministry cannot be over-emphasized, as the practical training of veterinarians is key to the expansion and continuation of this ministry.

Pray for:

a. The teaching of Christian morals and character traits

b. The Demonstration of God's love through our words, actions, and lifestyles

c. Training in science-based, useful, and practical veterinary medicine for Mongolian countryside veterinarians

d. Building lasting "mentor" or "colleague" relationships that develop into true friendships, leading non-believing individuals to a saving faith in Jesus Christ

e. That those who are believers or become believers will disciple the next generation of Christ followers and disciple-makers, and that they will take the Good News to the ends of the earth

f. A large veterinary training center and teaching hospital that will enable the expansion of the *Veterinary Continuing Education Program* to all veterinarians in Mongolia

6. *Small Animal Clinic/Training* Center

The clinic for the treatment of pets in Mongolia has opened its doors as an outreach to veterinary students, veterinarians, and pet owners. The care of pets is a new concept in Mongolia, where dogs were formerly for the protection of livestock and property, and cats were to be feared.

Pray for:

a. Our current location is very good, but it is associated with an apartment building. The noise from the animals can understandably cause frustration for other tenants of the building. Pray that we find a free-standing building, in a good location, that is zoned to allow a veterinary clinic, and is larger than our current building so that we can provide space for more training.

b. The professional development of the V.E.T. Net veterinarians. Their vision is to be able to expand the referral/training center to help elevate the care that can be provided in Mongolia. Currently the limitations on space make it difficult to provide normal veterinary services and perform the training that is desired.

c. For relationships with current veterinary students

d. Pray for the personal spiritual growth of our workers. Pray that they will daily be strengthened in their love and commitment to serving the Lord.

7. *Student Ministry*

The outreach to vet students through English training and pet and large animal clubs is a critical part of reaching these students with the Gospel.

Pray for:

a. Ways to encourage students to attend English and veterinary clubs
b. Cooperation from the veterinary school with these programs
c. More workers for this university harvest
d. Student's hearts to be prepared to accept Jesus as their personal Savior
e. Good mutual understanding and cooperation among this team
f. Discipleship and lifelong mentorships from this ministry

8. *Administration and Finance* Departments

The behind-the-scenes support people in these departments make the ministry of V.E.T. Net possible. Without these dedicated workers, all the other projects and programs would fail.

Pray for:

a. Each member's spiritual growth and closer relationship with God
b. Team unity and cooperation
c. That all finance and administrative work is done in an orderly and timely manner and with integrity
d. That each member and their families have good health and peace, and that they place God first in their lives
e. That all our work and relationships bring glory to God.

Thank you for your continuing prayers for all these specific ministries of V.E.T. Net. Prayer effects much and is vital to all that we do. Please see the last section of this book, "Website of Christian Veterinary Mission" for ways you can support these ministries.

I want to end with the following verses from the Apostle Paul in his Letter to the Philippians. It focuses on our future destiny in heaven with our Savior and Lord, Jesus Christ.

> *But our citizenship is in heaven. And we eagerly await a savior from there, the Lord Jesus Christ, who, by the power that enables him to bring everything under his control, will transform our lowly bodies so that they will be like his glorious body.*
>
> —Philippians 3:20—21, NIV

In Memoriam

Erica Dawn Geary, DVM

Figure 17.1. Erica Dawn Geary, DVM

June 14, 1988 to April 3, 2015

Every once in a while our lives are touched forever by the unexpected presence of another person. At Christian Veterinary Missions we found such a person in Erica Geary. Erica's beautiful smile and her love for life, people, animals, and her dear Lord left a deep and lasting impression on us all.

Erica grew up and was homeschooled in Damascus, Maryland, and came to faith in Jesus as her Savior at an early age. She graduated from Grove City College in 2010 with a degree in Molecular Biology, then went on to achieve her goal of receiving a *Doctor of Veterinary Medicine Degree* from Virginia-Maryland

Regional College of Veterinary Medicine in Blacksburg, Virginia in 2014. Erica loved her work as a doctor at the Ridge Animal Hospital in Farmville, Virginia.

Erica had the privilege of participating in many mission trips to far-flung places such as Haiti, Nicaragua and, most recently, Mongolia, where she planned to return as a full-time veterinary missionary. During her short-term mission trip to Mongolia to work with V.E.T. Net, Erica touched the hearts of both the Mongolian nationals and the international staff.

Erica died tragically in an automobile accident in Virginia on Good Friday, April 3, 2015. Although we were saddened by the news of her death and by the thoughts of a youthful life cut short, we rejoice in the assurance that she will share eternity with our Lord and Savior.

Testimonials

Testimonials of Mongolian Nationals

Many Mongolian nationals, both veterinarians and others, have served with V.E.T. Net and have been impacted for eternity by the work and ministry. They have also all been greatly blessed by the service and love of Frances and Gerald Mitchum.

These Mongolian nationals have made significant contributions to the development of this ministry and in service to their Mongolian people. Here are their testimonials. They have been edited but keeping their "character." [Joseph Lenard]

1) Testimonial of Puredorj Jamsram

Board Chairman of V.E.T. Net Mongolia NGO, from the very start
Former Bible School President
Senior Pastor of a Mongolian church

Practically, no one evangelized me. Here is how I came to faith in Jesus.

I was asked by a colleague to go with him to a meeting where he was invited. There were many who were invited. I accompanied him. It was Christmas day 1991.

An English man was talking in front. I could not understand anything, because I thought he was speaking in English, and I did not know English at that time. Later, I found out that he was speaking in Mongolian with a bad accent. At the end of the gathering, I was approached by a Mongolian man who asked me about my profession and invited me to a new place where they would gather again on Sunday. The reason he asked me to come was for me to accompany them with my accordion as they sang. I agreed.

At this other meeting, there was a Canadian man talking truly in English with a translator. However, no one could understand what he translated. Most of the time, they talked to each other and the guy who was translating told us roughly what this foreigner wanted to say. Seemingly, he was talking about God from a book called the Bible.

At that time, there was a NT translated into Mongolian. I bought a copy and read it for a whole week. I had much to say for the next Sunday meeting. I came to the gathering, bringing my accordion. After more incomprehensible talk, I wanted to stand up to challenge those gathered—about 12 young men and women—as to what they should be hearing. As soon as they finished talking, someone stood up and said that he read the Bible and thought that the translator was not translating understandably. This man who stood up talked about what Jesus in the Bible had done. I agreed with what he said. A few of us said that we should do better to understand what this foreign brother was trying to communicate.

After about a month time, with the leading of the Holy Spirit, I professed my faith in Jesus as my Savior and Lord. It was the time of the birth of Mongolian Church. There were about 20 of us.

I have been Chairman of V.E.T. Net since its start, and my service has been a great blessing to me. V.E.T. Net is one of the most respected and effective ministries in Mongolia. I am not a veterinarian, and I never thought that I would be part of this kind of amazing ministry. I do not understand the professional details about it, but I understand very well about its evangelistic activities. I am very thankful to God for V.E.T. Net and that I have had a part in it.

Over the years, I have seen Gerald and Frances encourage and lead many young professionals to become believers and followers of Jesus. What they have done in Mongolia will never be forgotten. They have impacted us for eternity.

Jesus has brought about many changes in my life, and I could write a very long time about it. In brief, **I was a good communist kid, but now I desire/strive to be a good child of God**. *"I was lost but now found; was blind but now I see,"* as the words of the famous song states.

I am very grateful to be a Bible teacher and pastor today. This is my life's calling and my joy!

2) Testimonial of Ragchaamaa Boldbaatar (Argia)

Head accountant at Mongolia V.E.T. Net NGO

My Name is Ragchaamaa B., and I go by Argia. I am working now as the head accountant at Mongolia V.E.T. Net NGO (*Non-Government Organization*).

In 2000, I started with V.E.T. Net right after I graduated from University when I was 22-years old.

I became a believer in Jesus Christ when I was 20 years old. At that time, my parents had divorced, and I really had a difficult time, feeling so hurt from my father. I participated in "Summer English Olympics" English-training program for students offered by the *English Language Institute* (*ELI*). Our class teacher was a Christian man, and he told me that if I want to know there is a Father who would never leave me, there is a way to do that. Through *ELI* teachers, I received Christ as my savior. I now have a heavenly Father, and He will be with me forever.

I started going to Holy Way Church, and I met Gerald and Frances who were going to that church. They invited me to their homegroup after church on Sundays, and I met many students and young people who came to that group. I really enjoyed those times, and they were very special in my life. I felt love and caring from them to me. I so much needed that in my life.

Gerald asked me to work with the V.E.T. Net Project of *Joint Christian Services International*, which V.E.T. Net was under at that time. I started working as a bookkeeper and became an accountant when we started Mongolia V.E.T. Net NGO. After awhile, I became the Chief Accountant and Internal Auditor. All those years, we had a great life as an organization. I saw God do many amazing things.

Just as with a healthy and fruitful tree, the foundation of V.E.T. Net started with good soil and the right seed, which the Mitchums planted in Mongolia 23 years ago. Mongolia V.E.T. NET now reaches into many different groups of people—kindergarten children, school pupils, teachers in countryside, government workers, herders, vets all over Mongolia, vet students, owners of start-up vet clinics, pet owners, and owners of race horses and other livestock.

Especially, Mongolian vets have become main beneficiaries of Mongolia V.E.T. Net. This is an ongoing, renewing process during every step of developing veterinary careers.

Who can create a ministry which continues to grow? Only God

can start that. Dr. Gerald Mitchum put Him first in everything when he started this ministry. I really so appreciate Gerald and Frances's love, heart, hospitality, commitment, leadership, vision, and concern for V.E.T. Net's future. I honor them.

Their financial support for the Mongolian people through V.E.T. Net and its Christian-ministry have played key roles in its success. I'm blessed to have a small part in this ministry. I really appreciate what they and others have done. Thank you!

[**Story in Text:** The story of how God used a fish to catch Ganzorig and his courtship with Argia is in Chapter 3; subsection: "The Right Bait"]

3) Testimonial of Ganzorig Bekn-Ochir (Ganzo)

Veterinarian and Executive Director of Mongolia V.E.T. Net (since 2011)

My name is Ganzorig Bekn-Ochir, and I go by the name "Ganzo." I am now the Executive Director of V.E.T. Net in Mongolia. Here is a little bit of my story of how I came to this position.

In 2001, when I was 23 years old, I started with V.E.T. Net as a veterinarian working in remote areas. I received Jesus Christ as my Savior in October of that year.

Since I came to V.E.T. Net, God started talking to my heart by my exposure to Bible verses. I began reading the Bible and seeking Him. **Thankfully, God has found me and I have found Him**—and He is still talking into my heart daily.

Through my work with V.E.T. Net, I have become a very happy person. The environment was a big attraction due to the staff and shuttles being very caring and helpful, which I had never seen before.

I took my first remote trip with V.E.T. Net after three months of working with them. We visited Jargalant and Bat-ulzi soums. I travelled with Dr. Glenn Gaines (shuttle vet), Dr. Ken Baker (shuttle physician), Nandia (translator), Batsukh and Zola (Mongolian vets), and Dermee (driver). We did training of local vets, visited herders, treated animals, and Dr. Baker was examining adults and children. It was a wonderful experience, and the daily devotional time was a blessing to me.

While on this remote trip, we went to Orkhon River for fishing. Zola came to me and said, "How are you doing? Any fish?" I said to her no fish. She said, "Ganzo, why don't you pray to God," and she left. After I prayed for fish, I caught my one and only fish. It was a nice one. I was so excited. At the evening Bible study, I said I am ready to come to accept Jesus Christ as my Savior! You can read more about this fishing experience in this book. There is more to the story.

V.E.T. Net is a unique model for many countries for how to reach out to people for Christ. We help vets, herders, livestock, children, and local communities. In the process, we build relationships with them and share our faith. **I think this is how Jesus and his disciples ministered.**

Frances and Dr. Gerald Mitchum are wonderful examples of how to be obedient and faithful in serving the Lord. I have found that God really blesses those who are faithful in small things. Gerald and Frances have greatly impacted my life and many other Mongolian people for Christ.

[**Story in Text:** The story of how God used a fish to catch Ganzorig and his courtship with Argia is in Chapter 3; subsection: "Hooked for Life"]

4) Testimonial of Undraa

Translator and reporter; married to Tsek; Teacher; but primary role is reporting to major funders—an enormous job—she is one of the few with the English skills to do this

My name is Undraa, and I am forty years old. I have been with V.E.T. Net from the very early days.

Before I became a believer, I relied on my own strength and efforts. Until I turned eleven-years old, Mongolia was a Socialist Country. Socialism promoted atheism. Therefore, I grew up thinking that there is no God.

In 1997, my parents accepted Jesus as their Savior, and then they shared their faith with me. Their miserable marriage was saved as they got to know that One True God exists. As this marriage was saved from divorcing, our family life turned into a paradise full of love, joy and hope.

I met Gerald and Frances in 1997 at our little local church named "Holy Way Fellowship," and I was invited to their home after church. That was a fun time with many college and university students who were discovering God with Gerald and Frances' help. In my opinion, this was the beginning of V.E.T. Net.

It has been 19 years since I joined V.E.T. Net in 1999 as a volunteer summer school teacher—actually a remote school teacher. I have held many responsible positions, and, currently, I am serving with V.E.T. Net as a translator and reporter while I also raise my small children.

I thank God for sending Gerald and Frances to Mongolia. They are enablers of the Christian missions by Mongolian-national professionals. They have discipled many young Mongolian first-generation Christians and have been role models to them to become servant leaders.

Mongolia V.E.T. Net was founded and developed by Gerald and Frances Mitchum. When I think of them, the words "leadership" and "vision" come to my mind.

Now, I am learning not to rely on my own strength and knowledge but to rely on God, and I think it is Mitchums' fault. It is definitely a good thing.

[**Story in Text:** The story of Undraa's courtship with Tserendorj is in Chapter 6; subsection: "A Veterinarian Changes Colors"]

5) Testimonial of Tserendorj (Tsek)

Husband of Undraa and one of the great spiritual and professional leaders at V.E.T. Net; Head of the *Continuing Education Department* of V.E.T. Net; Chief Veterinarian of the *Large Animal Clinic/Training Center*

My name is Tserendorj, and I go by "Tsek." I joined V.E.T. Net 16 years ago as a veterinarian.

I was not a Christian until I joined V.E.T. Net. To me, it was a foreign religion and Christians were crazy. It took years for me to believe in God and make the decision to follow Him. Now Christianity is my life.

My wife, Undraa, who is also with V.E.T. Net, helped me to believe in God. She answered my questions about God. However, she said:

> "You can not become God's child by knowledge, it is your heart that should be touched by Him. If or when that time comes—that time when God's Holy Spirit touches you—please do not harden your heart. Yield it to Him."

That time came, and I became a believer in early 2000's. I was baptized by a V.E.T. Net long-term missionary and friend from Canada.

Now, I am serving as the Head of the *Continuing Education Department* of Mongolia V.E.T. Net and the Chief Veterinarian of the *Large Animal Clinic and Training Center* in Ulziit, a suburb of Ulaanbaatar city.

During these 16 years of serving with V.E.T. Net, I have seen the development of modern veterinary practice in Mongolia. I feel blessed to be part of this effective ministry of veterinary professionals. Gerald fans the flame inside me of serving my people. He is an unceasing visionary.

Well, the major part of his successful ministry is Frances. Without Frances—his faithful helper, good listener, great communicator, cheerleader, wonderful cook and house-keeper—it would have been very hard for Gerald to accomplish all of this lasting ministry called Mongolia V.E.T. Net.

It is a blessing for Undraa and me to serve together at V.E.T. Net and raise our young children as believers in the Lord.

[Story in Text: The story of Tserendorj's courtship with Undraa is in Chapter 6; subsection: "A Veterinarian Changes Colors"]

6) Testimonial of Dorjpagam Aamjilsuren (Pagma)

Head of *Claim-a-County for Christ* Program [*CAC*] (since 2008)

I have a long name, but I go by "Pagma." I started work at V.E.T. Net in 2003 when I was 32 years old.

I first worked as an assistant coordinator and then as a coordinator of the *Claim-a-County for Christ* (*CAC*) program. In 2008, I became Head of the *CAC* program.

My parents worshiped Buddha from their childhood, and I followed them in their belief. Before working at V.E.T. Net, I worked as a countryside teacher, and after that, I studied at Teachers University in Ulaambaatar (UB). God used all this background to bring me to Himself and to prepare me for my future work at V.E.T. Net.

Two of my classmates at the university were my friends and they believed in Jesus Christ. Through attending Campus Crusade for Christ (now called "*Cru*") meetings, I first heard about Jesus, and I accepted Him as my Savior in December 2002 at Christmas time, at a *Cru* teachers event. I was 30 years old.

When I believed in Christ, I understood that He is the real God. Since that time, I have learned many things—who God is, why I believe in Christ, and what my ministry purpose is.

Before joining V.E.T. Net, I worked as a summer-school teacher for two years. During that time, I met Gerald and Frances. They discipled, advised, and encouraged me. I also learned Christian-leadership principles from them. My personal character has been changed, and the Mitchum's compassion and commitment to the Mongolian people has been an inspiring example.

After I started work at V.E.T. Net, my whole family came to Christ. Now, my husband and daughter and son are believers. This means everything to me. My husband also works with V.E.T. Net. Gerald and Frances have been a big blessing in my life and our family's ministry. I want to spread the gospel everywhere in Mongolia, and I am so happy to be working at V.E.T. Net.

Our teachers in *CAC* meet and develop friendships with people who live in the countryside and share the gospel with them. We are grateful that many have accepted the Lord. My vision is to spread the gospel through my service to reach Mongolian people and help to change their lives and to also reach other nations.

Our first initiative of V.E.T. Net was the ***Education-Development* program** which started in 1999. At that time, many children couldn't read and write. First, we started Mongolian training for reading and writing in two provinces, and we are continually expanding this initiative.

Our ***Claim-a-County* program** has grown each year, and now we are working in 128 counties in 12 states. Because of the *CAC* work, 82 churches and home groups have been started. In 2018 we are implementing the *CAC* program in 28 counties in 7 provinces. This program provides opportunity to build good relationships and share about God with many people. Every year, as part of *CAC* we organize **summer school training** for about 50 days in each county where we are working. Over 100 Christian teachers work with us to provide training for the countryside children.

Since 2009, we have organized a "***Shepherd's Conference***" in UB to help community leaders grow in their faith. 2018 was the 10th year, and 125 leaders attended the conference. All were encouraged by worshipping, studying, and sharing testimonies together during the week of training. The countryside leaders are so happy to come and learn new things and grow in their faith.

After *CAC* establishes a foothold for Christ in a community, our follow-up program called ***Watering-with-the-Word*** (*WWW*) continues with Christian teaching. Now, we have 112 *WWW* counties, and we have completed five states.

Our team ministry goal is to bring many families to Christ and to extend the Kingdom of God across Mongolia and other countries. What a blessing to be involved with this goal.

[**Story in Text:** The story of Dorjpagam's healed knee is in Chapter 9; subsection: "Leg Problem," and Chapter 11; subsection: "How It Works"]

[**For More Information on *Claim-a-County-for-Christ,*** see Chapter 11; subsections: "God's Strategic Plan" and "How It Works"]

7) Testimonial of Bayartsetseg Banbold (Bayraa)

A Chief Veterinarian at the *"Caring" Small Animal Clinic/ Training Center*; one of the spiritual leaders of V.E.T. Net

My name is Bayartsetseg Ganbold, and I go by "Bayraa." I started working at V.E.T. Net NGO (Non-Government Organization) in 2002 when I was 21 years old.

After I joined V.E.T. Net, I became a believer in 2002. I was introduced to V.E.T. Net at Vet School, where I attended English and veterinary-medical class from V.E.T. Net. Dr. Clay Ashley, the long-term veterinarian who taught Vet School students, was a kind of man I never met before—very different than the other men I knew.

Let me share with you some of my family story. When I was a child, my dad was alcoholic and did not care about his family. After my parents separated, my grandfather was the only man-role in my life. He was a very dictatorial man, and I always thought that I don't need men in my life because of the attitude and negative influences of my dad and grandfather. But Dr. Clay Ashley's attitude and kindness changed my view of men, and his true caring heart drew me to the living and loving God. Even though my dad rejected me and chose the alcoholic life—and I felt myself less valuable than a bottle of alcohol—the TRUE and LIVING GOD showed me that He would never reject or forsake me.

My wonderful story is that I have been able to share Jesus with both my mother and father, as well as all my siblings. All are dedicated believers now. My parents' marriage is restored. God has truly worked a miracle in my family.

Currently, I am working at the *"Caring" Small Animal Clinic/ Training Center* as a Chief Veterinarian. I help the "Pet Club" for Vet School students. They get medical teaching and practice at the clinic. In addition, urban and countryside vets, who run small-animal practices around the country, get small-animal training. I also help V.E.T. Net's Student Ministry by promoting fellowship and reaching their lives for Jesus.

I am thankful to God that He sent his faithful children, the Mitchums, to Mongolia. Their vision from God inspired me, and it has changed many lives in Mongolia. Their kindness and love guided me to walk with the Lord, and their encouragement gives me the strength to share His love and guide others to Jesus Christ.

God revealed to **me how He gives abundant life when we walk with Him. I have** now **blessed** my **family, parents, coworkers and** my **profession. Matthew 6:33 says,** *"Seek first the kingdom of God and His righteousness, and all these things will be added."* I have found this true in my life.

[Story in Text: The story of Bayraa's family is in Chapter 13; subsection: "*Gift-of-Love* in Action"]

Testimonials of Key Individuals and Short-Term Missionaries

Many key individuals at the very start of the Mitchum's ministry as well as short-term missionaries, including "shuttle vets"—who have come from around the world—have contributed much in the formation and service to N.E.T Net. In return, they have been impacted for eternity by their involvement in the work and ministry of V.E.T. Net and, specifically, by Dr. Gerald and Frances Mitchum. All have made significant contributions to the development of this ministry. Here are their testimonials. [Joseph Lenard]

1) Testimonial of Bill F. Korver, DMin

President of Carolina College of Biblical Studies, Fayetteville, NC; Former Pastor to Gerald and Frances and family in Southern Pines, NC

In the summer of 1995, our church enthusiastically commissioned and launched the Mitchums to serve Jesus through Christian Veterinary Mission (CVM). The results were remarkable—a God-sort-of-thing (Ephesians 3:20).

Both at home and in Mongolia, people were being changed. At home, **our church prayed for, gave to, and sent people to Mongolia** far more so than other fields where we supported missionaries. Our prayer times were far more passionate than before. People became more generous than ever before to meet needs in a far-away place that most had given no thought to before 1995. In Mongolia, young veterinary students and graduates were hearing the life-changing message of Jesus and coming to faith in Him!

I'm so glad I was able to witness firsthand a good bit of what you will read in this volume. I should also add, that when Gerald wrote his monthly newsletters, they were the best missionary newsletters I'd ever read! They were always compelling. I am very confident God will use his recollections to move you, as he is a very skilled written communicator.

It is my prayer that the story of V.E.T. Net will move you to whatever action God desires you to take for His glory and world evangelization.

2) Testimonial of Annie and Steve Kullberg
Engineer and COO of the Regional Food Bank of Oklahoma;
Leader of original "Senders Group" in Southern Pines, NC

My wife, Annie, and I had the privilege to be a part of the small church in Southern Pines, NC, where Gerald and Frances attended prior to leaving for Mongolia.

We hosted the "**Senders Group**" in our home, a group of five families that committed to pray and provide emotional and physical support to the Mitchums, as they started this ministry in Mongolia in 1995.

I will never forget the excitement of getting regular emails from Mongolia and praying over the specific requests. **We prayed fervently** for housing, staff selection, approval from government authorities, physical protection, good health, and God's blessing on this important work.

At first it was very difficult for Frances to get a number of food items, and in order to keep her equipped for her amazing hospitality ministry, we arranged for special transportation for several-hundred pounds of food that included southern staples like grits and maple syrup.

In my two trips to Mongolia, in 2001 and 2008, I have seen how hospitality by Frances and Gerald, in addition to all the other good service work of V.E.T. Net, has helped to grow the Kingdom of God in Mongolia.

3) Testimonial of Judy and Joseph Lenard, MBA, DDS
Private Practice of Orthodontics in Pinehurst, NC (retired);
Author of two books and Editor of this book, *Tend My Sheep–A Veterinarian in Mongolia*

We have been blessed to have known Frances and Gerald from the time they moved to Southern Pines, NC and Gerald opened his veterinary clinic in the 1980's—a friendship extending over 30 years.

They and their two sons, Kelly and Kevin, were also early members in a newly-founded church which we and three other couples started. For a time, Gerald taught a neighborhood Bible study in our home. Little did we know at that time that Gerald would go on to become a "Paul" in Mongolia.

The church "commissioned" Gerald and Frances to go to Mongolia as missionaries back in 1995, and we were part of the small "Senders Group" described in Steve Kullberg's testimonial. The church is now the largest church in the county and continues to have an active and vital missions program, which has supported the Mitchums for almost 25 years.

A team from the Christian Medical and Dental Association travelled to Mongolia in 1999 to evaluate the teaching and service needs of Mongolian physicians and dentists. While there, Judy and I also fellowshipped and worked with Frances and Gerald in Ulaanbaatar. We had the opportunity to see the early ministry of V.E.T. Net, including meeting with the young people in the Mitchum's apartment for Bible study.

It has been a blessing to pray for and support the Mitchums over these many years. Many have come to faith in Jesus through the ministry of V.E.T. Net. Praise God!

I pray that many will be blessed by reading this book's account of God's work in Mongolia. It is a remarkable story told by a remarkable story-teller.

4) Testimonial of Wes Harrison

Chairman, Red River Transportation, Inc. in Southern Pines, NC;
Coordinator with Mitchum's home church in Pinehurst, N.C.;
V.E.T. Net American Advisory Board Member

I made my first trip to work with V.E.T. Net in 2010. Since then, I have taken 7 trips over the last 8 years.

I have known Gerald and Frances since 1990, and they have consistently demonstrated their faithfulness and their desire to be used by God. They are a continuing inspiration to me.

My areas of service are teaching and discipleship. I have worked primarily with small groups of believers and churches in the countryside as well as discipling/mentoring the V.E.T. Net team. It has been my privilege to have taught in many small churches and to have shared my testimony with teachers and students in these remote areas.

I have become acutely aware that God is at work all over the world. I have experienced this in Mongolia where He is drawing Mongolians to Himself.

V.E.T. Net has the most all-inclusive, in-depth ministry that I have seen in my travels in Asia and Central/South America. By offering practical help to vets, herders, and teachers, V.E.T. Net wins the right to tell them about Jesus Christ—and they effectively do that using nationals. I love this ministry!

5) Testimonial of Morris N. Harper

Harper Trusts—Real-estate investments—Trustee, Houston, TX;
V.E.T. Net American Advisory Board member

In 2001, I made my first trip to Mongolia to teach business skills, and I may have been **the first non-veterinarian** that CVM permitted to go to serve with V.E.T. Net. I have returned 18 times over the past 17 years.

When I first met Gerald, I asked if he wanted my finances or if he wanted me in serving with V.E.T. Net. I am grateful for Gerald's response—he said he wanted both.

God has used me to teach the Bible as well as general business and mentoring skills. Most recently, He has used me and my real-estate background to assist in the search for a new and enduring property in Ulaanbaatar to secure the future of V.E.T. Net. In the process of these years of service, God has matured my faith and transformed my life as well.

I have had the opportunity to befriend Frances and Gerald. It has been their joint mission to minister to the entire population of Mongolia, one person at a time. Putting their feet under Frances' dinner table or learning to speak English with her N.C. accent have brought many to faith in Jesus. Others have been saved as Gerald witnessed to them in conjunction with his veterinary or business skills.

Frances and Gerald have worked to overcome the darkness of

Buddhism and Shamanism by sharing the light of Christ. I count it a privilege to call them my friends and to serve with them, and I look forward to reading their testimony in this book.

[**Story in Text:** The story of how God used a big-time real-estate investor to impact countryside people is in Chapter 11; subsection: "High-Flyer Lands in Mongolia"]

6) Testimonial of Al Dorminy

Nephew of Dr. Leroy Dorminy, founder of CVM effort which resulted in V.E.T. Net in Mongolia; Accountant and partner in Southeast Management and Leasing Corporation in Atlanta, Georgia;
V.E.T. Net American Advisory Board member;

In mid-2000, I asked my uncle, Dr. Leroy Dorminy—founder of CVM's efforts which resulted in V.E.T. Net in Mongolia—if he could use me as **a CVM-volunteer even though I was not a veterinarian**. He responded by referring me to Gerald Mitchum. I am grateful that Gerald welcomed my service.

In May 2001, I made my first of six trips to Mongolia. I consulted with Argia who was one of the first employees with V.E.T. Net and worked as the accountant. Argia has been a valuable and loyal long-term employee.

Because of my background in accounting and auditing, my tasks over the years have been reviewing financial statements, budgets, administration procedures, and internal controls—all essentials for running an efficient and above-reproach ministry.

The blessings I have received in serving Jesus in Mongolia have included the friendship of the Mitchums, the Ballengers, other missionary advisors, the V.E.T. Net staff, and the Advisory Board members.

In all that Gerald and Frances do, the love, hope, grace, and salvation of Jesus Christ brightly shines through.

[**Story in Text:** The story of how God uses non-vets in this ministry is in Chapter 11; subsection: "High Flyer Lands in Mongolia"]

7) Testimonial of Ed Neufeld, DVM

Veterinarian, retired from private practice, Canmore, Alberta, Canada; V.E.T. Net American Advisory Board member; and V.E.T. Net Canadian Representative

I first travelled to Mongolia in 2009, and I have returned every year for the past eight years.

In addition to teaching small-animal medicine in the *Distance Masters* program, I have helped to train young Mongolian veterinarians at **V.E.T. Net's *Enerekh Small Animal Clinic*** in Ulaanbaatar. Not only have these veterinarians become skilled veterinary surgeons handling a large case load of medical and surgical patients, but some have become followers of Jesus.

I am convinced of the value of V.E.T. Net's mission in Mongolia because it seeks to proclaim the whole gospel through a multifaceted ministry—this includes professional veterinary development, sharing the good news of Jesus, education of children in the countryside, and donating sheep for food to needy families. I have been blessed in my service with this ministry.

[**Story in Text:** The story of Shuttles contributing to the Small Animal Hospital training is in Chapter 10; subsections: "Animal Hospital," and "Animal Hospitals/Training Centers"]

8) Testimonial of Sarah and Paul Welch, DVM

Veterinary practice, including treatment of exotic pets in Tulsa, OK; V.E.T. Net American Advisory Board member;
Sarah has been a Mary Kay Cosmetics Director for many years.

Sarah and I have been to Mongolia to serve with V.E.T. Net seven times. My most vivid memory of Mongolia was on our first arrival in March of 2005. It was 11:00 p.m. in March, and as we left the airport we got to experience what -40^{0} F was like—bone chilling!

Our first introduction to V.E.T. Net was through Dr. Mary Ballenger. Mary was trying to talk me into coming to Mongolia to teach veterinarians how to treat some of the exotic pets that the pet stores were starting to sell—turtles, lizards, etc. Mary and my wife Sarah were friends and, as far as Mary thought, there was no reason we both couldn't come.

As we were preparing for our first trip, I was comfortable in what I would most likely be doing. I was a veterinarian, and I would be teaching other veterinarians. Sarah, however, wasn't sure how the Lord would use her. As I look back over my journal during that time, I see that I wrote down 1 Peter 4:10, *"Each of you should use whatever gift you have received to serve others, as faithful stewards of God's grace in its various forms."* Sarah has been a **Mary Kay Cosmetics Director** for many years, and as she and Mary Ballenger visited over the weeks, it was decided that Sarah would do "beauty hours" for the Mongolian women.

I have found that, although my veterinary mentoring is appreciated, the reaction of women in the countryside to Sarah's ministry has been astonishing. We have found that they will travel 20 miles over rough terrain to spend a fun afternoon with Sarah and the V.E.T. Net women. They are able to visit and have the opportunity to pamper themselves, sometimes for the first time in their lives.

Partnering with several of the V.E.T. Net team, Sarah teaches women about how to take care of their skin as well as other beauty tips. As they spend time together, the women are able to listen, sometimes for the first time, about Christ and how to receive Him into their lives. In a gentle and gradual way, Sarah and the V.E.T. Net women are able to show the countryside women that they are valuable and loved. In the process, they build relationships and share their faith.

We have learned that God can use everyone in His service to share in his plan to spread His gospel message to others, sometimes through surprising ways.

[**Story in Text:** The story of how God used a Mary Kay cosmetic director is in Chapter 9; subsections: "Makeover" and "Mary Kay, Anyone?"]

9) Testimonial of Bill Pratt, DDS

Retired from general dentistry practice in Puyallup, Washington;
V.E.T. Net American Advisory Board member

My wife, Peggy, and I have been blessed by our involvement with **dental missions** around the world. We formed our own small foundation and took 67 overseas mission trips, working in 21 countries over a 32-year period.

Our first trip to Mongolia to work with V.E.T. Net was in 2000, and we returned 13 additional times—the last being in 2014. Due to health reasons, our dental missionary work has been cut short.

Reflecting on why we worked in Mongolia more than anywhere else in the world, the answer is two-fold.

First, most of the Mongolians were unreached and had not heard the gospel, particularly in the countryside where we usually worked. Following the Russian rule, there was a hunger for the truth of the gospel. Other conditions made this to be a particularly fertile field for evangelizing. There was little or no TV, no movie theatres, and no libraries. Hence, unlike in the US, they had lots of spare time—so when they received Bibles, they read and discussed them. They were hungry to learn. God truly worked bad circumstances for spiritual growth and His glory.

Second, many Mongolians were living with chronic dental pain and dental needs. It was challenging setting up clinics in unique remote places, but it was rewarding to be welcomed and appreciated. There was little complaining and much gratitude for their dental treatment.

While receiving care, one man in his 80's trusted in Jesus and the salvation offered in Him. Before leaving, he asked, **"Why did I have to wait so long to hear this Good News?"** I'll never forget those words.

The Mitchums have done a great job of training Mongolians to take over the ministry they started. We thank the V.E.T. Net staff and Gerald and Frances for the opportunity to serve with them in Mongolia. Praise God for all that He has given to us.

[**Story in Text:** The story of how dentistry is used in countryside outreach is in Chapter 6; subsection: "Driver Education"]

10) Testimonial of Tom Juergens, DVM

Founder of Anoka Equine Clinic in Anoka, Minn.;
Founder of the V.E.T. Net *Fast Horse Workshop;* V.E.T. Net American Advisory Board member

I have traveled to Mongolia 20 times in 19 consecutive summers, spending from 2 to 9 weeks during each visit. My work has been focused on sharing the love of Christ through **equine** veterinary medicine.

I'm not the same person I was in 2000. Sure I'm older, but **the Holy Spirit has transformed me in my walk with Jesus in remarkable ways**. There are many influences to this transformation, but one very important and powerful influence has been my involvement in the V.E.T. Net ministry in Mongolia.

I had 25-years of equine practice when the Holy Spirit prompted me to go to Mongolia. It was my first mission trip, and I say I'm on my first mission trip 19 years later.

It was no accident that I was called to start an equine-specific ministry in Mongolia. There is no doubt that God had prepared me for this ministry through my practice, my faith, and the mentorship of Dr. Gerald Mitchum. The first years of my work in Mongolia involved starting the *Fast Horse Seminar*—a vet seminar teaching modern veterinary medicine to remote vets using the horse as a teaching model.

The ministry then extended into countryside trips to the remote regions of Mongolia, teaching vets and their herders improved health-care for their horses. At first, I thought that the ministry was all about veterinary medicine and making huge changes in the health care of the herders' animals. But after several frustrating years, I realized that all the veterinary work was only a path to establishing trusting relationships with the Buddhist Mongolians and sharing the Gospel of Jesus Christ. **Indeed, that was the mission**. This was part of my transformation from self-centered, high-powered equine practitioner to Christ-centered Kingdom builder—and that has made all the difference!

It became apparent that the way into the *lives* of these horse-oriented remote herders and their vets was through their horses. We would "earn the right to be heard," and then we could tell them of the Good News of Jesus Christ. Using culturally-relevant teaching materials that could be presented as follow-up by V.E.T. Net folks has proven very effective in teaching what it means to be a follower of Jesus. The key is using nationals to tell their own people about Jesus.

Hundreds of remote vets have now heard about Jesus and His saving grace and have been given Bibles. Some have become followers of Him. In addition, many remote herders have experienced His love and now know about Him.

Although my ministry work has been difficult, fatiguing and often frustrating, I have experienced great joy in knowing that God has guided me, protected me, and used me to share my faith through veterinary medicine. I thank God that He led me to Christian Veterinary Mission and V.E.T. Net to grow my faith and allow me to walk with Jesus.

[**Story in Text:** The story of how God used a short-term equine vet to help change equine medicine in Mongolia is in Chapter 9; subsections: "Long-term/ Short-term Shuttle Vet," and "The *Naadam Fast Horse Workshop*"]

11) Testimonial of Neil Dyer, DVM, PhD (Pathology)

Veterinary pathologist working at N. Dakota State U. in Fargo, N.D.; lives in Moorhead, Minnesota;
V.E.T. Net American Advisory Board member

My involvement with V.E.T Net began in the summer of 2006 when I attended the AVMA convention in Honolulu, Hawaii. It was there that I met Kit Flowers at the CVM booth. That initial meeting ultimately led me to Gerald Mitchum and a first visit to Mongolia in the summer of 2007.

My first trip was a tour of veterinary cases in Tuv Aimag, but before leaving Ulaanbaatar (UB), the beginnings of a program to develop distance educational materials for Mongolian vet students and veterinarians began. This was my introduction to the great blessing that the Lord was giving me through my new Mongolian family.

I returned to UB in the fall of 2009 as part of a plan to expand the distance education curriculum and do some teaching in the veterinary school. The success of this project was very encouraging. Again, I was moved by the way the Lord was able to use me in a university setting to teach pathology to the Mongolian vet students.

In 2012, I made a third trip and was again able to work with the vet students at the Mongolian State University of Life Sciences as well as complete some face-to-face instruction with students in the new V.E.T. Net Distance Masters project. With each trip, I was drawn closer to my Mongolian family and to the wonderful team of Western advisors that lived and worked in UB.

Yet, the most significant part of my ministry with V.E.T. Net came after 2012 when my wife, Lori, and I began hosting Mongolian vets at our home in Moorhead, Minnesota while they spent a month with me at North Dakota State U. I was able to rotate each veterinarian through the veterinary diagnostic lab, the veterinary technology program, the Department of Animal Sciences, as well as have them spend some time in a local vet clinic. This was most often done at Steele Veterinary Clinic in central North Dakota with Dr. Arlyn Scherbenske and his family. In the last six years, Lori and I have enjoyed visits from Ganzo, Tsek, Munkhtuul, Ariuna, Nergui and Alta. Each of them blessed us for a month in the spring and brought something new and wonderful from the Lord. It was fantastic to have my family involved in their visits. As my grandchildren grew up, they came to believe that everyone had Mongolian visitors in the spring!

So, I have been blessed by V.E.T Net on both sides of the ocean—as a short-term advisor in UB and as a host in Minnesota.

In total, the experience with V.E.T. Net has been a completely unexpected and thrilling gift from God. The beauty of this ministry is in how it draws on all aspects of animal health from many countries to enlarge God's Kingdom. It has enriched my life in many, many ways.

12) Testimonial of Caroline and David Beischer, DVM

Mixed animal vet with interest in dairy medicine and production;
Heads a V.E.T. Net *Dairy Residency Program* (2018) in Wonthaggi, Victoria, Australia, where they live; V.E.T. Net Advisory Board member; and Australian V.E.T. Net Representative

David & Caroline Beischer live in Wonthaggi, Victoria, Australia, where David is a mixed-animal vet.

We have made three trips to Mongolia to work with V.E.T. Net—in 2006, 2008, and 2017. In 2006, the whole family came for three-months, including our three boys, aged 4–11 at the time.

Particularly, the experiences from our 2006 trip has had a lasting impact on all members of our family. Dealing with challenging circumstances taught us valuable lessons on dependence and trust in God. He is always faithful! The wonderful relationships that have developed with members of the V.E.T. Net family remain very special to us. God has placed a special love in our hearts for Mongolia and V.E.T. Net.

During our three stays in Mongolia, we made countryside veterinary trips and worked with *Claim-a-County* program. In 2018, we started a *Dairy Residency* program in our home town in Australia to teach vets how to run a dairy operation and treat dairy animals.

Christ's love is visible within the organization through their care for one another and outwardly as they practically train, help and share God's Word with vets, herders and families in the countryside. God has clearly blessed the ministry as it has grown from humble beginnings to its current stature, drawing Christian vets, medical practitioners, dentists, pharmacists, teachers and business people from around the globe.

The contributions of Gerald and Frances to this ministry have been immense. A love for God and the Mongolian people provided the right ingredients to craft a veterinary ministry out of nothing!

The Mitchums have amazing gifts for hospitality, compassion for struggling Mongolian vets, and passion to share God's hope through Christ with the Mongolian people. All this lit the fuse for this amazing work of God!

Recruitment of faithful co-workers and continued vision and wisdom to see and implement God's possibilities for the ministry have also been vitally important in the development of V.E.T. Net.

It has been an honor to serve with the Mitchums, and we have been blessed as we have worked to be a blessing to others.

NOTE: The story of how God has used short-term missionaries after their involvement in Mongolia is in the Epilogue.

Testimonials of Long-Term Missionaries

This category includes those who have been led by the Holy Spirit to move to Mongolia and work as long-term missionaries with V.E.T. Net. All have made significant contributions to the development of this veterinarian-based ministry, and I can't thank them enough for their service, friendship, and their fellowship. Here are their testimonials. [Gerald Mitchum]

1) Testimonial of Richard and Mary G. Ballenger, DVM

Long-term staff; Mary is Advisor to the *Continuing-Education-Extension* program, and she is advisor to the large-animal group; prior work was as vet in Tulsa, Oklahoma;
Richard is strategic advisor to the finance and accounting groups

Over ten-years ago, my husband, Richard, and I moved to Mongolia to work as **full-time missionaries** with the Mitchums in V.E.T. Net. We have seen so many wonderful things happen.

As Veterinary-*Continuing-Education* Advisor and advisor to the large-animal group, I have seen extraordinary professional growth within our V.E.T. Net veterinarians.

Richard has been instrumental in advising the V.E.T. Net finance and accounting group as well as wearing many hats in helping in the ministry.

Most importantly, we have seen everyone in V.E.T. Net grow spiritually and learn how to pray fervently. Many Mongolians are committing their lives to Christ and living for Him.

Gerald and Frances, thank you for saying "Yes" to God and moving to Mongolia in 1995. Your obedience has changed the whole veterinary profession in Mongolia and is transforming the nation by helping to lead many to faith in Jesus Christ.

[**Story in Text:** The story of a long-term vet and financial advisor is in Chapter 10; subsections: "*Continuing-Education-Extension* Program," and "V.E.T. Net's Finances"]

2) Testimonial of Michael and Hillary Mincher, DVM

Long-term staff working with large animals; Hillary's prior work was with horses and other livestock in rural West Tennessee;
Michael is the V.E.T. Net counselor and advisor to *Shepherd's Conference*

Our first introduction to V.E.T. Net was at the CVM short-course in the fall of 2015, followed by our vision trip in December of that year.

After that two-week trip to Mongolia, Michael and I knew V.E.T. Net was where God was calling us to serve as **full-time missionaries**, and we were back in Mongolia the following November of 2016.

Hillary is a member of the large-animal continuing-education team and works in the internship program and clinical practice of the large-animal clinic, in addition to discipleship training of the V.E.T. Net team.

Michael is serving as the V.E.T. Net counselor as well as doing discipleship training, developing biblical-training materials, and teaching English. He also works closely with the teachers to put on the annual *Shepherd's Conference* for countryside herders and church leaders.

Gerald and Frances have lived out Jesus' command in Matt. 22:37–38 to love God completely and to love your neighbor as yourself. It is an honor and inspiration to serve with them.

[**Story in Text:** The story of a long-term veterinarian with large animals and the internship program; and a Christian consultant is in Chapter 10; subsections: "Animal Hospitals/Training Centers," and "The *Shepherd's Conference*"]

3) Testimonial of Helen and Justin Woolsey, DVM

Long-term staff working with small animals with the *"Caring" Small Animal Clinic/Training Center* (*CAC*); prior work as a vet in Greenville, Tennessee; Helen is a teacher and advisor to *CAC*; Helen and Justin are active with outreach to vet students visiting V.E.T. Net

In 2014, my wife and I met Gerald and Frances, and we knew we would never be the same.

With their encouragement and the Lord's guidance, we all—including my wife, Helen, and my two children, Caleb and Caroline—moved to Mongolia in 2016 to work as long-term missionaries alongside the Mitchums and V.E.T. Net. By working with them, hearing their stories, speaking with those whose lives had been transformed, and seeing evidence of how veterinary medicine has changed in Mongolia, we have seen firsthand how God has used them to impact the people of this country. We are continually amazed.

I have now worked two years as a veterinarian advisor with the *Enerekh Small Animal Clinic.* This clinic, along with all the other entities of V.E.T. Net, continue to improve the lives of animals *and* nationals—all with the love of Christ.

The work that the Mitchums have done in Mongolia is unparalleled, yet you can find them humbly giving all the glory to God and recounting the ways only He has sustained, supported, and provided for them. The Mitchums are our inspiration, and they are true heroes of the Christian faith.

Our lives are counted among the ones that Gerald, Frances, and the V.E.T. Net organization have changed. May their vision and work carry on to the ends of Mongolia, until all of God's sheep have been tended.

[**Story in Text:** The story of Justin's work at the small animal clinic is in Chapter 10; subsection: "Animal Hospitals/Training Centers"]

4) Testimonial of Chris and Andrew Spence, DVM

Long-term staff working with *Large Animal Hospital/Training Center;* Andrew's prior work was as a vet in the South Island of New Zealand; Chris has homeschooled their children and is presently the Advisor to the *Gift-of-Love* program

In November/December 2006, Andrew traveled to Mongolia for a one-month trip to work with V.E.T. Net and investigate the possibility of bringing our family to Mongolia for long-term service.

Andrew is a veterinarian from New Zealand with mixed practice experience—predominantly dairy, also sheep/beef, deer, camelids and horses—and has a special interest in small animal orthopedics.

In 2013, the Lord opened the door for us to come with 8 of our 9 children (Simon, Ben, Jonathan, Rebekah, Caleb, Peter, David and Nathan). We arrived in August and spent the next few months helping to build a large animal-training building at V.E.T. Net's *Large Animal Clinic* site at Olziit which has also become our home—big enough to house our family.

Andrew has been involved with the large animal vets and *Continuing Education* as well as helping at the *Small Animal Clinic* especially in teaching and assisting with orthopedic cases. He has been involved in student and intern ministries as well as the V.E.T. Net *Master's Program*.

The rest of the family has helped with teaching English in various degrees in the student ministry, *Claim-a-County* work and various professional veterinary organizations. Our whole family has made our home a center of hospitality and friendship. We have also been involved in the *Gift-of-Love* program which began in 2017.

V.E.T. Net has a unique niche ministry providing practical help that opens hearts to the Gospel of Christ. We have been blessed to be a part of this Mongolian organization with the many different ways it reaches out and serves their countrymen—providing training to upskill the local people as well as building bridges to share the Hope that is within us.

Gerald and Frances have been an inspiration to all of us. They are devoted to the Lord and committed to the people of Mongolia. As more of our family returns to New Zealand to marry and start having children, we can better appreciate the personal sacrifice the Mitchums have made over the past 25-years in being here as full-time missionaries. God knows and will reward them richly.

[**Story in Text:** The story of the *Large Animal Hospital/Training Center* is in Chapter 10; subsection: "Animal Hospitals/Training Centers"]

About the Author

Figure 18.1. Gerald Mitchum, DVM

Gerald Mitchum was born on May 15, 1942 in Monroe, North Carolina. He graduated from East Carolina State University with a major in biology.

In fulfillment of his dream to be a veterinarian, Gerald graduated from the U. of Georgia School of Veterinary Medicine and interned at Colorado State University. Later, he completed a master's degree from Massey University Veterinary Department in the town of Palmerston North, New Zealand. He has held teaching positions in the veterinary departments at Kansas State U. and Massey University in New Zealand, and he has owned veterinary practices in Bozeman, Montana; Sparta, North Carolina; Galax, Virginia; and in Southern Pines, North Carolina.

Gerald and Frances have been married for 54 years and have two sons, Kelly and Kevin, and six grandchildren.

Gerald grew up with Godly parents and accepted Jesus as his personal Savior and Lord at an early age. He has a love for the people of Mongolia and has a passion for helping them with physical needs, presenting the gospel, and leading them to salvation in Jesus Christ.

Website
of Christian Veterinary Mission

Figure 19.1. Logo of CVM

www.cvmusa.org

Christian Veterinary Mission (CVM) exists to share the love of Christ through veterinary medicine. Working in communities worldwide, CVM equips and encourages veterinary professionals and students to build relationships with others through the use of veterinary knowledge and skills so that lives are transformed.

Dr. Gerald and **Frances Mitchum** have served in Mongolia with **Christian Veterinary Mission** since 1995. Through an organization which they founded—known as V.E.T. Net—the Mitchums provide much-needed veterinarian education by bringing to the country both long-term and short-term veterinary missionaries of many different specialties.

They have also made it possible for the Mongolian veterinarians to purchase high quality drugs for their animals, and V.E.T. Net's veterinary work has allowed them to expand into supporting schools and providing Christian teachers for children in even the remotest parts of Mongolia. All of their work is done with a very strong Christian witness, including Bible training for Mongolians in most "aimags" (provinces) of the country. This ministry has been extremely effective since the fall of the country's former communist government in the early 1990's.

To **financially support V.E.T. Net** in general or specific programs which you have read about in this book (*Gift-of-Love, Claim-a-County for Christ, Watering-with-the-Word, Herder Training,*

Shepherd's Conference), please make contributions through CVM on their website or these contributions can be mailed to *Christian Veterinary Mission*, 19303 Fremont Ave. N, Seattle, Washington 98133. Related to the *Gift-of-Love* Program, detailed feedback-reports will be sent to you to keep you informed of how your *Gift-of-Love* contributions are being used.

We also greatly value your **prayers**—see the Epilogue for a full discussion of prayer requests. Thank you.

Website for Tend My Sheep

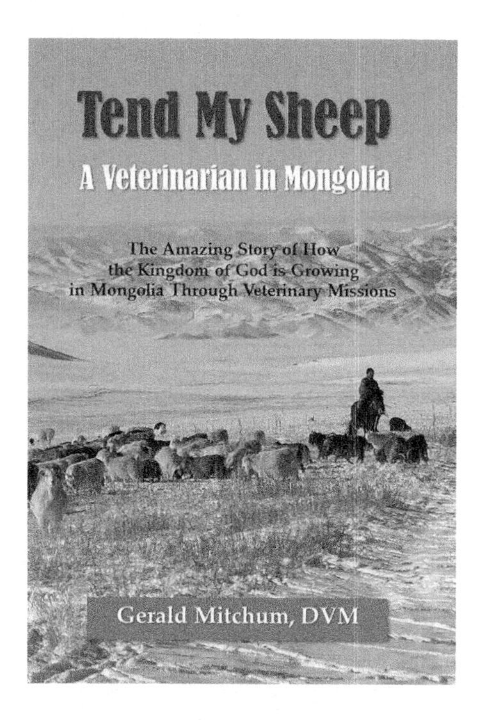

Figure 20.1. Bookcover

For additional information related to ***Tend My Sheep–A Veterinarian in Mongolia***, please visit our book website:

www.tendmysheep.net

Discover:

- Overview of the book.
- Summary descriptions of each of the 16 chapters.
- Videos of V.E.T. Net, *Gift-of-Love* Program, and other ministries
- Collection of drawings by Tamir Dugermaa used in the book.
- Collection of photographs of Mongolia.
- Testimonials of Mongolian nationals affiliated with V.E.T. Net.

- Prayer requests of V.E.T. Net staff serving in Mongolia.
- Opportunity to leave feedback under "**Contact**." The email address related to the book is **TendMySheep@VetNetmn.org**

Acknowledgement:

Our website is designed and maintained by Bob Brown. I am grateful for all that Bob has done and continues to do to help with this book and the promotion on the website.